Excel® 2007 Data Analysis

Your visual blueprint™ for creating and analyzing data, charts, and PivotTables

by Denise Etheridge

BICENTENNIAL

1807

WILEY

2007

BICENTENNIAL

Wiley Publishing, Inc.

Excel® 2007 Data Analysis: Your visual blueprint™ for creating and analyzing data, charts, and PivotTables

Published by
Wiley Publishing, Inc.
111 River Street
Hoboken, NJ 07030-5774

Published simultaneously in Canada

Library of Congress Control Number: 2007925985

ISBN: 978-0-470-13229-6

Manufactured in the United States of America

10 9 8 7 6 5 4 3 2 1

Trademark Acknowledgments

Contact Us

For general information on our other products and services please contact our Customer Care Department within the U.S. at 800-762-2974, outside the U.S. at 317-572-3993, or fax 317-572-4002.

For technical support please visit www.wiley.com/techsupport.

PRAISE FOR VISUAL BOOKS...

"This is absolutely the best computer-related book I have ever bought. Thank you so much for this fantastic text. Simply the best computer book series I have ever seen. I will look for, recommend, and purchase more of the same."

—David E. Prince (NeoNome.com)

"I have several of your Visual books and they are the best I have ever used."

—Stanley Clark (Crawfordville, FL)

"I just want to let you know that I really enjoy all your books. I'm a strong visual learner. You really know how to get people addicted to learning! I'm a very satisfied Visual customer. Keep up the excellent work!"

—Helen Lee (Calgary, Alberta, Canada)

"I have several books from the Visual series and have always found them to be valuable resources."

—Stephen P. Miller (Ballston Spa, NY)

"This book is PERFECT for me — it's highly visual and gets right to the point. What I like most about it is that each page presents a new task that you can try verbatim or, alternatively, take the ideas and build your own examples. Also, this book isn't bogged down with trying to 'tell all' – it gets right to the point. This is an EXCELLENT, EXCELLENT, EXCELLENT book and I look forward to purchasing other books in the series."

—Tom Dierickx (Malta, IL)

"I have quite a few of your Visual books and have been very pleased with all of them. I love the way the lessons are presented!"

—Mary Jane Newman (Yorba Linda, CA)

"I am an avid fan of your Visual books. If I need to learn anything, I just buy one of your books and learn the topic in no time. Wonders! I have even trained my friends to give me Visual books as gifts."

—Illona Bergstrom (Aventura, FL)

"I just had to let you and your company know how great I think your books are. I just purchased my third Visual book (my first two are dog-eared now!) and, once again, your product has surpassed my expectations. The expertise, thought, and effort that go into each book are obvious, and I sincerely appreciate your efforts."

—Tracey Moore (Memphis, TN)

"Compliments to the chef!! Your books are extraordinary! Or, simply put, extra-ordinary, meaning way above the rest! THANK YOU THANK YOU THANK YOU! I buy them for friends, family, and colleagues."

—Christine J. Manfrin (Castle Rock, CO)

"I write to extend my thanks and appreciation for your books. They are clear, easy to follow, and straight to the point. Keep up the good work! I bought several of your books and they are just right! No regrets! I will always buy your books because they are the best."

—Seward Kollie (Dakar, Senegal)

"I am an avid purchaser and reader of the Visual series, and they are the greatest computer books I've seen. Thank you very much for the hard work, effort, and dedication that you put into this series."

—Alex Diaz (Las Vegas, NV)

Credits

Project Editor
Sarah Hellert

Acquisitions Editor
Jody Lefevere

Copy Editor
Lauren Kennedy

Technical Editor
Namir Shammas

Editorial Manager
Robyn Siesky

Business Manager
Amy Knies

Media Projects Supervisor
Laura Moss-Hollister

Media Development Specialist
Josh Frank

Manufacturing
Allan Conley
Linda Cook
Paul Gilchrist
Jennifer Guynn

Book Design
Kathryn Rickard

Production Coordinator
Adrienne Martinez

Layout
Carrie A. Foster
Jennifer Mayberry
Melanee Prendergast
Heather Ryan
Amanda Spagnuolo

Screen Artist
Jill A. Proll

Cover Illustration
Elizabeth Cardenas-Nelson

Proofreader
Laura L. Bowman

Quality Control
Cynthia Fields

Indexer
Broccoli Information

Wiley Bicentennial Logo
Richard J. Pacifico

Special Help
Barbara Moore

Vice President and Executive Group Publisher
Richard Swadley

Vice President Publisher
Barry Pruett

Composition Director
Debbie Stailey

About the Author

Denise Etheridge is a certified public accountant as well as the president and founder of Baycon Group, Inc. She publishes Web sites, provides consulting services on accounting-related software, and authors computer-related books. You can visit www.baycongroup.com to view her online tutorials.

Author's Acknowledgments

I would like to thank all of the people at Wiley who assisted me in writing this book, with particular thanks to Jody Lefevere, Sarah Hellert, Namir Shammas, and Lauren Kennedy.

I would also like to thank Malinda McCain for her assistance on this and many other projects.

This book is dedicated to my parents, Frederick and Catherine Etheridge.

TABLE OF CONTENTS

CHAPTER 4: USING FINANCIAL FUNCTIONS 62

CHAPTER 5: USING STATISTICAL FUNCTIONS AND TOOLS 82

CHAPTER 6: ORGANIZING WORKSHEET DATA 104

TABLE OF CONTENTS

CHAPTER 10: USEFUL DATA ANALYSIS TOOLS AND TECHNIQUES 182

CHAPTER 11: SHARING YOUR WORKBOOK WITH OTHERS 208

CHAPTER 12: AUTOMATING WITH MACROS 234

TABLE OF CONTENTS

HOW TO USE THIS BOOK

Excel 2007 Data Analysis: Your visual blueprint for creating and analyzing data, charts, and PivotTables uses clear, descriptive examples to show you how to analyze data with Excel. If you are already familiar with Excel, you can use this book as a quick reference for many Excel tasks.

Who Needs This Book

This book is for the experienced computer user who wants to find out more about Excel. It is also for more experienced Excel users who want to expand their knowledge of the different features that Excel has to offer.

Book Organization

Excel 2007 Data Analysis: Your visual blueprint for creating and analyzing data, charts, and PivotTables has 12 chapters and 3 appendixes.

Chapter 1, "Getting Started," introduces you to Excel worksheets. You learn how to enter, edit, and format your data.

Chapter 2, "Creating Formulas," shows you how to create and use formulas. You learn how to create mathematical equations that automatically compute, name cells and ranges, create constants, and check formulas for errors.

Chapter 3, "Creating and Using Functions," introduces you to the function wizard and shows you how to use some of Excel's most popular functions such as ROUND, LOOKUP, and LARGE.

Chapter 4, "Using Financial Functions," teaches you how to use some of Excel's many financial functions. You learn how to compute present value, future value, internal rate of return, depreciation, and more.

Chapter 5, "Using Statistical Functions and Tools," focuses on some of Excel's many statistical functions. You learn how to compute an average, median, mode, standard deviation, and more.

Chapter 6, "Organizing Worksheet Data," teaches you how to work with data that is structured as a list. Among other things, you learn to sort, filter, and count your data.

Chapter 7, "Working with PivotTables," teaches you how to use a PivotTable to analyze your data. PivotTables enable you to look at how your data is distributed across categories.

Chapter 8, "Charting Data," teaches you how to create a visual representation of your data by using a chart. You learn how to create a chart, edit a chart, add trendlines, and more.

Chapter 9, "Working with External Data," teaches you how to exchange data between Excel and other products.

Chapter 10, "Useful Data Analysis Tools and Techniques," introduces you to a number of tools and techniques you may find useful, such as what-if analysis, goal seek, and consolidation.

Chapter 11, "Sharing Your Workbook with Others," provides you with a number of tools that are useful if you need to share your workbook with others.

Chapter 12, "Automating with Macros," shows you how automate the tasks you perform in Excel by using macros.

The three appendixes, "Excel Keyboard Shortcuts," "Excel Function Quick Reference," and "Formula Basics" provide you with a quick reference to each of these topics.

What You Need to Use This Book

To perform the tasks in this book, you need a personal computer that meets the minimum requirements for any Microsoft Office 2007 product:

- Microsoft Windows XP with Service Pack (SP) 2, Windows Server 2003 with SP1, or later operating system

- 256 megabyte (MB) RAM or higher

- 500 megahertz (MHz) processor or higher

- 2 GB of available hard disk space

- CD-ROM or DVD drive

- Keyboard and pointing device, such as a mouse

- 1024x768 or higher resolution monitor

The Conventions in This Book

A number of styles have been used throughout *Excel 2007 Data Analysis: Your visual blueprint for creating and analyzing data, charts, and PivotTables* to designate different types of information.

Courier Font

Indicates the use of code such as tags or attributes, scripting language code such as statements, operators, or functions, and code such as objects, methods, or properties.

Bold

Indicates information that you must type.

Italics

Indicates a new term.

•

Apply It

An Apply It section takes the code from the preceding task one step further. Apply It sections allow you to take full advantage of code.

Extra

An Extra section provides additional information about the preceding task. Extra sections contain the inside information to make working with Excel easier and more efficient.

What's on the Web Site

The Web site www.wiley.com/go/exceldata2007vb has example files that you can use to see the tasks illustrated in *Excel 2007 Data Analysis: Your visual blueprint for creating and analyzing data, charts, and PivotTables*. These files also have extra information that can aid you in your understanding of the tasks performed in this book.

Introduction to Data Analysis with Excel

This book is about using Microsoft Excel to analyze your data. Microsoft Excel is an electronic worksheet you can use to maintain lists; perform mathematical, financial, and statistical calculations; create charts; analyze your data with a PivotTable; and much more. Excel can help you locate data, find trends in your data, and present your data to others.

Each Excel file is a workbook. Each workbook can have multiple worksheets. Worksheets are made up of rows and columns of cells you use to enter information. One of the many useful features of Excel is the ability to calculate. When you enter a formula into Excel, Excel can automatically calculate the result, and when you make changes to your worksheet, Excel can automatically recalculate.

You can also use Excel to create charts. A chart is a graphical representation of your data. When using Excel,

you can choose from several types of charts, including Column, Line, Pie, Bar, Area, and Scatter. Charts can make your data easier to read, easier to understand, and easier to compare.

A *PivotTable* is an interactive worksheet table you can use to analyze data. A PivotTable gives you an easy way to summarize and view large amounts of data. Using a PivotTable, you can rotate rows and columns of data so you can see different views of your data easily. You can use Excel to create PivotTables.

Excel provides a way for you to create and maintain lists. A list is a series of rows and columns. Each column has a label — for example, name, address, telephone number. Each row under a column has information pertaining to the column label. You can sort, filter, and analyze your lists in Excel.

Introduction to Data Analysis with Excel

OPEN A NEW WORKBOOK

1. Click the Office button.

   A menu appears.

2. Click New.

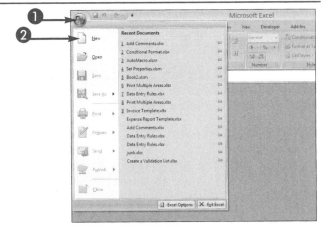

The New Workbook dialog box appears.

3. Double-click Blank Workbook.

   Excel opens a new workbook.

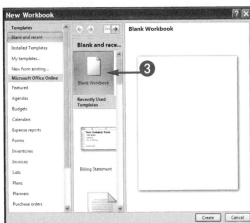

Understanding the Excel Window

When you open an Excel workbook, Excel presents the Excel window. Your window should be similar to the one in the illustration. It may not be quite the same because Excel renders windows based on the size of your screen, the resolution to which your screen is set, and the other screen display options.

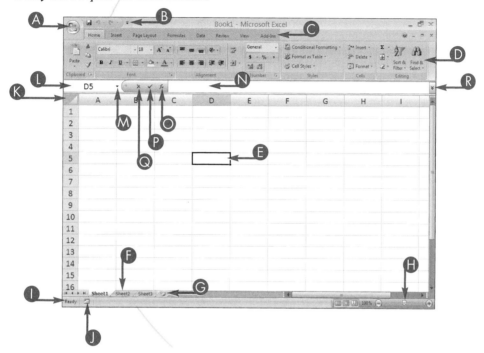

A **OFFICE BUTTON**

Click the Office button to open, save, print, prepare, send, publish, and close files.

B **QUICK ACCESS TOOLBAR**

Place commands you use often on the Quick Access toolbar.

C **TABS**

Click a tab to view Ribbon options.

D **RIBBON**

Click the buttons in the Ribbon to execute Excel commands.

E **CELL**

Enter data into cells.

F **SHEETS**

Each workbook has multiple sheets. You can enter data into each sheet.

G **INSERT SHEET**

Click to insert a new sheet.

H **ZOOM**

Drag to adjust the magnification of your worksheet.

I **STATUS BAR**

Right-click to adjust what appears on the status bar.

J **RECORD MACRO BUTTON**

Click to begin recording a macro.

K **SELECT ALL BUTTON**

Click to select everything in your worksheet.

L **NAME BOX**

Displays the name of the active cell.

M **DROP-DOWN LIST**

Displays a list of defined range names.

N **FORMULA BAR**

Use the formula bar to enter and edit data.

O **INSERT FUNCTION**

Opens the Insert Function dialog box.

P **ENTER BUTTON**

Click to accept a cell entry.

Q **CANCEL BUTTON**

Click to cancel a cell entry.

R **EXPAND FORMULA BAR**

Click to make the formula bar larger.

Enter Data

Worksheets divide information into rows and columns of data. People often use worksheets to calculate financial, statistical, or engineering data. Microsoft Excel is an electronic worksheet. You can use it to enter, display, manipulate, analyze, and print the information you organize into rows and columns.

Each Excel 2007 worksheet has more than 1 million rows and more than 16,000 columns. Excel labels each row in numerical order, starting with 1. Excel labels each column in alphabetical order, starting with A. When Excel reaches the letter Z, it begins ordering with AA, AB, AC, and so on. You refer to the intersection of a row and column as a cell. The intersection of a cell also forms the cell name. For example, you refer to the first row in column A as cell A1 and the seventh row in column C as cell C7. When using Excel, you enter your data into worksheet cells.

To move to a cell, move your mouse pointer to the cell and then click. The cell becomes the active cell and Excel surrounds it with a black border. Once in a cell, you can use the arrow keys on your keyboard to move up, down, left, and right. You can enter text, numbers, dates, and formulas into cells.

Alphabetic characters and numerical data you do not use in mathematical calculations are text. Any sequence of characters that contains a letter, Excel considers text. By default, Excel considers all numerical data numbers. If you wish to enter numerical data as text, precede your entry with an apostrophe.

As you type, the data you enter into a cell appears on the formula bar. You can press the check mark on the formula bar or you can press the Enter key to enter your data into a cell.

Enter Data

ENTER TEXT

1. Move to the cell in which you want to enter text.

2. Type the text you want to enter.

3. Press Enter.

   Excel enters the text into the cell and then moves down to the next cell.

- Alternatively, you can click the check mark on the formula bar to enter data.

ENTER NUMBERS

1. Move to the cell in which you want to enter a number.

2. Type the number you want to enter.

3. Press Enter.

   Excel enters the number into the cell and then moves down to the next cell.

- You can also click the check mark on the formula bar to enter data.

ENTER NUMBERS AS TEXT

① Move to the cell in which you want to enter a number as text.

② Type an apostrophe followed by the number you want to enter.

③ Click the check mark.

Excel enters the number into the cell.

Alternatively, press Enter.

If you receive an error, click the Error button (⬦) and then click Ignore Error.

ENTER DATES

① Move to the cell in which you want to enter a date.

② Type the date you want to enter.

③ Click the check mark.

Excel enters the date into the cell.

Alternatively, press Enter.

C2	③	✓	ƒₓ	'4569275

	A	B	C	D
1		Employee Name	Employee Number	Hire Date
2		James Love ① →	'4569275	← ②
3				
4				
5				
6				

D2	③	✓	ƒₓ	05/23/2007

	A	B	C	D
1		Employee Name	Employee Number	Hire Date
2		James Love	4569275	① → 05/23/2007
3				②
4				
5				
6				

Extra

When you enter numbers as text, an Error button (⬦) may appear. Excel is checking to see if you entered the number as text by mistake. You should click the button and then click Ignore Error.

When you press Enter after typing an entry into a cell, by default Excel moves down one cell. If you want Excel to move to the cell to the right, press the right-arrow key or the Tab key. If you want Excel to move up, press the up-arrow key. If you want Excel to move to the left, press Shift+Tab or the left-arrow key.

By default, when you press the Enter key after typing an entry, Excel moves down one cell. You can change the default location to which Excel moves. Click the Office button. A menu appears. Click Excel Options in the lower-right corner. The Excel Options dialog box appears. Click Advanced. Make sure the After Pressing Enter check box is selected and then choose Right, Up, or Left in the Direction field to cause Excel to move right, up, or left when you press Enter.

Format Numbers

Formatting makes your data easier to read and helps you conform to company, country, or industry standards for formatting. Excel provides a variety of options for formatting numbers, dates, and times. By applying formatting, you change the way a number, date, or time appears. For example, you can use Excel's formatting options to tell Excel you want to separate the month, day, and year of a date with slashes.

The Number group on the Home tab has several buttons you can use to format numbers quickly. Click the down arrow next to the Accounting Number Format button to choose to apply a United States currency format, a United Kingdom currency format, a Euro format, or another currency format. Use the Percent Style button to display the value in a cell as a percent. Use the Comma Style button to display the value in a cell with a thousands separator. Use the Increase Decimal and Decrease Decimal buttons to increase and decrease the number of decimal places.

The Number Format box is located on the Home tab in the Number group. You can use it to format numbers quickly. Just click the down arrow to display a menu of options. Then click a format option to apply it to a cell or cell range. Click the More Number Formats option to open the Format Cells dialog box. You can also click the launcher in the Number group to open the Format Cells dialog box.

The Format Cells dialog box has four categories you can use to format numbers: General, Number, Currency, and Accounting. The General format is the default format. It displays numbers exactly the way you type them.

Format Numbers

GENERAL NUMBER FORMAT

1 Type numbers.

The numbers appear in the format you type them.

2 Click and drag to select the cells you want to format.

3 Click the Home tab.

4 Click the Comma Style button in the Number group.

- Excel separates the thousands in the numbers.

- Excel adds two decimal places.

- Negative numbers appear in parentheses.

- Zeros are represented by a dash.

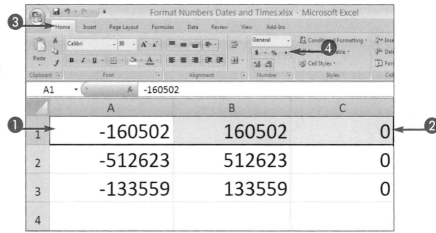

ACCOUNTING NUMBER FORMAT

1 Select the numbers to format.

2 Click the Accounting Number Format button in the Number group.

● Excel adds a dollar sign, aligned with the left side of the cell. Excel reserves space for a right parenthesis for negative values.

3 Click the Decrease Decimal Place button. Each click removes a decimal place.

● If you click the Increase Decimal Place button, each click adds a decimal place.

CURRENCY FORMAT

1 Select the numbers to format.

2 Click the Number group's launcher.

3 In the Number tab of the Format Cells dialog box, click Currency.

4 Click here and set the number of decimal places.

5 Click here and select a currency symbol.

6 Click to select a number format for negative numbers.

7 Click OK.

● Excel formats your numbers.

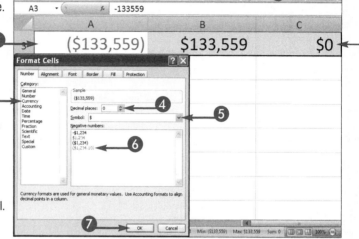

Extra

Changing a number format can increase the contents of the cell. If your number is too long to fit in its cell, Excel fills the cell with pound signs (#####). To view the number, double-click the line at the top of the column that separates columns, or click and drag the line to make the cell wider.

You can use the Text format in the Format Cells dialog box to convert a number to text. Numbers formatted as text are not used in mathematical calculations. Certain numbers — for example, employee numbers — are never used in mathematical calculations and should be formatted as text. If you want to format a number as text as you type it, precede the number with an apostrophe (').

If you right-click in any cell that contains a number, you can choose number formatting options from the mini-toolbar or you can click Format Cells from the context menu to open the Format Cells dialog box.

continued →

When using the Format Cells dialog box, you can use the Number format option to apply special formats to your numbers. You can set the number of decimal places, specify whether your number should display a thousands separator, and determine how to display negative numbers. You can choose from four formats for negative numbers: preceded by a negative sign (–), in red, in parentheses, or in red and parentheses.

The Currency format offers you the same options as the Number format except you can choose to display a currency symbol. The currency symbol you choose determines the options you have for displaying negative numbers. If you choose the dollar sign ($), thousands are separated by commas by default.

Excel designed the Accounting format to comply with accounting standards. When using the Accounting format, if you use the dollar sign symbol ($), the dollar sign aligns with the left side of the cell, decimal points are aligned, a dash (–) displays instead of a zero, and negative values display in parentheses.

Countries vary in the way they display dates and times. Use the Date and Time format option to choose a locale. If you choose English (U.S.), you have more than 15 ways to display a date and a variety of ways to display time. To learn more about dates and times, see Chapter 3.

The Percentage option converts numbers to a percent. You can choose the number of decimal places you want to display. The Fraction option converts numbers to a fraction. If your locale is English (U.S.), you can use the Special format option to format ZIP codes, phone numbers, and Social Security numbers.

Format Numbers (continued)

PERCENTS

① Click and drag to select the numbers you want to format.

② Click the Percent Style button in the Number group.

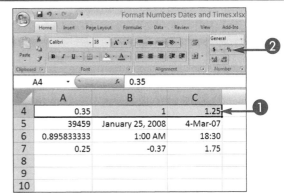

● Excel converts the numbers to percentages.

DATES

① Click and drag to select the cells you want to format.

② Click the Number group's launcher.

③ In the Number tab of the Format Cells dialog box, click Date.

④ Click to choose a format.

⑤ Click OK.

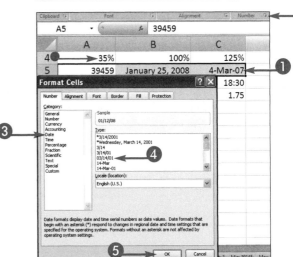

- Excel formats the dates.

TIMES

1. Click and drag to select the cells you want to format.

2. Click the Number group's launcher.

3. In the Number tab of the Format Cells dialog box, click Time.

4. Click to choose a format type.

5. Click OK.

- Excel formats the time.

FRACTIONS

1. Click and drag to select the cells you want to format.

2. Click the Number group's launcher.

3. In the Number tab of the Format Cells dialog box, click Fraction.

4. Click to choose a format type.

5. Click OK.

Excel formats the numbers as fractions.

These cells show how Excel formats the numbers.

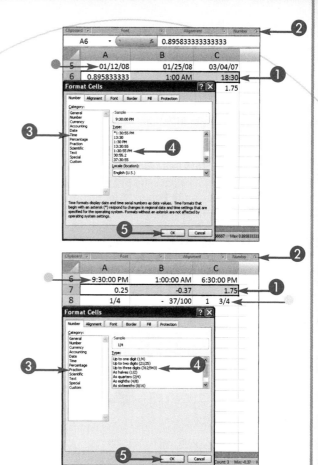

Extra

Excel has several special formats you can use to format Social Security numbers, ZIP codes, and phone numbers. To apply the Social Security number special format, type nine digits into a cell. Click in the cell. Click the launcher in the Number group. The Format Cells dialog box opens to the Number tab. Click Special in the Category box. Click Social Security number in the Type box. Click OK. Excel formats the digits you entered as a Social Security number.

You can preformat cells so that when you enter data into a cell, Excel automatically formats it. To preformat the cells, select the cells you want to preformat and then apply the format to them. When you type data into the preformatted cells, Excel automatically applies the format to your data.

You can set the default number of decimal places Excel applies when you type a number into a worksheet. Click the Office button. A menu appears. Click Excel Options in the lower-right corner. Click Advanced. Make sure the Automatically Insert Decimal Point check box is checked. Type the number of decimal places you want in the Places field. Click OK.

Format Cells

Formatting enhances the presentation of reports. Rows and column headings give your data a visual orientation and highlight important information about the structure and content of your data.

You can use the Home tab to format cells in a variety of ways. Clicking the launcher in the Font or Alignment group opens the Format Cells dialog box; here, you can format numbers, align data within or across cells, apply a variety of formats to fonts, add borders, and fill cells with color. Many of the options available to you in the Format Cells dialog box are also available in the Ribbon. When you use the Ribbon, you can frequently apply a format with a single click.

You can set off cells by applying a colored background and changing the font color. Use a fill to create a colored background for a cell. You can set off columns or other important information by applying borders. A border adds color to the lines that surround a cell. You can choose the type and thickness of the border line, and you can choose to apply your border only to the sides of the cell you specify. When applying a border, you can choose the color, style, and placement of the border.

On the Home tab, in the Font group, Excel provides an Increase Font Size button and a Decrease Font Size button. You can click the Increase Font Size button to make your font larger. You can click the Decrease Font Size button to make your font smaller. You can also enter a font size directly into the Ribbon and/or select a new font.

Format Cells

CREATE A FILL

1. Click the Home tab.

2. Click and drag to select the cells you want to format.

3. Click here and then select a fill color.

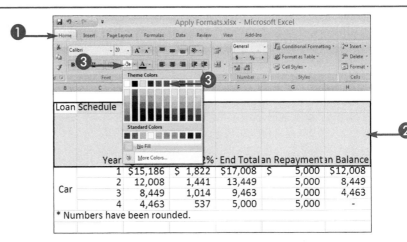

- Excel applies a fill color to the cells you selected.

CHANGE THE TEXT COLOR

1. Click and drag to select the cells you want to format.

2. Click here and select a font color.

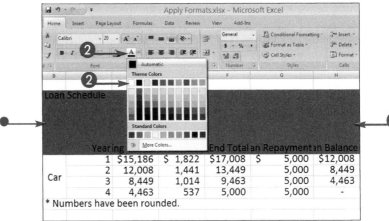

- Excel applies a font color to the cells you selected.

ADD A BORDER

① Click and drag to select the cells you want to format.

② Click the down arrow next to the Borders button.

③ Click here and select a color.

④ Click to select a border style.

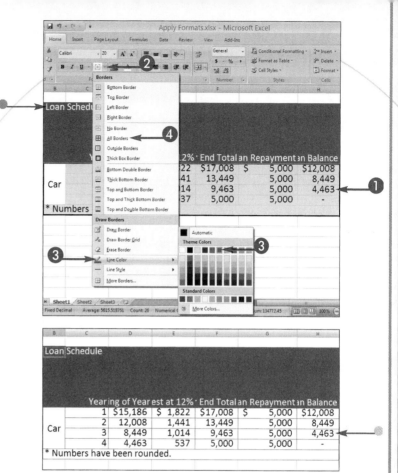

- Excel adds a border to your cells.

	Year	ing of Year	est at 12%	End Total	an Repayment	an Balance
Car	1	$15,186	$ 1,822	$17,008	$ 5,000	$12,008
	2	12,008	1,441	13,449	5,000	8,449
	3	8,449	1,014	9,463	5,000	4,463
	4	4,463	537	5,000	5,000	-

* Numbers have been rounded.

Extra

You can set the default font and font size for all of your workbooks. Click the Office button. A menu appears. Click Excel Options in the lower-right corner. The Excel Options dialog box appears. Click Popular. In the Use this Font field, select the font you want to use. In the Font Size field, select the font size you want to use. Click OK. The next time you open a workbook, it will use the font and font size you selected.

If you want text to stand out, you can change the font. If you want to adjust the size of your text so it fits in a cell, you can adjust the font size. You can click the down arrow next to the Font field to change the font for the selected range. Click the down arrow next to the Font Size field to change the font size in the selected range. You can also right-click and then use the mini-toolbar to change the font and font size.

continued →

Format Cells
(continued)

I f the text you enter is too long to fit in a single cell, Excel allows the text to spill over into an adjacent cell. If you place text or data in the adjacent cell, Excel cuts off the text in the original cell and you cannot see all of it. If you want to display the text in the original cell on multiple lines in a single cell, use the Excel Wrap Text feature.

By default, data or text you enter in a cell displays from left to right. You can change this by clicking the Orientation button and selecting a new orientation. You can angle your text or show your text vertically.

Titles provide a brief summary of your data and you may want to center them over the data they summarize. You

can center text within a cell by using the Center button. To center text across several cells, you can use the Merge and Center button. In addition to being able to merge and center, you can merge cells in Excel 2007 without centering and you can merge several rows and columns of cells into a single cell. If you want to return merged cells to their original state, you can select the cells and then click the Unmerge Cells option.

The Excel Ribbon also has several options you can use to align text within a cell. You can align text with the top, middle, or bottom of a cell and/or with the left, right, or center of a cell.

Format Cells *(continued)*

MERGE AND CENTER

1. Click the Home tab.

2. Click and drag to select the cells you want to merge and center.

3. Click the Merge and Center button in the Alignment group.

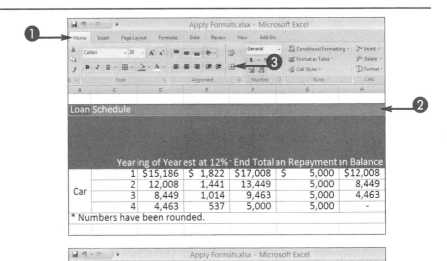

- Excel merges and centers your text.

WRAP TEXT

1. Click and drag to select the cells whose text you want to wrap.

2. Click the Wrap Text button in the Alignment group.

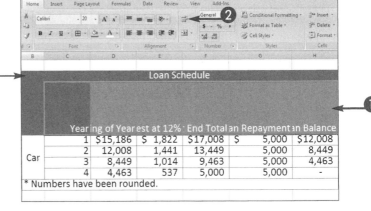

- Excel wraps your text.

ORIENTATION

1 Click the cell or cells whose orientation you want to change.

2 Click here and select an orientation.

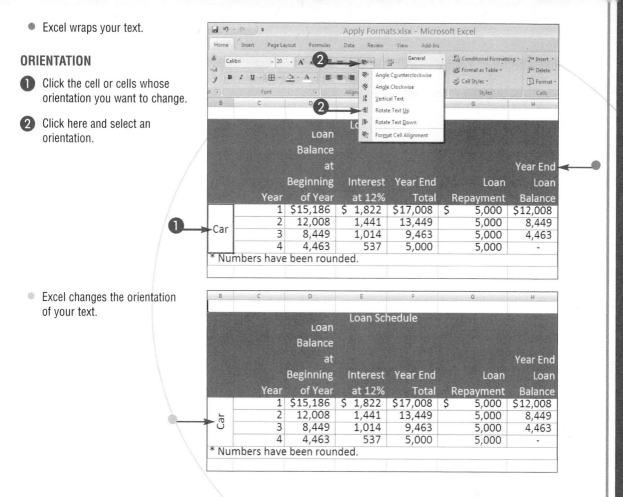

- Excel changes the orientation of your text.

Extra

Excel has several buttons you can use to align data within a cell. Use the Align Left button (⊞) to align your data with the left side of the cell, use the Align Right button (⊞) to align data with the right side of the cell, and use the Center button (⊞) to center data in the cell.

Excel has buttons you can use to place data at the top, bottom, or middle of the cell. Use the Top Align button (⊞) to place data at the top of the cell, use the Middle Align button (⊞) to place data in the middle of the cell, and use the Bottom Align button (⊞) to place data at the bottom of the cell.

To set data off, you may want to put it in a cell but indent it. You can use the Increase Indent button (⊞) to increase the amount of the indent in a field and the Decrease Indent button (⊞) to decrease the amount of the indent in a field.

Select
Data

Before you can execute an Excel command, you must select the cells to which you want the command to apply. For example, if you want to add a blue fill to several columns of cells, you start the process by selecting the cells. The most common way to select cells is to click and drag. Excel highlights the selected cells. The range of cells you select does not have to be contiguous. You can hold down the Ctrl key as you click and drag to select noncontiguous groups of cells. If you do not hold down the Ctrl key, Excel deselects the first range of cells when you begin to select a new range of cells. If you select multiple ranges of cells, Excel highlights each selected range.

You can select a single cell or the entire worksheet. To select a single cell, click in the cell. To select every cell in a worksheet, click the Select All button or press Ctrl+A.

To select an entire row or an entire column, simply click the row or column identifier. For example, to select all of the cells in column C, click the C identifier for the column. To select multiple columns, click the first column and then continue holding down the mouse button as you drag to the other columns you want to select. To select entire rows, you click the row identifiers on the left side of the rows.

You can quickly select a large range of cells by clicking in the first cell you want to select, holding down the Shift key, and then clicking in the last cell you want to select.

Select Data

SELECT THE ENTIRE WORKSHEET

① Click the Select All button.

Alternatively, press Ctrl+A.

SELECT CONTIGUOUS CELLS

① Click the first cell you want to select.

② Drag to the last cell you want to select.

Alternatively, click the first cell, hold down the Shift key, and then click the last cell.

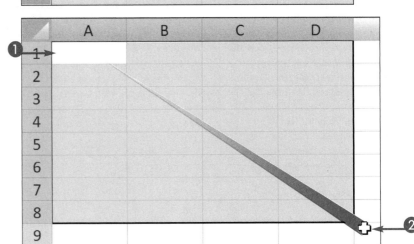

SELECT NONCONTIGUOUS CELLS

1 Click the corner of the first block of cells.

2 Drag the mouse to highlight the desired cells.

3 Press Ctrl.

4 Select the next block of cells.

Repeat Steps 3 and 4 to select additional cell blocks.

SELECT COLUMNS OR ROWS

1 Click the label for the first column or row you want to select.

2 Drag to the last column or row you want to select.

● Excel selects the columns or rows.

Extra

You can format multiple worksheets at the same time. For example, say you are collecting data for three different regions and want to present your data in three worksheets that use the same format. Select three worksheets and type the formatting once to have it appear on all three worksheets. You select multiple worksheets by holding down the Ctrl key as you click the tab of each worksheet you want to select. When you enter data or make changes to any one of the selected worksheets, Excel changes all of the other selected worksheets as well. To deselect multiple worksheets, click a tab for an inactive worksheet while not holding down the Ctrl key.

You can also use the arrow keys to select cells. Click in any cell, hold down either the Shift key or the F8 key, and then use the left, right, up, and down arrow keys to expand your selection.

To select noncontiguous ranges of cells, select the first range of cells. Click Shift+F8, and then select the next range of cells.

You can press Ctrl+Shift+an arrow key to select everything from the active cell to the next blank cell that is to the right, to the left, above, or below the active cell.

Copy, Cut, and Paste Cells

f you want to use the same values in multiple locations, you can copy and paste instead of retyping. For example, you can copy a list of data in one worksheet to another worksheet, or you can copy a formula to multiple other cells. When you copy and paste a cell or range of cells, Excel duplicates everything in the cell — including the cell values, formulas, formatting, comments, and data validation — and leaves the original cell values unchanged. You can select, copy, and paste multiple cells only if the cells are adjacent.

If you want to move information from one location to another, you can select, cut, and paste. Cutting and pasting removes data from the original location and

places it in a new location. When you apply the Cut or Copy command to a range of cells, Excel surrounds the cells with a dotted line. The selected cells remain marked until you paste or press the Esc key to deselect the cells.

After you cut or copy a range of cells, you can paste the cell contents to any location within your current workbook, another Excel workbook, or any other Microsoft Windows program. When you paste to an Excel workbook, Excel replaces the content of the cells into which you paste with the cut or copied values. For that reason, be careful when you paste, because you can overwrite other data. The best method is to select the first cell into which you want to paste the contents and then apply the Paste command.

Copy, Cut, and Paste Cells

COPY AND PASTE

① Select the cells you want to copy.

② Click the Home tab.

③ Click the Copy button in the Clipboard group.

A dotted line appears around the copied cells.

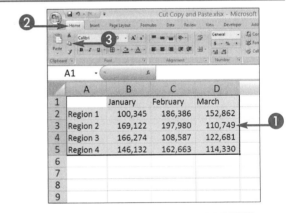

④ Place the mouse pointer where you want to paste the cells.

⑤ Click Paste in the Clipboard group.

● Excel places a copy of the copied cells in the new location.

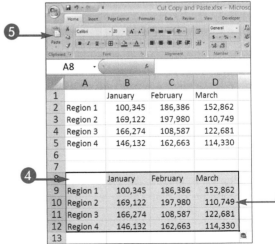

CUT AND PASTE

① Select the cells you want to move.

② Click the Home tab.

③ Click the Cut button in the Clipboard group.

A dotted line appears around the selected cells.

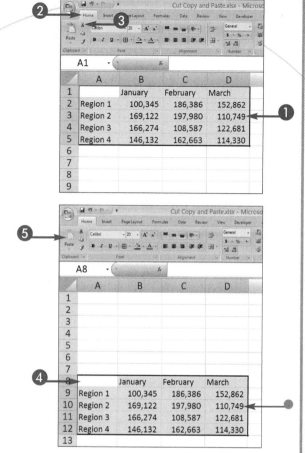

④ Place the mouse pointer where you want to paste the cells.

⑤ Click Paste in the Clipboard group.

● Excel places the data in the new location.

Extra

To use your mouse to move a range of cells, select the cells you want to move and then point to the border of your selection. When your mouse pointer turns to a ⬚, drag your selection to a new location.

To use your mouse to copy a range of cells, select the cells you want to copy and then hold down the Ctrl key while you point to the border of your selection. When your mouse pointer turns to a ⬚, drag your selection to a new location.

You can select cells and press Ctrl+C to copy or Ctrl+X to cut and then press Ctrl+V to paste.

When you cut or copy a range of cells that have hidden rows or columns and then paste, Excel includes the hidden rows and/or columns when it pastes.

If you want to copy only visible cells, select the cells you want to copy. Click the Home tab. Click Find & Select in the Editing group. A menu appears. Click Go To Special. The Go To Special dialog box appears. Click Visible Cells Only. Click OK. Press Ctrl+C. Move to the Paste area. Press Ctrl+V.

Copy with the Office Clipboard

With Office 2007, you can place content into a storage area called the Clipboard and then paste the content into Excel or another Office application. Cut and copied content stays on the Clipboard until you close all Office applications. The Office Clipboard can store up to 24 cut or copied items. When you add the 25th item, Office deletes the first item. You can store text and graphics on the Clipboard. As you add items to the Clipboard, they appear at the top of the Clipboard task pane. All the items on the Clipboard are available for you to paste to a new location in Excel or into another Office document.

The Clipboard is not visible until you access it. In Excel, you access the Clipboard by clicking the launcher in the Clipboard group of the Home tab. Each item on the Clipboard appears with an icon that tells you the Office application the information originated from and shows a portion of the text or a thumbnail if the item is a graphic. You can also use the Clipboard to store a range of cells. The Office Clipboard pastes the entire range, including all the values, but any formulas in the cells are not included when you paste. You can paste everything on your Clipboard into your worksheet by clicking the Paste All button. You can clear the Clipboard by clicking the Clear All button.

After you paste an item from the Clipboard, Excel provides the Paste Options icon menu. You can use the menu to choose whether you want to use the source formatting or the destination formatting for the pasted data.

Copy with the Office Clipboard

① Click and drag to select the cells you want to copy.

② Click the Home tab.

③ Click the Copy button in the Clipboard group.

Excel places a copy of the information on the Office Clipboard.

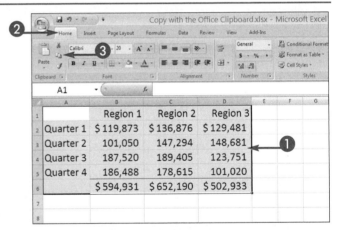

④ Click the launcher in the Clipboard group.

● The Clipboard task pane appears.

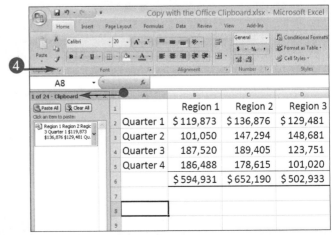

⑤ Click the destination cell.

⑥ Click the item you want to paste.

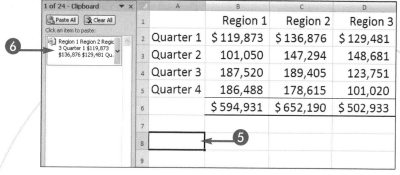

● The content is pasted into the new location.

● In the Paste Options icon menu, choose whether to keep the formatting of the copied item or change it to match the formatting of the new location. The default is to match the formatting of the new location. Press Esc to accept the default and remove the menu.

Extra

You can set the following options by clicking the Options button in the Clipboard task pane.

OPTION	DESCRIPTION
Show Office Clipboard Automatically	Shows the Office Clipboard automatically when you copy.
Show Office Clipboard When Ctrl+C Pressed Twice	Shows the Office Clipboard when you press Ctrl+C twice.
Collect Without Showing Office Clipboard	Prevents the Clipboard task pane from appearing while you are copying.
Show Office Clipboard Icon on Taskbar	When the Office Clipboard is active, displays an icon on the Windows taskbar.
Show Status Near Taskbar When Copying	Shows the number of items collected out of 24 when you add an item to the Office Clipboard.

Insert and Delete Cells

As you develop your worksheets, you will sometimes want to make changes to the layout. For example, as you modify your worksheet, you may find that you need to insert or delete cells or even insert or delete entire rows or columns of cells. In Excel, you can shift a cell or group of cells up, down, left, or right. You can also add or delete rows and columns.

When you insert cells, rows, or columns, Excel automatically adjusts any formulas that reference the cells, whether they are relative or absolute. See Appendix C to learn more about relative and absolute cell references. When you delete cells, rows, and columns, the same is true; however, when you delete a cell that you

directly reference in a formula, Excel cannot adjust the formula and displays a #REF error instead.

If you want to insert columns, select the number of columns to the left of where you want the new columns and then select the Insert Column option. For example, if you want to insert three columns, select three columns and then select the Insert Column option. If you want to insert rows, select the number of rows above where you want the new rows and then select the Insert Row option. For example, if you want to insert three rows, select three rows and then select the Insert Row option. If you want to insert nonadjacent columns or rows, hold down the Ctrl key as you select where you want to place the rows or columns.

Insert and Delete Cells

INSERT CELLS

①　Click the point at which you want to insert cells.

　　Select multiple cells if you want to insert multiple cells.

②　Click the Home tab.

③　Click the down arrow next to Insert in the Cells group.

　　A menu appears.

④　Click Insert Cells.

●　The Insert dialog box appears.

⑤　Click the direction in which you want to shift cells (○ changes to ◉).

⑥　Click OK.

●　Excel shifts the number of cells you selected.

Note: *If you want to delete cells, select the cells, click Home, click the down arrow next to Delete, click Delete Cells, choose the direction in which you want to shift the cells, and then click OK.*

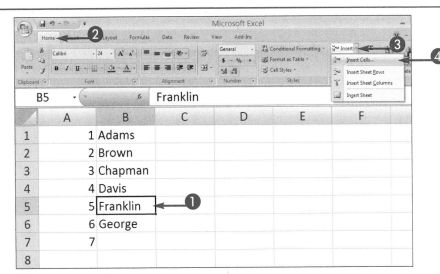

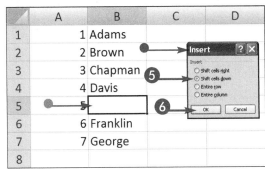

INSERT COLUMNS OR ROWS

① Click and drag column or row labels where you want to insert columns or rows.

This example uses rows.

② Click the Home tab.

③ Click Insert in the Cells group.

	A	B	C	D	E	F
1		January	February	March		
2	Region 1	100,345	186,386	152,862		
3	Region 2	169,122	197,980	110,749		
4	Region 3	166,274	108,587	122,681		
5	Region 4	146,132	162,663	114,330		
6						
7						

◈ Excel inserts the columns or rows.

	A	B	C	D	E	F
1						
2						
3		January	February	March		
4	Region 1	100,345	186,386	152,862		
5	Region 2	169,122	197,980	110,749		
6	Region 3	166,274	108,587	122,681		
7	Region 4	146,132	162,663	114,330		
8						

Extra

You can delete the contents of cells by selecting the cells and then pressing the Delete key. You can also use Excel's Clear options to remove everything or to delete formats, contents, or comments from a cell. To remove everything from a cell or group of cells, select the cells and then click the Home tab. Click Clear (☑) in the Editing group and then click Clear All. To remove formats while leaving the contents intact, select the cells and then click the Home tab. Click Clear in the Editing group, and then click Clear Formats. To remove contents while leaving the formatting intact, select the cells and then click the Home tab. Click Clear in the Editing group, and then click Clear Contents.

You can use comments to annotate your worksheet. To add a comment, click the cell to which you want to add a comment, click the Review tab, and then click Comment. You can then type your comment in the block provided. To remove a comment, select the cell with the comment, click the Home tab, click Clear, and then click Clear Comments. To learn more about comments, see Chapter 11.

Find and Replace

As worksheets get larger, finding the information you want can be difficult. You can use Excel's Find feature to locate information. If you want to replace the found information with new information, use Excel's Find and Replace feature. Use the Find tab in the Find and Replace dialog box to find information. Use the Replace tab in the Find and Replace dialog box to find and replace information.

You can use substitutions in the Find and Replace dialog box. You can use the asterisk (*) as a substitute for any sequence of characters. You can use the question mark (?) as a substitute for any single character. For example, typing ***ber** finds September, October, November, and December. Typing **J?ne** finds Jane and June.

When you click the Find All button, Excel by default finds every instance of the value you are looking for in the active worksheet and lists the workbook, worksheet, cell name, cell address, value, and formula for each found value at the bottom of the Find and Replace dialog box. When you click Find Next, Excel moves to the first instance of the value, and Excel moves to the next instance with every additional click of the Find Next button. If you want to replace the values you find with a new value, click Replace All on the Replace tab to replace every instance of the value. Click Replace to replace the selected instance of the values and then move to the next instance. Click Find Next if you want to move to the next instance without replacing the selected instance.

In the Find and Replace dialog box, you can use the Options button to set additional options.

Find and Replace

FIND

1. Click the Home tab.

2. Click Find & Select in the Editing group.

   A menu appears.

3. Click Find.

- The Find and Replace dialog box appears.

4. Type what you want to find into the Find What field.

5. Click Find All to find all instances. Click Find Next to find the first instance.

   This example uses Find All.

6. If you clicked Find All, click an instance to move to that instance.

- Excel moves to the instance you clicked.

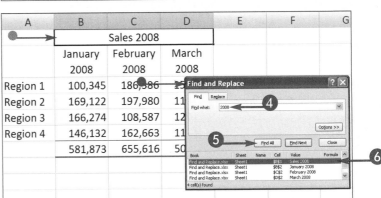

REPLACE

① Repeat Steps 1 to 3 under Find.

② In the Find and Replace dialog box, click the Replace tab.

③ Enter what you want to find.

④ Enter your replacement.

● Click the Replace All button to replace all instances.

This example uses Replace All.

● Click Find and then Replace to find and replace the first instance; then click Find Next to find the next instance.

● Excel replaces the data.

A message box appears telling you Excel made replacements.

⑤ Click OK.

⑥ Click the Close button to close the Find and Replace dialog box.

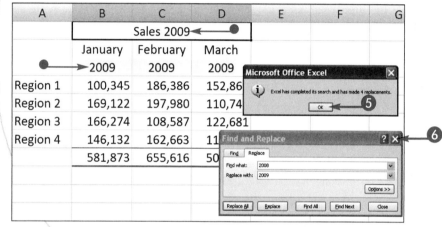

	A	B	C	D	E	F	G
			Sales 2008				
		January 2008	February 2008	March 2008			
	Region 1	100,345	186,386	152,862			
	Region 2	169,122	197,980	110,749			
	Region 3	166,274	108,587	122,681			
	Region 4	146,132	162,663	11			
		581,873	655,616	50			

	A	B	C	D	E	F	G
			Sales 2009				
		January 2009	February 2009	March 2009			
	Region 1	100,345	186,386	152,86			
	Region 2	169,122	197,980	110,74			
	Region 3	166,274	108,587	122,681			
	Region 4	146,132	162,663	11			
		581,873	655,616	50			

Microsoft Office Excel
Excel has completed its search and has made 4 replacements.
OK

Find and Replace
Find what: 2008
Replace with: 2009
Options >>
Replace All   Replace   Find All   Find Next   Close

Extra

You can click the Options button on the Find and Replace tabs of the Find and Replace dialog box to set several options. In the Within field, select Sheet if you want to search only the active worksheet. Select Workbook if you want to search the entire workbook.

In the Search field, select By Rows if you want to search right to left across the rows. Select Column if you want to search top to bottom down the columns.

Select the check box in the Match Case field (☐ changes to ☑) if you want your match to be case sensitive. For example, if this option is not selected, abc is considered the same as ABC or aBc.

Select the check box in the Match Entire Cell Contents field (☐ changes to ☑) if you want what you type in the Find What field to match the cell contents and not contain any extraneous information. For example, say one cell contains the value Jane Smith and another cell contains the value Smith. If you select Match Entire Cell Contents, Excel will find Smith but not Jane Smith.

Find and Replace Formats

Cells can contain numbers, text, formats, and formulas. With Excel, you can search for any of these elements to view them, replace them, or perform some other action. You may, for example, find and replace values to correct mistakes, or perhaps you need to return to a value to add a comment or apply formatting.

You can access the Excel Find and Replace dialog box on the Home tab in the Editing group or by pressing Ctrl+H. The Find feature is part of Find and Replace and is available on the Home tab in the Editing group or by pressing Ctrl+F.

To find and replace formats, specify what you are seeking and with what you want to replace the item you are seeking. Click the Options button in the Find and Replace

dialog box to specify additional details. Use the Within drop-down menu to indicate whether to search the current worksheet or the current workbook.

In the Find and Replace dialog box, clicking a Format button opens the Find Format or Replace Format dialog box. You can use these dialog boxes to specify the Number, Alignment, Font, Border, Fill, or Protection you want to find and/or replace. Use the Formatting button to restrict your search to characters formatted in a certain way, such as bold or percentages.

Before you start a new Find and/or Replace for formats, make sure you clear all formats by clicking the down arrow next to the two Format buttons and then clicking Clear Find Format and Clear Replace Format.

Find and Replace Formats

① Click the Home tab.

② Click Find & Select in the Editing group.

③ Click Replace.

Alternatively, you can press Ctrl+H to open the Find and Replace dialog box.

④ In the Find and Replace dialog box, click Options if your dialog box does not look like the one shown here.

Note: The Options button allows you to toggle between the short and long forms of the dialog box.

⑤ Click here and select Choose Format From Cell.

⑥ Click in a cell that has the format you want to replace.

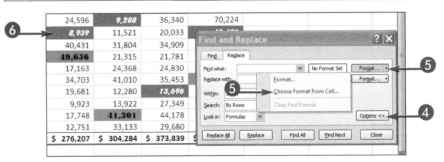

- A preview of the format you selected appears.

7 Click here and select Choose Format From Cell.

8 Click in a cell that has the format you want to use as a replacement.

- A preview of the format you selected appears.

9 Click Replace All.

- You can click Replace to make one change at a time.

- If you want to find instead of replace formats, click Find All or Find Next to highlight cells in the worksheet without replacing formats.

- Excel replaces the formats.

10 A message box appears, telling you Excel made replacements. Click OK.

11 Click Close.

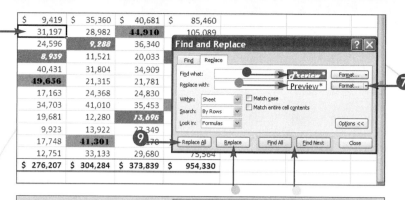

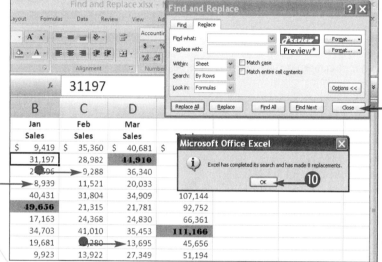

Extra

On the Home tab, when you click Find & Select in the Editing group, Excel presents a menu of options. If you click Formulas, Comments, Conditional Formatting, Constants, or Data Validation, Excel finds all the formulas, comments, conditional formatting, constants, or data validations in your worksheet and selects them. You can use the Tab key and Shift+Tab keys to move among the cells.

If you want to move around your worksheet quickly, you can use the Go To dialog box. Press Ctrl+G or click the Home tab, click Find & Select in the Editing group, and then click Go To to open the Go To dialog box. In the Go To field, you can double-click a range name to move to the named range. In the Reference field, type a cell address and then click OK to move to a cell.

Understanding Formulas

n Excel, you use formulas. A *formula* is an equation that performs a calculation. A formula can consist of operators, functions, numbers, text, and cell references. You place formulas in cells. You can click a cell and then type your formula into the formula bar or you can type your formula directly into a cell. You start most formulas by typing an equal sign (=).

Operators

You use operators to tell Excel the type of calculation you want to perform. There are four types of operators: arithmetic, comparison, text concatenation, and reference.

Arithmetic Operators

Use arithmetic operators to perform mathematical calculations such as addition (+), subtraction (–), multiplication (*), division (/), percent (%), and exponentiation (^). For example, the formula = 3 * 2 + 1 - A4 multiplies 3 times 2, adds 1, and then subtracts the contents of cell A4. If cell A4 is equal to 3, the equation returns 4.

OPERATOR	KEY	PURPOSE	EXAMPLE	ANSWER
+	Plus sign	Adds	=1+1	2
–	Minus sign	Subtracts	=3–2	1
–	Minus sign	Negates	–1	–1
*	Asterisk	Multiplies	=3*2	6
/	Forward slash	Divides	=6/2	3
%	Percent sign	Converts to a percent	.10	10%
^	Caret	Raises to a power	=3^2	9

Comparison Operators

Use comparison operators to compare values. The result of a comparison operation is either the logical value TRUE or the logical value FALSE. For example, the formula =A1=B1 compares the value in cell A1 to the value in cell B1 and returns the value TRUE if they are equal and FALSE if they are not equal.

OPERATOR	PURPOSE	EXAMPLE	ANSWER
=	Determines if values are equal	=1=1 =2=1	TRUE FALSE
<>	Determines if values are unequal	=1<>1 =2<>1	FALSE TRUE
>	Determines if one value is greater than another value	=1>2 =2>1	FALSE TRUE
<	Determines if one value is less than another value	=1<2 =2<1	TRUE FALSE
>=	Determines if one value is greater than or equal to another value	=1>=2 =2>=1	FALSE TRUE
<=	Determines if one value is less than or equal to another value	=1<=2 =2<=1	TRUE FALSE

Text Concatenation Operator

There is only one text concatenation operator — the ampersand (&). Use the ampersand to join values together to produce one continuous text value. For example, if the text "John" is in cell A1 and the text "Smith" is in cell B1, the formula = A1 & " " & B1 returns John Smith.

Reference Operators

Use reference operators to specify the range of cells you want to use in your formula. There are three reference operators: the colon (:), the comma (,), and the space. Excel refers to them as the *range operator*, the *union operator*, and the *intersection operator*, respectively. The colon references every cell included in and between the referenced cells. For example, A1:C3 includes cells A1, A2, A3, B1, B2, B3, C1, C2, and C3. The comma enables you to reference two or more cells or values. For example, A1, B2, 25 references cells A1 and B2, and the number 25. The intersection operator references all the cells two range operators have in common. For example, the reference B1:C3 C1:D3 references cells C1 to C3. You can use more than one reference operator in a single formula.

OPERATOR	PURPOSE	EXAMPLE
:	References every cell included in and between two cell references	A1:C3
,	References two or more values	A1, B3, C5, 15
space	References all the cells two range operators have in common	B1:C3 C1:D3

Operator Precedence

When you perform a mathematical calculation in Excel, you must be careful of precedence — the order in which Excel performs calculations. For example, Excel performs calculations from left to right, performing multiplication and division before addition and subtraction. The formula = 3 + 4 * 2 returns 11. Excel multiplies 4 times 2 and then adds 3. If you want to change the order of precedence, add parentheses. Excel calculates numbers in parentheses first. The formula = (3 + 4) * 2 returns 14. Excel adds 3 plus 4 and then multiplies the result by 2.

The following table shows the precedence order, from highest to lowest, that Excel uses to evaluate operators in formulas. If the operators in the formula have the same order of precedence, Excel evaluates the equation from left to right.

PRECEDENCE	OPERATORS	SYMBOL
1	Parentheses	( )
2	Reference operators	: (space) ,
3	Minus sign	– (negates a number before any calculations)
4	Percent sign	%
5	Exponentiation	^
6	Multiplication and division	*, /
7	Addition and subtraction	+, –
8	Concatenation	&
9	Comparison operators	=, <, >, <=, >=, <>

Functions

A function is a formula that Excel has predefined. You can use a function to do such things as add numbers, find an average, or find the highest number in a list. Excel provides you with more than 300 functions that are divided into the following categories: Financial, Date and Time, Math and Trig, Statistical, Lookup and Reference, Database, Text, Logical, Information, Engineering, and Cube. You supply values — called *arguments* — to the function; Excel returns the result. Excel's Function Wizard steps you through the process of adding a function to your worksheet. See Chapter 3 for more information on this wizard. You can also type functions directly into a worksheet. You start by typing an equal sign following by the function name. As you begin to type the function name, the formula AutoComplete list appears. Double-click the function you want to add to your formula. Excel adds the function and an open parenthesis. Type your arguments. A comma must separate each argument. End your function with a close parenthesis. The following is an example of a valid function: =SUM(25, B1, B5:D5).

You can nest a function within another function and arithmetic formulas can contain functions.

Create Formulas

xcel provides you with tools for storing numbers and other kinds of information. However, the real power of Excel comes from its ability to manipulate information. You can use formulas and functions to perform myriad calculations in Excel.

You can carry out calculations in many ways. One method is to use operators such as the plus (+), minus (–), multiplication (*), and division (/) signs. You start by typing an equal sign and the values you want to add, subtract, multiply, or divide, each separated by an operator. For example, type =6*3/2+25-B6, press Enter, and Excel does the math and displays the answer in the same cell. You can also type an equal sign, click in a cell that contains the value you want to perform an operation on, and then type the operator.

A second method involves functions. Functions perform calculations on your information and make the results available to you. To use a function, type an equal sign followed by the function name and parentheses; for example, =SUM(). Place the values on which you want to perform the calculation inside the parentheses, separating them with commas. If the values are on the worksheet, click the cells they are in or type the cell address.

A third method is to use Excel's AutoSum feature, which offers a point-and-click interface for several functions, such as SUM, AVERAGE, MIN, MAX, and COUNT. You simply select the feature you want from Excel's AutoSum menu and Excel tries to guess the cells on which you want to perform the function by selecting them. You can press Enter to accept Excel's selection or you can click and drag to select the cells you want.

Create Formulas

CALCULATE WITH AN OPERATOR

1 Type =.

2 Click the cell with the number you want to use in your calculation or type the first number.

3 Type an operator, such as plus (+), minus (–), multiply (*), or divide (/).

4 Click a cell with the number you want to use in your calculation or type the next number.

5 Press Enter.

● The result appears in the cell in which you typed your formula.

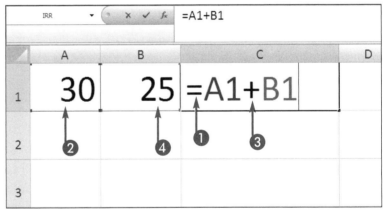

CALCULATE USING A FUNCTION AND CELL ADDRESSES

1 Type the numbers you want to calculate into adjacent cells.

2 In another cell, type = followed by the first few letters of the function.

3 Double-click the option you want to use.

4 Click and drag to select the numbers you want to calculate.

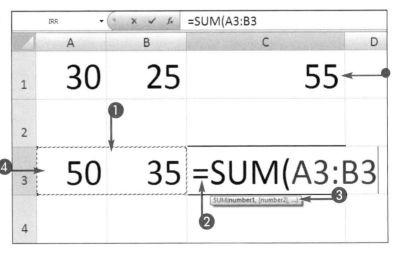

● The result appears in the cell.

CALCULATE USING AUTOSUM

① In adjacent cells, type numbers.

② Click the cell in which you want the result.

③ Click the Formulas tab.

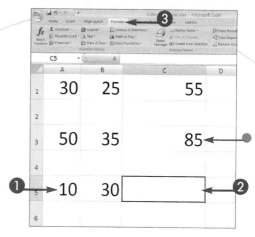

④ Click here and select an option.

● This example uses Sum.

You can select from Sum, Average, Count Numbers, Max, and Min.

Excel places =SUM() in the cell, with the cell addresses for numbers you may want to add.

⑤ To accept the cell addresses Excel has selected, press Enter.

To select other addresses, click and drag and then press Enter.

The result appears in the cell selected in Step 2.

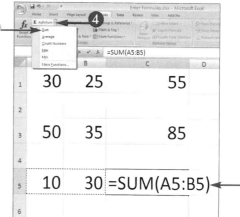

Extra

By default, when you create a formula, Excel references the cells on the active worksheet. If you want to reference cells on another worksheet, precede the cell address with the sheet name followed by an exclamation point (!). For example, you can use the following to sum cells on Sheet2 and have the result appear in a cell on Sheet1: =SUM(Sheet2!A1:A5). If you change the sheet name, Excel automatically updates the formula.

Expanding the formula bar lets you enter longer formulas. You can click the chevron (⬦) at the end of the formula bar or press Ctrl+Shift+U to expand and collapse the formula bar.

You can right-click on the status bar, which is located at the bottom of the Excel window to display the Customize Status Bar menu. If you select Average, Count, Minimum, Maximum, and Sum from the menu that appears, when you click and drag over two or more cells, Excel automatically places the average, a count, the lowest number, the highest number, and the sum of the values on the status bar.

Edit Formulas

After creating a formula, you can update it to accommodate new data or you can change it. You can modify the cells your formula references, change its arguments, or move your formula to a new location.

You can modify your formula directly, or, if your formula includes a function, you can modify it using the Function Arguments dialog box. To edit a formula, double-click the cell containing the formula, type your changes or click the cell containing the formula, and then use the formula bar to make your edits. When Excel is in edit mode, it highlights the cells that the formula references. Each value in the formula displays in a different color, and Excel outlines range references in the same color, making it easy for you to identify each part of your formula.

You can change a function argument by clicking the cell that contains the function and then clicking the Insert Function (fx) button to open the Function Arguments dialog box, which enables you to select new cell ranges for each argument. When you accept the changes, Excel updates the cell references.

When you move a formula to a new cell on your worksheet, all cell references in the formula, whether absolute or relative, remain the same. For example, if you move the formula =SUM(A1:A5), which has a relative reference and is located in cell A6, into cell A7, the cell references in the formula do not change. You can move a formula simply by dragging it to a new cell. Run your mouse pointer over the border of the cell; when you see a four-sided arrow, drag the cell to a new location. Excel moves any formatting with the data.

Edit Formulas

MODIFY A FORMULA

1 Double-click the cell containing the formula you want to edit.

Alternatively, you can click the cell and then press F2.

Excel color-codes the referenced cells.

2 Highlight the cell reference you want change.

3 Click a new cell reference.

Excel changes the cell reference in the formula.

4 Press Enter to update the formula.

CHANGE ARGUMENTS

1 Click the cell containing the formula you want to edit.

2 Click the Insert Function button.

• The Function Arguments dialog box appears.

3 Type the desired changes to the formula arguments.

4 Click OK to update the formula.

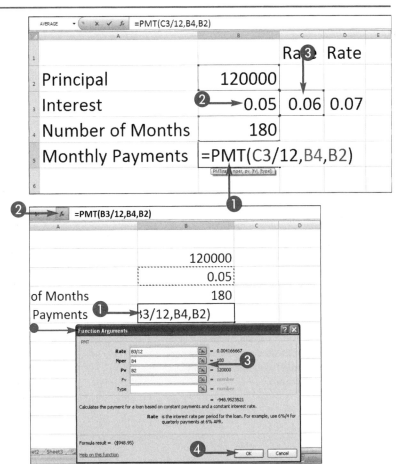

MOVE A FORMULA

1 Click the cell containing the formula you want to move.

2 Click the edge of the border and drag to a new cell.

Excel outlines the new location with a dotted line.

B14	▾	*fₓ*	=SUM(B2:B13)

	A	B	C
1	Month	Sales	
2	January	137,543	
3	February	174,645	
4	March	199,658	
5	April	124,104	
6	May	103,899	
7	June	194,498	
8	July	124,882	
9	August	146,609	
10	September	171,250	
11	October	175,077	
12	November	135,087	
13	December	159,436	
14	❶	1,846,688	
15	TOTAL		❷

Release the mouse button.

● Excel pastes the formula in the new cell.

◐ All cell references remain the same.

B15	▾	*fₓ*	=SUM(B2:B13)

	A	B	C
1	Month	Sales	
2	January	137,543	
3	February	174,645	
4	March	199,658	
5	April	124,104	
6	May	103,899	
7	June	194,498	
8	July	124,882	
9	August	146,609	
10	September	171,250	
11	October	175,077	
12	November	135,087	
13	December	159,436	
14			
15	TOTAL	1,846,688	

Extra

You can use cut, copy, and paste to move a formula from one location in your worksheet to another location. When you cut and paste a formula, the cell references do not change. This is true for formulas with relative cell addresses and for formulas with absolute cell addresses. When you copy and paste a formula, the cell references may change depending upon the type of cell reference. See Chapter 1 to learn how to cut, copy, and paste.

To use the same formula in multiple cells, you can use the Fill Handle to copy the formula to adjoining cells in the same row or column. This changes all relative cell references within the formula. For example, copying =SUM(A1:A5) from cell A6 to cell B6 results in =SUM(B1:B5). The Fill Handle is the black box on the bottom-right corner of a selected cell. You simply drag it to an adjacent range of cells. Excel outlines the cells where the formula will copy to with a dotted line. Excel copies the formula and any cell formatting to the new cells.

To delete a formula, click the cell that contains the formula and then press the Delete key.

Name Cells and Ranges

In Excel, you can name individual cells and groups of cells, called *ranges*. A cell named Tax or a range named Northern_Region is easier to remember than the corresponding cell address. You can use named cells and ranges directly in formulas to refer to the values contained in them. When you move a named range to a new location, Excel automatically updates any formulas that refer to it.

When you name a range, you determine the scope of the name by telling Excel whether it applies to the current worksheet or the entire workbook. You can name several ranges at once by using Excel's Create from Selection option. You can use the Name Manager to delete named ranges.

Excel range names must be fewer than 255 characters. The first character must be a letter, underscore (_), or backslash (\). You cannot use spaces or symbols. You can use the period or underscore as a separator. It is best to create short, memorable names. Each range name must be unique within it scope. Range names are not case sensitive. Excel considers the name profit the same as the name PROFIT.

There is a down arrow located on the left side of the formula bar. When you click the down arrow, a list of named ranges appears. If you click a named range, you will move to the cells it defines. When you are creating a formula, if you click and drag to select a group of cells that have a range name, Excel automatically uses the range name instead of the cell address.

To learn how to use a named range, see the task "Create Formulas that Include Names" later in this chapter.

Name Cells and Ranges

NAME A RANGE OF CELLS

1. Click and drag to select the cells you want to name.

   Alternatively, click a cell with a value to create a named cell.

2. Click the Formulas tab.

3. Click Define Name in the Defined Names group.

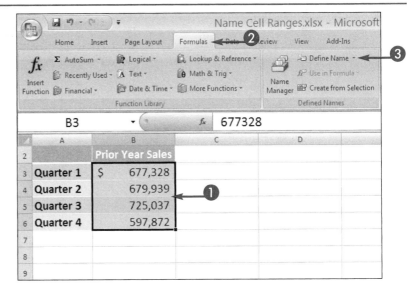

- The New Name dialog box appears.

4. Type a name for the range.

5. Click here and then select the scope of the range.

- The range you selected in Step 1 appears here.

6. Click OK.

   Excel creates a named range.

   The defined name is now available to use in a formula.

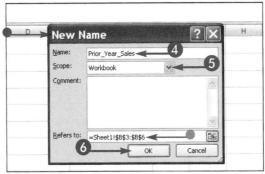

CREATE NAMED RANGES FROM A SELECTION

① Click and drag to select the cells you want to include in the named range.

Include the headings. They become the range names.

② Click the Formulas tab.

③ Click Create from Selection in the Defined Names group.

● The Create Names from Selection dialog box appears.

④ Click the location of the range names (☐ changes to ☑).

⑤ Click OK.

The defined names are now ready for use in a formula.

● You click here to move to a named range.

⑥ Click Name Manager in the Defined Names group.

● The Name Manager dialog box appears.

⑦ Click a name.

⑧ Click Delete.

Excel deletes the named range.

Note: See the next task to learn more about constants.

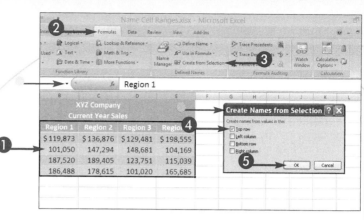

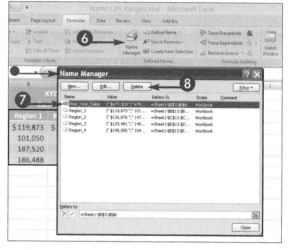

Extra

You can use Excel's Name Manager to rename, edit, or delete named ranges and constant values. On the Formula tab, click Name Manager. The Name Manager dialog box appears. Double-click the name you want to edit. The Edit Name dialog box appears. Make the changes you want and then click OK. To delete a range name or constant, click the name in the Name Manager dialog box and then click the Delete button. If you want to create a new range name or constant, click the New button in the Name Manager dialog box. The New Name dialog box appears. You can use it to make your entries. In addition to formulas, you can also enter text as a constant value. Simply type the text into the Refers To field.

If you have a worksheet that includes formulas that reference cells or ranges that are named, you can convert the cell or range references to range names. Select the cells containing the formulas and then click the down arrow next to Define Names on the Formulas tab. A menu appears. Click Apply Names. The Apply Names dialog box appears, displaying all of the range names that exist within the workbook. Click OK. Excel updates the formulas in the selected cells to include the range names.

Define and Display Constants

Use a constant whenever you want to apply the same value in different contexts. With constants, you can refer to a value by simply using the constant's name.

You can use constants many ways. For example, the sales tax rate is a familiar constant that, when multiplied by the subtotal on an invoice, results in the tax owed. Likewise, income tax rates are the constants used to calculate tax liabilities. Although tax rates change from time to time, they tend to remain constant within a tax period.

To create a constant in Excel, you need to type its value in the New Name dialog box, the same dialog box you use to name ranges, as shown in the previous task, "Name Cells and Ranges." When you define a constant,

you determine the scope of the constant by telling Excel whether it applies to the current worksheet or the entire workbook. To use the constant in any formula in the same workbook, simply use the name you defined.

The rules that apply to naming a range also apply to naming a constant. Excel constant names must be fewer than 255 characters. The first character must be a letter, underscore (_), or backslash (\). You cannot use spaces or symbols. You can use the period or underscore as a separator. It is best to create short, memorable names. Each name must be unique within its scope. Constant names are not case sensitive. Excel considers the name profit the same as the name PROFIT.

To learn how to use a constant, see the next task, "Create Formulas that Include Names."

Define and Display Constants

DEFINE A CONSTANT

1 Click the Formulas tab.

2 Click Define Name in the Defined Names group.

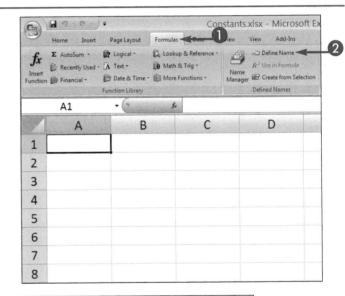

The New Name dialog box appears.

3 Type a name for your constant.

4 Click here and select the scope of your constant.

5 Type an equal sign (=) followed by the constant's value.

6 Click OK.

You can now use the constant.

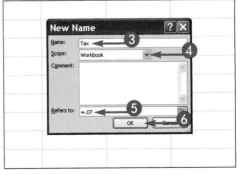

DISPLAY A CONSTANT

1 Click a cell.

2 Type an equal sign followed by the first letter or letters of the constant's name.

A menu appears.

Note: *If you do not know the constant's name, click the Formulas tab and then click Use in Formula. A menu appears. Click the name and then press Enter.*

3 Double-click the name of the constant.

4 Press Enter.

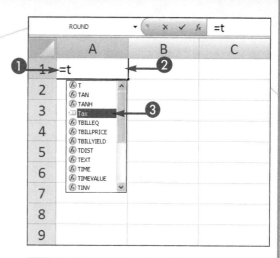

● The constant's value appears in the cell.

Note: *To learn how to use named constants and named ranges in formulas, see the next task, "Create Formulas that Include Names."*

Extra

When you have a large number of named ranges and constants in your workbook, you may find it difficult to keep track of them all. Excel provides a feature that quickly creates a list of all names and the corresponding cell ranges. To create the list, press F3. The Paste Name dialog box appears. Click the Paste List button. Excel creates a list with the first column containing the range names, and the second column identifying the corresponding cell ranges. For example, if cells B2 through B10 contain your advertising expenses, Excel pastes values similar to the following:

```
Advertising    =Sheet1!$B$2:$B$10
```

The range reference simply identifies the cells within the named range. Excel first lists the name of the worksheet containing the range and then the cells within the range.

Excel places the list in your active worksheet, starting in the cell in which your cursor is located. Before creating your list, place your cursor in a blank cell with plenty of blank cells below it. Excel does not create a link to the list, so to keep your list up-to-date, you must re-create it whenever you change the named ranges.

Create Formulas that Include Names

onstructing formulas can be complicated, especially when you use several functions in the same formula or when multiple arguments are required in a single function. Using named constants and named ranges can make creating formulas and using functions easier by enabling you to use terms you have created that clearly identify a value or range of values.

An *argument* is information you provide to the function so the function can do its work. A *named constant* is a name you create that refers to a single, frequently used value. See the previous task, "Define and Display Constants," for more information. A named range is a name you assign to a group of related cells. See the task "Name Cells and Ranges," earlier in this chapter, for more information. To insert a name into a function or use it in a formula or as a

function's argument, you must type it, access it by using Use in Formula on the Formulas tab, or select it from the Function AutoComplete list.

When you name a range, the name must be unique within its scope. When you define the same range name globally and/or for multiple worksheets, by default Excel uses the definition you created for the active worksheet. If you want to use the global definition, you must precede the name with the workbook name followed by an exclamation point (!); for example, `WorkBookName!RangeName`. If you want to use a definition created for another worksheet, you must precede the name with the worksheet name followed by an exclamation point (!); for example, `WorkSheetName!ConstantName`.

Create Formulas that Include Names

USE A CONSTANT OR RANGE NAME IN A FORMULA

1 Place the cursor in the formula.

2 Type the name of the constant or range.

As you type, a list of possible values appears. Double-click a value to place it in the formula.

3 Press Enter.

● The cell displays the result.

USE A CONSTANT OR RANGE NAME IN A FORMULA

Note: Use this technique if you forget the name of a constant or range.

① Begin typing your formula.

② Click the Formulas tab.

③ Click Use in Formula in the Defined Names group.

A menu appears.

④ Click the constant or range name you want to use.

If necessary, continue typing your formula.

⑤ Press Enter.

● Excel feeds the selected constant or range name into the formula, which then displays a result based on it.

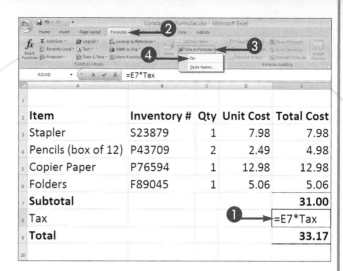

Check Formulas for Errors

When you create formulas, you can nest a formula within another formula. Because there are so many intermediate steps when you nest formulas, determining the accuracy of your results may be difficult. You can use the Evaluate Formula dialog box to check the result of intermediate calculations to determine if your result is correct.

When you open the Evaluate Formula dialog box, you see your formula. The Evaluate Formula dialog box steps you through the calculation one expression at a time so you can see how Excel evaluates each argument. Click the Evaluate button to begin the process. When your formula includes a function, Excels solves for each argument in the function, and then solves the rest of the formula. Excel underlines individual expressions. You can click the Evaluate button to see the results of an expression. The results of expressions appear in italics.

If you based the reference on another formula, you can click the Step In button to display the formula. Click the Step Out button to return to the reference. When you have stepped through the entire formula, Excel displays the result and a Restart button. Click the Restart button to evaluate your expression again.

You cannot modify your formula while you are in the Evaluate Formula dialog box. If you find a mistake and you want to change to your formula, exit the Evaluate Formula dialog box to make the change.

If you want to examine all of the formulas in your worksheet, click the Show Formulas button in the Formula Auditing group of the Formulas tab. To return to displaying results, click the Show Formulas button again.

Check Formulas for Errors

1 Click the cell that contains the formula.

2 Click the Formulas tab.

3 Click the Evaluate Formula button in the Formula Auditing group.

The Evaluate Formula dialog box appears.

4 Click Evaluate.

● Excels displays the results of the evaluation.

5 Continue clicking Evaluate to review each expression.

6 Click Step In to review the detail of an expression.

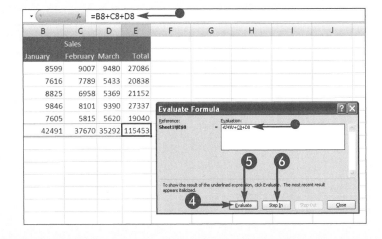

⑦ Click Step Out to return to the expression.

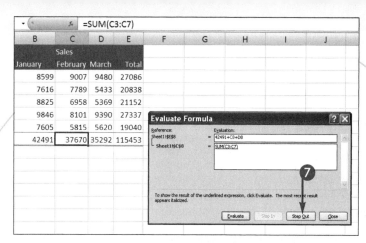

● When Excel reaches the end of the formula, it displays the results.

⑧ Click Restart to evaluate the formula again.

⑨ Click Close to close the dialog box.

Excel closes the dialog box.

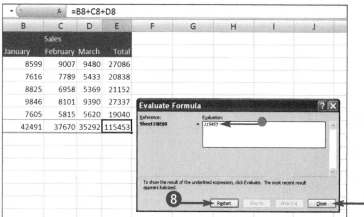

Trace Precedents and Dependents

When you create a formula, Excel evaluates all the values in the formula and returns a result. If Excel cannot calculate the formula, it displays an error message in the formula cell. You can use the Excel trace features to help you locate your error.

Typically, an error occurs when your formula refers to an invalid cell value. For example, if the cell contains the formula =A1/A2 and cell A2 contains the number 0, Excel returns the error message #DIV/0!, which indicates that the formula attempted to divide by zero.

You can view a graphical representation of the cells a formula refers to by clicking the cell and then clicking Trace Precedents in the Formula Auditing group on the Formulas tab. This option draws blue arrows to each cell referenced in the formula. By selecting this option, you can identify the exact cells used in your formula.

If you want to find out which formulas use a specific cell, you can view a graphical representation by clicking in the cell and then clicking Trace Dependents in the Formula Auditing group on the Formulas tab. This option draws blue arrows to each cell that contains a formula that uses the active cell as an argument. By displaying the dependent cells for a formula, you can visually identify the cells that require the formula. If you perform this option before deleting a value, you can quickly determine if your deletion will affect any formula on your worksheet.

You can remove arrows Excel draws to dependents or precedents by clicking Remove Arrows in the Formula Auditing group on the Formulas tab.

Trace Precedents and Dependents

TRACE PRECEDENTS

① Click the cell containing the formula for which you want to trace precedents.

● If the cell has an error, an Error icon displays next to the formula.

② Click the Formulas tab.

③ Click Trace Precedents in the Formula Auditing group.

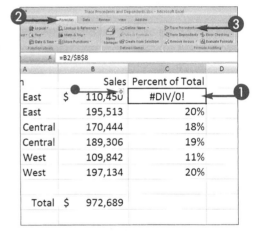

● Excel draws arrows between the cells on which the formula is based and the formula's cell.

④ Make the appropriate modifications to the correct the error in the formula.

⑤ Click Remove Arrows.

Excel removes the arrows.

Note: Click the down arrow next to Remove Arrows to choose from Remove Arrow, Remove Precedent Arrows, or Remove Dependent Arrows.

TRACE DEPENDENTS

① Click the cell for which you want to trace dependents.

② Click the Formulas tab.

③ Click Trace Dependents in the Formula Auditing group.

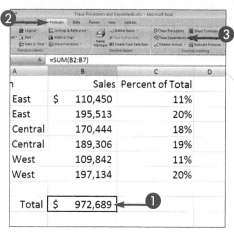

● Excel draws arrows between the formula's cell and the dependent cells.

④ Click Remove Arrows.

Excel removes the arrows.

Note: Click the down arrow next to Remove Arrows to choose from Remove Arrow, Remove Precedent Arrows, or Remove Dependent Arrows.

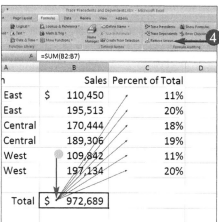

Extra

The following table lists the formula error messages.

ERROR	DESCRIPTION
#####	Either the column is not wide enough to display the result, or an argument contains a negative date or time value.
#VALUE!	An argument contains the wrong type of value; for example, an attempt to add cells containing text.
#DIV/0	Excel attempted to divide a number by zero.
#NAME?	Excel does not recognize the name of a function or range. This typically occurs when you misspell a function name.
#N/A	A specified cell reference is not available to the formula.
#REF!	A cell reference is not valid.
#NUM!	Formula contains invalid numeric values. This can occur when a number contains a character, such as a dollar sign, as a value in a formula.
#NULL!	The cell ranges do not intersect.

Understanding the Function Wizard

Excel's Function Wizard simplifies the use of functions. You can take advantage of the wizard for every one of Excel's functions, from the SUM function to the most complex statistical, mathematical, financial, or engineering function.

You can access the Function Wizard two ways. One way involves selecting the cell where the result is to appear, clicking the Insert Function button (fx), and using the Insert Function dialog box to find a function. The Insert Function dialog box provides you with two methods you can use to find the function you want. You can type a description of the function in the Search for a Function field and then click Go. Excel retrieves all of the relevant functions and lists them in the Select a Function field. You can also use the Or Select a Category field to select

the category in which your function falls. When you do, Excel lists all the functions in that category in the Select a Function field. You double-click to select the function you want.

Another way to access the Function Wizard, which is a bit quicker, makes sense when you know the name of your function. Start by selecting a cell for the result. Type an equal sign and the beginning of the function name. In the list of functions that appears, double-click the function you want and then click the Insert Function button.

Both methods bring up the Function Arguments dialog box, where you can type the values you want to use in your calculation, type the range that contains the values, or click the cells containing the values you want.

Understanding the Function Wizard

① Type your data into your worksheet.

② Click the cell in which you want the results to appear.

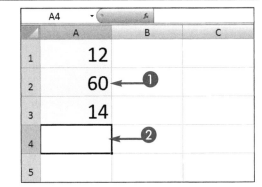

③ Click the Insert Function button.

● The Insert Function dialog box appears.

④ Click here and select All to list all functions.

⑤ Double-click the function you want to use.

Note: *This example demonstrates the* SUM *function.*

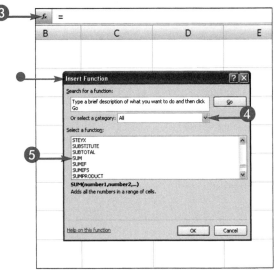

The Function Arguments dialog box appears.

6 Click the cell(s) or type the values requested in each field.

7 Click OK.

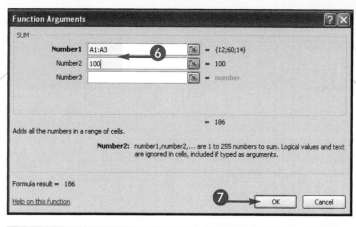

● The results appear in the cell you selected in Step 2.

Extra

When you select a function in the Select a Function field of the Function Arguments dialog box, a brief explanation of the function appears below the field. If you need more information, click Help on This Function. Excel will take you directly to a help screen with detailed information on how the function works. Excel also provides an example, which you can copy and paste into your worksheet.

The more than 300 functions built into Excel enable you to perform tasks of every kind, from adding numbers to calculating the internal rate of return for an investment. You can think of a function as a black box. You put your information into the box, and out come the results you want. You do not need to know any obscure algorithms to use functions. Excel calls each bit of information an argument, and its Function Wizard provides guidance for every argument for every function.

Round a Number

Frequently, when you are creating a worksheet you will need to round numbers. Excel has several functions to aid you. The most commonly used one is the ROUND function. This function rounds to the number of digits you specify. It takes two arguments: Number, the number you want to round, and Num_digits, the number of digits to which you want to round your number. If Num_digits is 1 or higher, Excel rounds to the number of decimal places you specify. If Num_digits is 0, Excel rounds to the nearest integer. If Num_digits is –1 or lower, Excel rounds to the number of digits you specify that are to the left of the decimal point. The function =ROUND(3512.5847,2) rounds to 3512.58, the function =ROUND(3512.5847,0) rounds to 3513, and the function =ROUND(3512.5847,-2) rounds to 3500.

When you use the ROUND function, if the digit you are rounding to is 5 or higher, Excel rounds up. If the digit is 4 or lower, Excel rounds down. If you only want Excel to round up, use the ROUNDUP function. If you only want Excel to round down, use the ROUNDDOWN function. Both ROUNDUP and ROUNDDOWN take the same two arguments as ROUND: Number and Num_digits.

Do not confuse rounding with number formatting. Rounding works by evaluating a number in an argument and rounding it to the number of digits you specify. When you format numbers, you simplify the appearance of numbers in the worksheet, making them easier to read. The underlying numbers do not change.

Round a Number

1 Type the number you want to round into your worksheet.

2 Click the cell in which you want the result to appear.

3 Click the Insert Function button.

The Insert Function dialog box appears.

4 Click here and select All to list all the functions.

5 Double-click ROUND.

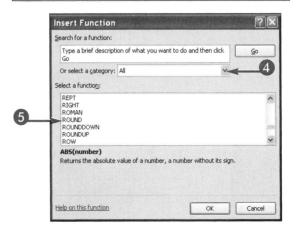

The Function Arguments dialog box appears.

⑥ Click the cell that contains the number you want to round or type the cell address.

Alternatively, if the number is not in a cell, you can type the number into the Number field.

⑦ Type the number of decimal places to which you want to round.

A negative number rounds to the left of the decimal point. A 0 rounds to the integer. A positive number rounds to the number of decimal places specified.

⑧ Click OK.

● The result appears in the cell.

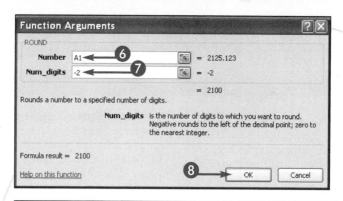

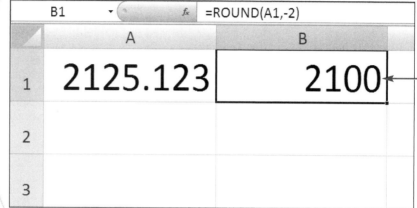

Extra

The following functions relate to the rounding.

FUNCTION	DESCRIPTION
INT	Rounds down to the nearest integer. The INT function takes one argument: the number you want to round. The formula =INT(7.9) rounds the number 7.9 down to 7. The formula =INT(-7.9) rounds the number -7.9 down to -8, the next lowest integer.
TRUNC	Truncates to the number of digits you specify. The TRUNC function takes two arguments: Number, the number you want to truncate, and Num_digits, the number of digits to which you want to truncate your number. The formula =TRUNC(7.9,0) truncates the number 7.9 to 7. The formula TRUNC(-7.9,0) truncates to number -7.9 to -7. The TRUNC function differs from the INT function in that when you are working with negative numbers, the TRUNC function does not round down.

Determine the Nth Largest Value

Sometimes you want to identify and characterize the top values in a series, such as the Runs Batted In (RBIs) of the top three hitters in major-league baseball or the average purchases, in a given period, for your five largest customers.

The LARGE function evaluates a series of numbers and determines the highest value, second highest, or Nth highest in the series, with N being a value's rank order. LARGE takes two arguments: Array, the range of cells you want to evaluate, and K, the rank order of the value you are seeking, with 1 being the highest, 2 the next highest, and so on. The result of the LARGE function is the value you requested.

Another way to determine the first, second, or following number in a series is to sort the numbers from largest to smallest and then simply read the results, as shown in Chapter 6. This technique is less useful when you have a long list or when you want to use the result in another function, such as summing the top five values.

Other useful functions work in a similar manner to the LARGE function. SMALL evaluates a range of values and returns the smallest value, second smallest, or Nth smallest in a series. SMALL also takes two arguments: Array, the range of cells you want to evaluate, and K, the rank order of the value you are seeking, with 1 being the lowest, 2 the next lowest, and so on. For example, if you enter 1 as the K value, it returns the lowest number, 2 for next lowest, and so on. The MIN and MAX functions return the lowest and highest values in a series, respectively. They take one argument: a range of cell values.

Determine the Nth Largest Value

① Type the values from which you want to identify the highest number, or second highest, or other value.

② Click the cell in which you want the results to appear.

③ Click the Insert Function button.

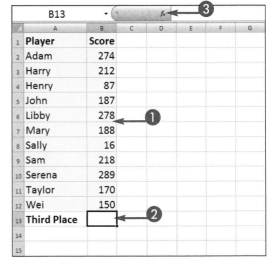

The Insert Function dialog box appears.

④ Click here and select Statistical.

⑤ Double-click LARGE.

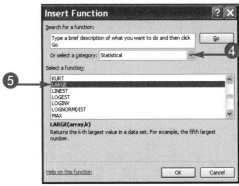

The Function Arguments dialog box for the LARGE function appears.

⑥ Click and drag to select the cells you want to evaluate or type the range.

⑦ Type a number indicating what you are seeking (1 for highest, 2 for second highest, 3 for third highest, and so on).

⑧ Click OK.

● The cell displays the value you requested.

If K in Step 7 is greater than the number of cells, a #NUM error appears in the cell instead.

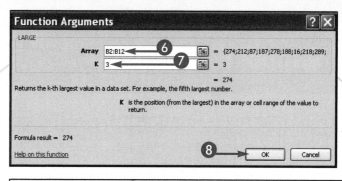

	B13	▾		fx	=LARGE(B2:B12,3)

	A	B	C	D	E	F	G	H
1	**Player**	**Score**						
2	Adam	274						
3	Harry	212						
4	Henry	87						
5	John	187						
6	Libby	278						
7	Mary	188						
8	Sally	16						
9	Sam	218						
10	Serena	289						
11	Taylor	170						
12	Wei	150						
13	**Third Place**	274						
14								

Extra

If you have a number and you want to determine how it ranks in relationship to a list of numbers, use the RANK function. The RANK function takes three arguments: Number, a number for which you want to find its rank in a list; Ref, the list of numbers; and Order, a number specifying whether you want to rank from highest to lowest or lowest to highest. Use the number 0 or leave the Order option blank if you want to rank from highest to lowest. Use the number 1 or any number greater than 1 if you want to rank the order from lowest to highest.

If the numbers 11, 51, 6, 46, 35, 4, 10, 32, 88, and 42 are in cells B2 to B11 respectively, the formula =RANK(11,B2:B11,0) returns the number 7. This is because Excel orders the numbers as follows: 88, 51, 46, 42, 35, 32, 11, 10, 6, 4, and the number 11, the number for which you are seeking the rank, is in the seventh position. The formula =RANK(11,B2:B11,1) returns the number 4. Excel ranks the numbers from lowest to highest. The number 11 is in the fourth lowest position.

Create a
Conditional Formula

With a conditional formula, you can perform calculations on numbers that meet a condition. For example, you can find the highest score for a particular team from a list that consists of more than one team. You can create a formula that only evaluates the scores for players on Team 1.

A conditional formula often uses two functions. The first function, IF, defines the condition, or test, such as players on Team 1. To create the condition, you use a comparison operator, such as greater than (>), less than (<), greater than or equal to (>=), less than or equal to (<=), or equal to (=). The second function in a conditional formula performs a calculation on numbers that meet the condition. Excel carries out the IF function

first and then calculates the values that meet the condition defined in the IF function.

IF is an array function. It compares every number in a series to a condition and keeps track of the numbers that meet the condition. To create an array function, you press Ctrl+Shift+Enter instead of pressing the Enter key or clicking OK to complete your function when using the Function Arguments dialog box. You must surround arrays with curly braces ({ }). Excel enters the curly braces automatically when you press Ctrl+Shift+Enter but not when you press Enter or OK.

IF has an optional third argument. Use the third argument when you want to specify what happens when the condition is not met.

Create a Conditional Formula

1 Type your data into your worksheet.

2 Click the cell in which you want your results to appear.

3 Click the Insert Function button.

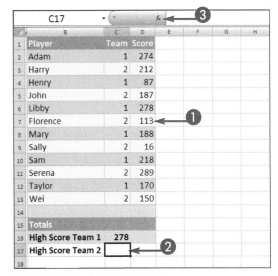

The Insert Function dialog box appears.

4 Click here and select All.

5 Double-click the function on which you want to base your conditional function.

Note: *This example uses* MAX, *which finds the highest value in a list.*

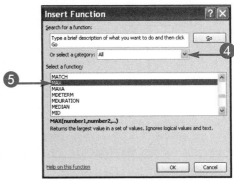

48

The Function Arguments dialog box appears.

6 Type **IF(**.

7 Type the range or range name for the series you want to evaluate.

Note: See Chapter 2 to learn more about naming ranges.

8 Type a comparison operator, the condition, and then a comma.

9 Type the range or range name for the series that you want to calculate.

10 Type **)**.

11 Press Ctrl+Shift+Enter.

● The result appears in the cell with the formula.

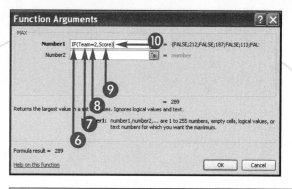

	B	C	D	E	F	G	H	I
1	Player	Team	Score					
2	Adam	1	274					
3	Harry	2	212					
4	Henry	1	87					
5	John	2	187					
6	Libby	1	278					
7	Florence	2	113					
8	Mary	1	188					
9	Sally	2	16					
10	Sam	1	218					
11	Serena	2	289					
12	Taylor	1	170					
13	Wei	2	150					
14								
15	Totals							
16	High Score Team 1	278						
17	High Score Team 2	289						
18								

C17 ▼ fₓ {=MAX(IF(Team=2,Score))}

Apply It

You can use the IF function to execute one command if a condition is true and another command if a condition is false. For example, you can use the formula that follows to create a function that calculates bonuses. If a salesperson's sales are equal to or greater than $100,000, the formula calculates a bonus of 10 percent; otherwise, it calculates a bonus of 5 percent. The cell B2 contains the salesperson's sales.

```
=IF(B2>=100000,B2*.1,B2*.05)
```

In this case, the IF function take three arguments: Logical_test, the condition for which you are testing; Value_if_true, the operation you want to perform if the cell being analyzed meets the condition; and Value_if_false, the operation you want to perform if the cell being analyzed does not meet the condition. The statement B2>=100000 is the Logical_test argument. The statement B2*.10 is the Value_if_true argument. It calculates a bonus of 10 percent. The statement B2*.05 is the Value_if_false argument. It calculates and bonus of 5 percent.

Calculate a Conditional Sum

You can use conditional sums to identify and sum investments whose growth exceeds a certain rate or to identify values that meet some other condition and sum them. The SUMIF function combines the SUM and IF functions into one easy-to-use function.

SUMIF is simple, when compared to a formula that uses both SUM and IF. SUMIF enables you to avoid complicated nesting and to use the Function Wizard without making one function an argument of the other. However, using two functions (SUM and IF) gives you more flexibility. For example, you can use IF to create multiple complex conditions.

SUMIF takes three arguments: Range, a range of values; Criteria, the condition you want to apply to the values; and Sum_range, the range to which the condition applies. Excel adds the values that meet the condition together.

For example, you can create a function that evaluates a list to determine the team a person is on, and for all persons on Team 1, it can add the scores. The third argument, the range to which the condition applies, is optional. If you exclude it, Excel sums the range you specify in the first argument.

You can apply conditions to numbers or text. For example, you can sum all scores where the team is equal to 1, or you can sum all scores where the team is equal to Team One, "Team One".

The COUNTIF function works like SUMIF. It combines two functions (COUNT and IF) and takes two arguments: Range, a series of values; and Criteria, the condition by which Excel tests the values. Whereas SUMIF sums the values, COUNTIF returns the number of items that passed the test.

Calculate a Conditional Sum

① Create a list of values to sum conditionally.

Note: Excel tests each value to see whether it meets a condition. If it does, Excel adds it to the other values that meet the condition.

② Click the cell in which you want the results to appear.

③ Click the Insert Function button.

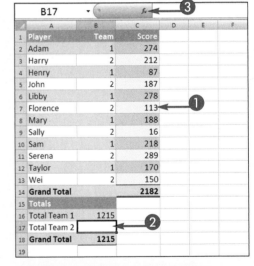

The Insert Function dialog box appears.

④ Click here and select All.

⑤ Double-click SUMIF.

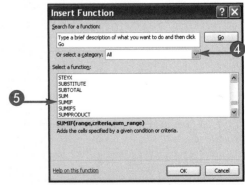

The Function Arguments dialog box appears.

6 Click and drag to select the range or type the range name for the series you want to evaluate.

7 Type a comparison operator and a condition.

8 Click and drag to select the range or type the range name you want to sum if your condition is met.

9 Click OK.

● The result appears in the cell with the formula.

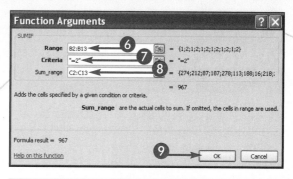

	A	B	C	D	E	F	G	H	I
								B17	▾		fx =SUMIF(B2:B13,"=2",C2:C13)

	A	B	C	D	E	F	G	H	I
1	Player	Team	Score						
2	Adam	1	274						
3	Harry	2	212						
4	Henry	1	87						
5	John	2	187						
6	Libby	1	278						
7	Florence	2	113						
8	Mary	1	188						
9	Sally	2	16						
10	Sam	1	218						
11	Serena	2	289						
12	Taylor	1	170						
13	Wei	2	150						
14	**Grand Total**		**2182**						
15	**Totals**								
16	Total Team 1	1215							
17	Total Team 2	967							
18	**Grand Total**		**2182**						
19									

Extra

In the example, if the team names were text — ''Team One'' and ''Team Two'' — you would use the following formula to add the scores for all the players on Team One: =SUMIF(B2:B13,"Team One",C2:C13). See Sheet2 of the example file Conditional Sum.xlsx for a demonstration.

You can use the question mark (?) and asterisk (*) wildcards when creating your condition. A ? will match a single character, and an * will match any series of characters. For example, 123?98 will match any value that starts with 123, ends with 98, such as 123X98, 123-98, or 123A98. *son will match any value that ends with son, such as Jackson or Johnson.

You can use the Conditional Sum Wizard, an Excel add-in. The Conditional Sum Wizard has four self-explanatory steps. The last step diverges from the SUMIF Function Wizard in that both the condition and the result appear on your worksheet. You can thus display conditions and results side by side to compare them.

Calculate Products and Square Roots

Many Excel users are familiar with the basic operations that are available when they click the AutoSum button: addition, subtraction, minimum, maximum, and count. Fewer are familiar with two other basic operations that are available when they use a mathematical function. By using the PRODUCT function, you can multiply two or more numbers. By using the SQRT function, you can find the square root of a number.

You can use PRODUCT or SQRT by entering the values you want to use in the function into your worksheet. If you do not want the values to appear in the worksheet, start by clicking the cell where the result is to appear and typing an equal sign, the function name (PRODUCT or SQRT), and an open parenthesis. Click the Insert Function button to enter the formula values.

Excel can only calculate the square roots of positive numbers. If a negative number is the argument, as in SQRT(-9) Excel returns #NUM in the cell. If you want to calculate the positive square root of a negative number, find the absolute value of the number first by using the ABS function. The ABS function returns a number without its sign. The following formula would return 3, the positive square root of –9: =SQRT(ABS(-9)).

Each argument in the PRODUCT function can have more than one value. An argument can be a number, a cell range, or an array. In Excel, an array is a series of values enclosed in curly braces; for example, {2, 3, 4}. Excel multiplies each value in the array; the product of {2, 3, 4} is 24. Excel also multiplies each value in a cell range.

Calculate Products and Square Roots

CALCULATE A PRODUCT

① Type the values to multiply.

② Click where you want the result to appear.

③ Type **=PRODUCT(** in the cell.

Note: *Typing the function directly into a cell or into the formula bar preceded by an equal sign is an alternative to choosing it from the Function Wizard.*

④ Click the Insert Function button.

⑤ In the Function Arguments dialog box, type the range or click and drag the cells you want to multiply.

Note: *Optionally, you can type values directly into the Number1 field.*

⑥ Type the value you want to multiply by directly into the Number2 field.

Note: *Optionally, you can click and drag the cells or type the range.*

● Excel multiplies each value in the range. The interim answer appears here.

⑦ Click OK.

● The product appears in the cell you clicked in Step 2. In this example, 2 * 3 * 4 = 24 and 24 * 2 = 48.

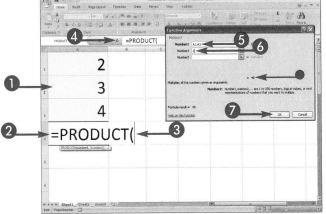

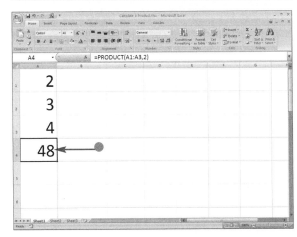

CALCULATE A SQUARE ROOT

① Click the cell in which you want the result to appear.

② Type **=SQRT(** in the formula bar or in the cell in which you want the result to appear.

As you begin to type, the Function AutoComplete list appears. Double-click an option to select it.

③ Click the Insert Function button.

● The Function Arguments dialog box appears.

④ Type the value for which you want the square root.

Note: *Optionally, you can click a cell containing the value.*

● Notice that the Function Arguments dialog box displays the interim answer.

⑤ Click OK.

● The square root appears in the cell.

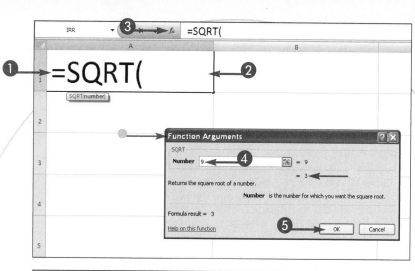

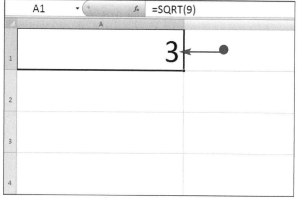

Apply It

Related to PRODUCT and SQRT is POWER. To find the power of any number, such as 3 to the second power, use the POWER function. The POWER function takes two arguments: the number you want to raise to a power and the power to which you want to raise it. The formula =POWER(3,2) raises the number 3 to the second power, yielding the number 9.

The PRODUCT function can take up to 255 arguments. Each argument can consist of a number, range, or array of numbers you want to multiply. TRUE and FALSE are logical values. In Excel, TRUE is equal to 1 and FALSE is equal to 0. You can also use TRUE and FALSE as arguments in the PRODUCT function.

FORMULA	RESULT
=PRODUCT({2,3,4},2)	48
=PRODUCT(2,3,TRUE)	6
=PRODUCT(2,3,FALSE)	0

Look Up
Information

VLOOKUP searches the first column in your list, and when it finds the value that you are looking for, it returns another value in the same row. For example, you have a list, and in the first column, there are names; in the second column, there are addresses; and in the third column, there are phone numbers. You have a name and you want to find the phone number. VLOOKUP can search for the name and return the phone number.

The first column of your list must contain the values you want to use to retrieve another value and you must sort the first column in ascending order. In the VLOOKUP function, you specify the column from which you want to retrieve the corresponding value.

You can use the Function Wizard to enter your VLOOKUP arguments. You must enter three required arguments: Lookup_value, the value or the cell address containing the value you want to use to retrieve another value;

Table_array, the list's cell range; and Col_index_num, the column that contains the value you want to retrieve. For simplicity, call the first column in the list 1, the second column 2, and so on.

The VLOOKUP function has an optional fourth argument called Range_lookup. If you enter TRUE or leave the argument blank, the function looks for the closest match to the value you seek. If you enter FALSE, the function returns exact matches only.

If you are searching text data, make sure the column you are searching does not contain any leading spaces, trailing spaces, inconsistent use of curly and straight quotation marks, or nonprinting characters. These situations can cause VLOOKUP to bring back an incorrect result. For the same reason, if you are searching dates, make sure you format your dates as dates and not text.

Look Up Information

1 Type the value you want to use to retrieve another value.

2 In an adjacent cell, type **=VLOOKUP(**.

As you begin to type, the Function AutoComplete list appears. Double-click an option to select it.

3 Click the Insert Function button.

The Function Arguments dialog box appears.

4 Click the cell with the value you entered in Step 1.

5 Click and drag to select all the values in your list or type a cell range.

6 Type the number of the column containing the value you want to retrieve.

7 Click OK.

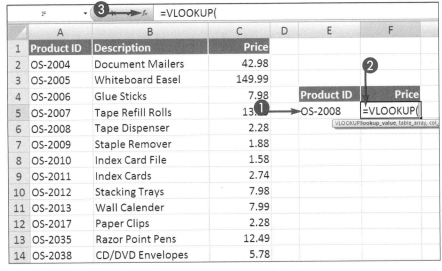

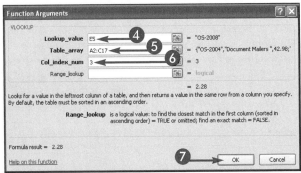

● The cell containing the formula displays the value corresponding to the lookup value.

	E5	▾	⨍	OS-2008		
	A	B	C	D	E	F
1	Product ID	Description	Price			
2	OS-2004	Document Mailers	42.98			
3	OS-2005	Whiteboard Easel	149.99			
4	OS-2006	Glue Sticks	7.98		Product ID	Price
5	OS-2007	Tape Refill Rolls	13.99		OS-2008	2.28
6	OS-2008	Tape Dispenser	2.28			
7	OS-2009	Staple Remover	1.88			
8	OS-2010	Index Card File	1.58			
9	OS-2011	Index Cards	2.74			
10	OS-2012	Stacking Trays	7.98			
11	OS-2013	Wall Calender	7.99			
12	OS-2017	Paper Clips	2.28			
13	OS-2035	Razor Point Pens	12.49			

⑧ Type another lookup value.

● The cell containing the formula displays the value corresponding to the lookup value.

	F5	▾	⨍	=VLOOKUP(E5,A2:C17,3)		
	A	B	C	D	E	F
1	Product ID	Description	Price			
2	OS-2004	Document Mailers	42.98			
3	OS-2005	Whiteboard Easel	149.99			
4	OS-2006	Glue Sticks	7.98		Product ID	Price
5	OS-2007	Tape Refill Rolls	13.99		OS-2011	$2.74
6	OS-2008	Tape Dispenser	2.28			
7	OS-2009	Staple Remover	1.88			
8	OS-2010	Index Card File	1.58			
9	OS-2011	Index Cards	2.74			
10	OS-2012	Stacking Trays	7.98			
11	OS-2013	Wall Calendar	7.99			
12	OS-2017	Paper Clips	2.28			
13	OS-2035	Razor Point Pens	12.49			

Extra

HLOOKUP is the opposite of VLOOKUP. It searches for a value in a row and returns a value in the same column. For example, you may have names, addresses, and telephone numbers. Your names are listed across the first row, your addresses are listed across the second row, and your phone numbers are listed across the third row. HLOOKUP scans the first row to find the name. Then it returns the related phone number.

Like VLOOKUP, HLOOKUP takes four arguments: Lookup_value, the cell address containing the value you want to use to retrieve another value; Table_Array, the table's cell range; Row_index_number, the row that contains the value you want to retrieve; and the Range_lookup value. If the Range_lookup value is set to true, the values in the first row of your table must be in ascending order. Setting the Range_lookup value to true tells Excel you want to return approximate matches. With HLOOKUP, the first row of your table must contain the values you want to use to retrieve another value. When specifying the row that contains the value you want to retrieve, call the first row in your table 1, the second row 2, and so on.

Determine the Location of a Value

To determine the location of a value within a row or column of your worksheet, you can use the MATCH function. For example, if you have a list and you want to find where in the list information for a particular salesperson is located, you can use the MATCH function.

The MATCH function takes three arguments: Lookup_value, Lookup_array, and Match_type. The Lookup_value is the value you want to find. The Lookup_array is the cell range against which you want to match. The Match_type is a number that tells Excel how to match values from the Lookup_value argument to the Lookup_array argument.

The Match_type argument is optional. If you omit the argument, or you enter a value of 1, Excel finds the largest value that is less than or equal to the

Lookup_value. If you enter 0, Excel finds an exact match. If you enter –1, Excel returns the smallest value that is greater than or equal to the Lookup_value. If you omit the Match_type or enter a Match_type of 1, you must sort the Lookup_array in ascending order by the lookup value. If you enter a Match_type of 0, the Lookup_array can be in any order. If you enter a Match_type of –1, you must sort the Lookup_array in descending order by the Lookup_value. See Chapter 6 for more on sorting your data.

The MATCH function returns an integer value that identifies the location of the value within the specified range of cells. For example, if Excel returns the value 2 and the specified range of cells in A4 through A24, cell A5 contains the value, or the closest match.

Determine the Location of a Value

1 Create your list of data.

This example locates an exact match. To find the closest match, you must sort the list in ascending or descending order.

Note: See Chapter 6 for more information on sorting your data.

2 Type the value for which you want to retrieve the location.

3 Click the cell in which you want your results to appear.

4 Click the Insert Function button.

The Insert Function dialog box appears.

5 Click here and select all.

6 Double-click MATCH.

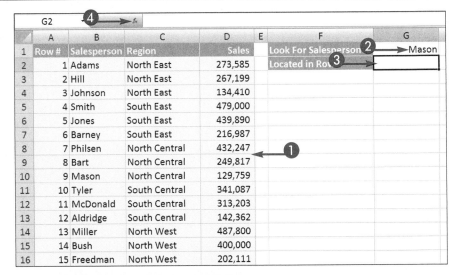

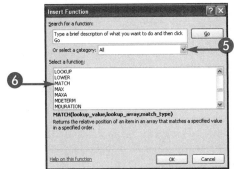

The Function Arguments dialog box appears.

7 Click the cell that contains the value you want to look up or type the cell address.

8 Click and drag to select the column you want to search.

● Optionally, type 0 to find an exact match, 1 to find the largest value less than the one you specified, or −1 to find the smallest value greater than the one you specified.

9 Click OK.

● Excel returns the row location of the value you entered in Step 2.

Type a new value to retrieve a new row location.

The row location is relative to the top of the Lookup_array. The first row of the Lookup_array is 1, the second row is 2, and so on.

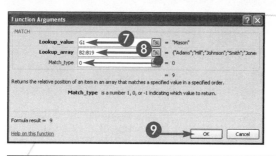

Function Arguments

MATCH
Lookup_value	G1		=	"Mason"
Lookup_array	B2:B19		=	{"Adams";"Hill";"Johnson";"Smith";"Jone
Match_type	0		=	0

= 9

Returns the relative position of an item in an array that matches a specified value in a specified order.

Match_type is a number 1, 0, or -1 indicating which value to return.

Formula result = 9

Help on this function   OK   Cancel

G2   =MATCH(G1,B2:B19,0)

	A	B	C	D	E	F	G
1	Row #	Salesperson	Region	Sales		Look For Salesperson =	Mason
2	1	Adams	North East	273,585		Located in Row #	9
3	2	Hill	North East	267,199			
4	3	Johnson	North East	134,410			
5	4	Smith	South East	479,000			
6	5	Jones	South East	439,890			
7	6	Barney	South East	216,987			
8	7	Philsen	North Central	432,247			
9	8	Bart	North Central	249,817			
10	9	Mason	North Central	129,759			
11	10	Tyler	South Central	341,087			
12	11	McDonald	South Central	313,203			
13	12	Aldridge	South Central	142,362			
14	13	Miller	North West	487,800			
15	14	Bush	North West	400,000			
16	15	Freedman	North West	202,111			

Apply It

The MATCH function retrieves the relative position of the value for which you are looking. If you want to retrieve the actual value, use the INDEX function in conjunction with MATCH. The INDEX function has two forms. In this example, we use the Array form. The Array form takes three arguments: Array, the list of values from which you want to retrieve a value; Row_num, the position of the row you want to retrieve if you list values down a column; and Col_num, the position of the column you want to retrieve if you list your values across a row.

In the following formula, =INDEX(D2:D19,G2), D2:D19 represents the range that contains the values from which you want to retrieve a value. Cell G2 contains the row number of the value you want to retrieve. The MATCH function retrieved the value in cell G2. If you include Row_num in your function, Col_num is optional and vice versa. For a demonstration of the INDEX function, refer to the file Match.xlsx Sheet2, which you can download from the Web page for this book.

Perform Time Calculations

Using Excel formulas and functions, you can perform calculations with dates and times. You can find, for example, the number of hours worked between two times or the number of days between two dates. Date and time functions convert every date and time into a serial value that Excel can add and subtract and then convert back into a recognizable date or time.

Excel calculates a date's serial value as the number of days after January 1, 1900, and represents each date with a whole number. Excel calculates a time's serial value in units of 1/60th of a second. Each time can be represented as a serial value between 0 and 1.

A date and time, such as January 1, 2000, at noon, consists of the date to the left of the decimal and a time to the right. Take the example August 25, 2005, at 5:46 p.m. The date and time serial value is 38589.74028.

Subtracting one date or time from another involves subtracting one serial value from another and then converting the result back into a date or time. Showing a time or date in the General format displays its serial value. Use a Time or Date format to display a recognizable date or time. To display a time in hour:minute format, right-click the cell that contains the time, click Format Cell, click Time, and then click the 13:30 format.

When subtracting times that cross midnight, such as 11 p.m. to 2 a.m., you need a programming function called modulus, or MOD. The formula is =MOD(later time - earlier time, 1). If subtracting times or dates yields a negative time or date, Excel displays a series of pound signs (######).

Perform Time Calculations

FIND THE DIFFERENCE BETWEEN TWO TIMES

① Type the first time in a cell.

Note: If you do not include AM or PM, Excel defaults to a.m. If you want p.m., you must type PM.

② Type the second time in a cell.

③ Click the cell in which you want the results to appear.

④ Type an equal sign (=).

⑤ Click the cell with the later time.

⑥ Type a minus sign (−).

⑦ Click the cell with the earlier time.

⑧ Press Enter.

	A	B	C
1	Departure Time	Arrival Time	Travel Time (hours: mins)
2	2:20 AM	11:15 PM	
3	6:35 AM	7:45 AM	1:10
4	10:22 AM	12:30 PM	2:08
5	11:55 AM	4:26 PM	4:31
6	11:30 PM	3:00 AM	3:30
7			
8			

	A	B	C
1	Departure Time	Arrival Time	Travel Time (hours: mins)
2	2:20 AM	11:15 PM	= B2 - A2
3	6:35 AM	7:45 AM	1:10
4	10:22 AM	12:30 PM	2:08
5	11:55 AM	4:26 PM	4:31
6	11:30 PM	3:00 AM	3:30
7			
8			

	A	B	C
1	**Departure Time**	**Arrival Time**	**Travel Time (hours: mins)**
2	2:20 AM	11:15 PM	0.871527778
3	6:35 AM	7:45 AM	1:10
4	10:22 AM	12:30 PM	2:08
5	11:55 AM	4:26 PM	4:31
6	11:30 PM	3:00 AM	3:30
7			
8			

- The result may appear as a serial value.

CONVERT A SERIAL VALUE TO A TIME

1. Click the Home tab.

2. Click the Number group's dialog box launcher.

- The Format Cells dialog box appears.

3. Click the Number tab.

4. Click Time.

5. Click a format type.

   The 13:30 format displays hours:minutes.

6. Click OK.

- The cell displays the number of hours and minutes between the two times.

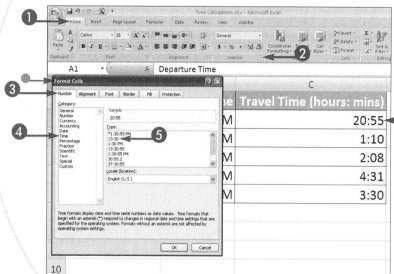

Extra

Excel has a number of functions you can use to format serial time values.

FUNCTION	DESCRIPTION
HOUR	Returns the hour portion of a time value. The HOUR function returns values from 0 to 23. The value 0 represents 12:00 a.m. The value 23 represents 11 p.m. You can enter text, a serial number, a cell address, or the results of a formula into the function.
MINUTE	Returns the minutes portion of a time value. The MINUTE function returns values from 0 to 59. You can enter text, a serial number, a cell address, or the results of a formula into the function.
SECOND	Returns the seconds portion of a time value. The SECOND function returns values from 0 to 59. You can enter text, a serial number, a cell address, or the results of a formula into the function.
TIME	Returns the serial value of a time. The TIME function takes three arguments: HOUR, MINUTE, and SECOND.

Perform Date Calculations

With Excel, finding the number of days between two dates is as simple as subtracting one date from another. For example, by using Excel's date calculation feature you can easily find the number of days between the date you start a project and the date you end it. You simply subtract the start date from the end date. If the start date is in cell A1 and the end date is in cell A2, the formula to calculate the number of days between the start date and the end date is =A2-A1. When performing date calculations, if your first date is later than your second date, Excel returns a negative number.

A special-purpose Date & Time function, NETWORKDAYS, enables you to find the number of workdays between two dates. Like other Excel functions, date and time functions make use of the Function Wizard. As with all functions, the wizard works with data you type into it, such as a specific date, or with data you type into cells.

To calculate the number of workdays between two dates, use the NETWORKDAYS function. The function's arguments include a start date, an end date, and optionally, any intervening holidays that automatically reduce the number of workdays between the two dates. Excel automatically deducts the number of weekend dates.

In Windows, Excel can perform date arithmetic on any date after January 1, 1900. If you use dates before then, Excel treats them as text and does not perform a calculation on them. Instead, it gives you a #VALUE! error.

Perform Date Calculations

FIND THE NUMBER OF WORK DAYS BETWEEN TWO DATES

1 Type the start date.

2 Type the end date.

• If you want the calculation to consider holidays, type the dates of holidays between the start and end dates.

3 Click the field in which you want the result to appear.

4 Click the Insert Function button.

The Insert Function dialog box appears.

5 Click here and select Date & Time.

6 Double-click NETWORKDAYS.

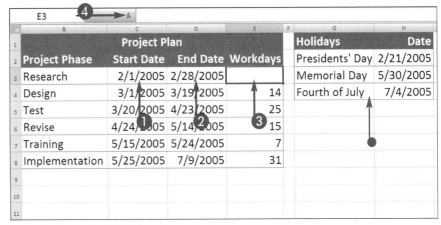

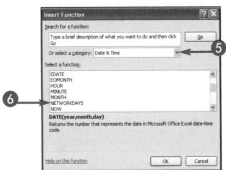

The Function Arguments dialog box appears.

⑦ Click the cell containing the start date or type the cell address.

⑧ Click the cell containing the end date or type the cell address.

● Optionally, click and drag the range of holidays or type the range.

⑨ Click OK.

● The cell with the formula displays the net workdays between the two dates.

FIND THE NUMBER OF DAYS BETWEEN TWO DATES

① Click the cell in which you want your results to appear.

② Type =.

③ Click the cell containing the end date or type the cell address.

④ Type –.

⑤ Click the cell containing the start date or type the cell address.

⑥ Press Enter.

● The results appear in the cell you clicked in Step 1.

Function Arguments

NETWORKDAYS

Start_date	C3 ⑦	= 38384
End_date	D3 ⑧	= 38411
Holidays	H2:H4	= {38404;38502;38537}
		= 19

Returns the number of whole workdays between two dates.

Holidays is an optional set of one or more serial date numbers to exclude from the working calendar, such as state and federal holidays and floating holidays.

Formula result = 19

Help on this function ⑨ → OK   Cancel

E11   fx   =D11-C11 ← ⑤

Project Plan			
Project Phase	**Start Date** ④③	**End Date**	**Workdays**
Research	2/1/2005	2/28/2005	19 ←
Design	3/1/2005	3/19/2005	14
Test	3/20/2005	4/23/2005	25
Revise	4/24/2005	5/14/2005	15
Training	5/15/2005	5/24/2005	7
Implementation	5/25/2005	7/9/2005	31
Project	**Start Date**	**End Date**	**Total Days**
	2/1/2005	7/9/2005	158 ←

Extra

When performing date arithmetic, if you need to type a date directly into a formula or function, use the DATE function. Excel may not calculate properly if you use text. The DATE function returns the date you specify. It takes three arguments: the year, the month, and the day, in that order. To subtract July 9, 2005, from February 1, 2005, and retrieve the result, 158, use the following formula:

=DATE(2005, 7, 9) – DATE(2005,2,1)

In Excel, you can enter the current date simply by clicking in the cell in which you want the date to appear and pressing the Ctrl and semicolon keys at the same time.

Typing =TODAY() returns the current date also. You can use the TODAY function to perform date arithmetic. Typing =TODAY() + 5 returns the date five days in the future. Typing =TODAY() – 5 returns the date five days in the past.

There are more than 15 ways you can format a date, including, August 1, 1956; Aug 1, 1956; 01-Aug-56; Wednesday, August, 1956; 8/1; and 8/1/56. To format a date, click the launcher in the Number group on the Home tab. Then in Category field on the Number tab, click Date.

Calculate Future Value

I f you have $1,000 and you plan to invest it at 10 percent interest, compounded annually for ten years, the amount you will receive at the end of ten years is called the future value (FV) of $1,000. You can use Excel's FV function to calculate the amount you will receive.

An *annuity* is a series of payments where each payment is the same amount, the period between payments is the same, the interest rate for each period is constant, and the interest is compounded. If you deposit $1,000 per year for five years and receive 10 percent interest, compounded annually, the amount you receive at the end of five years is the future value of an annuity. You can also use Excel's FV function to compute the future value of an annuity.

When you are working with the FV function, negative numbers are *cash outflows* and positive numbers are *cash inflows*. Enter a negative number when you are making a payment. Enter a positive number when you are receiving cash. Although the transaction is called a *payment,* note that there are two sides to the transaction. For example, when you make a payment to the bank, the bank considers the transaction a receipt. When you receive money from the bank, the bank considers the transaction a payment.

Excel's FV function takes five arguments: the interest rate, the number of payment periods, the amount of each payment, the value for which you are trying to find the future value, and a number, Type, indicating when payments are due. If you make your payments at the beginning of the period, enter a 1 as the Type argument. If you make your payments at the end of the period, leave the Type argument blank or enter 0.

Calculate Future Value

CALCULATE FUTURE VALUE

1 Click the cell in which you want to place the future value.

2 Type =FV(.

Alternatively, select FV from the AutoComplete list that appears after you begin typing.

3 Click the Insert Function button.

4 In the FV Function Arguments dialog box, enter the interest rate.

Note: *If you make payments more than once annually, divide the interest rate by the number of payments per year.*

5 Enter the number of periods you are investing.

Note: *If you make payments more than once annually, multiply the number of years by the number of payments per year.*

6 Enter the value for which you want to find the future value.

7 Click OK.

● Excel calculates the future value.

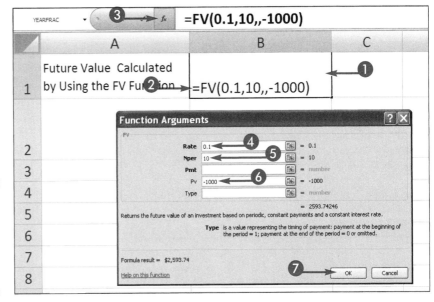

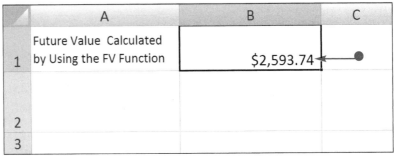

CALCULATE THE FUTURE VALUE OF AN ANNUITY

1. Click the cell in which you want to place the future value.

2. Type **=FV(**.

   Alternatively, select FV from the AutoComplete list that appears after you begin typing.

3. Click the Insert Function button.

4. In the FV Function Arguments dialog box, enter the interest rate.

5. Enter the number of periods you are investing.

6. Enter the payment amount.

7. Enter **1** in the Type field.

Note: Enter **1** in the Type field if you make payments at the beginning of the period. Leave the Type field blank if you make payments at the end of the period.

8. Click OK.

- Excel calculates the future value of the annuity.

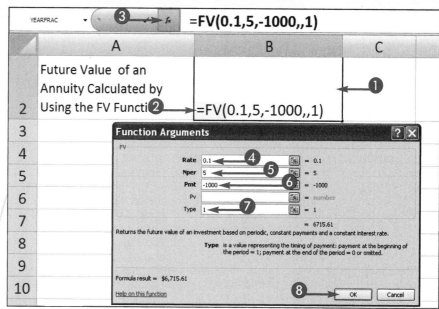

YEARFRAC f_x =FV(0.1,5,-1000,,1)

	A	B	C
	Future Value of an Annuity Calculated by		
2	Using the FV Functi ❷ →=FV(0.1,5,-1000,,1)		
3			

Function Arguments   ? X

FV

Rate 0.1   ❹   = 0.1
Nper 5   ❺   = 5
Pmt -1000   ❻   = -1000
Pv   = number
Type 1   ❼   = 1

= 6715.61

Returns the future value of an investment based on periodic, constant payments and a constant interest rate.

Type is a value representing the timing of payment: payment at the beginning of the period = 1; payment at the end of the period = 0 or omitted.

Formula result = $6,715.61

Help on this function   ❽ →   OK   Cancel

	A	B	C
	Future Value of an Annuity Calculated by		
2	Using the FV Function	$6,715.61	
3			
4			

Apply It

When you are calculating future value, be careful of the amount you enter in the Rate and Nper, number of periods, fields. You should divide the annual interest rate by the number of payments per year. If payments are monthly, you should divide the annual interest rate by 12. If your rate is 8 percent, enter **.08/12** in the Rate field. You should also multiply the number of payments in a year by the number of years of payments. If payments are monthly for five years, multiply 5 by 12 to get 60 and enter **60** in the Nper field.

You can use the following formula to calculate the future value of an investment: $fv = a*((1+i)\wedge n)$ where fv equals the future value, a equals the amount for which you want to find the future value, i equals the annual interest rate, and n equals the number of periods. To find the future value of $1,000 at 10 percent for ten years, enter **=1000*((1+.10)^10)** or use Excel's FV function. For a detailed example of how to calculate future value, refer to the file Future Value.xlsx, which is on the Web site for this book.

Calculate Present Value

I nvestors use the concept of present value (PV) to recognize the time value of money. Because an investor can receive interest, $1,000 today is worth less than $1,000 ten years from today. For example, if an investor invests $1,000 today at 10 percent interest per year, compounded annually, in ten years the investor will have $2,593.74. Therefore, the present value of $2,593.74 at 10 percent, compounded annually, for 10 years is $1,000. Or, worded differently, $1,000 today is worth $2,593.74 ten years from today. You can use the following formula to calculate the present value of an investment: pv = a/((1+i)^n) where pv equals the present value, a equals the amount for which you want to find the present value, i equals the annual interest rate, and n equals the number of periods. To find the present value of the $2,593.74 given in the example,

enter the formula =2593.74/((1+.10)^10) or use Excel's PV function.

An *annuity* is a series of payments where each payment is the same amount, the period between payments is the same, the interest rate for each period is constant, and the interest is compounded. For example, a payment of $1,000 per year for five years at 10 percent interest compounded at the end of each year is an annuity. The present value of an annuity is equal to the sum of the present value of each payment. To find the present value, you can add the present values of each payment or you can use Excel's PV function. Excel's PV function takes five arguments: the interest rate, the number of payment periods, the amount of each payment, the value for which you are trying to find the present value, and a number indicating when payments are due.

Calculate Present Value

CALCULATE PRESENT VALUE

1. Click the cell in which you want to place the present value.

2. Type **=PV(**.

   Alternatively, select PV from the AutoComplete list that appears after you begin typing.

3. Click the Insert Function button.

4. In the PV Function Arguments dialog box, type the interest rate.

Note: *If you make payments more than once annually, divide the interest rate by the number of payments per year.*

5. Enter the number of periods you are investing.

Note: *If you make payments more than once annually, multiply the number of years by the number of payments per year.*

6. Enter the value for which you want to find the present value.

7. Click OK.

● Excel calculates the present value.

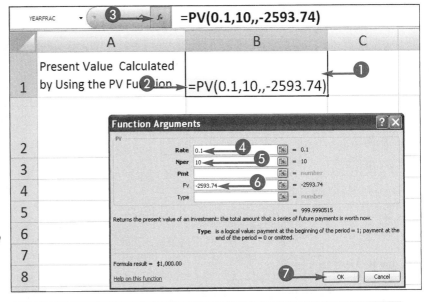

CALCULATE THE PRESENT VALUE OF AN ANNUITY

1 Click the cell in which you want to place the present value.

2 Type **=PV(**.

Alternatively, select PV from the AutoComplete list that appears after you begin typing.

3 Click the Insert Function button.

4 In the PV Function Arguments dialog box, enter the interest rate.

5 Enter the number of periods you are investing.

6 Enter the payment amount.

7 Click OK.

● Excel calculates the present value of an annuity.

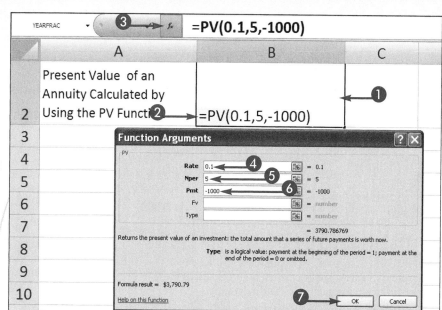

	A	B	C
2	Present Value of an Annuity Calculated by Using the PV Function	$3,790.79	
3			
4			

Extra

Car loans and mortgages are annuities. The money you receive when you take out the loan is the present value of the loan.

When you are calculating present value, be careful of the amount you enter in the Rate and Nper fields. You should divide the annual interest rate by the number of payments per year. If payments are monthly, you should divide the annual interest rate by 12. If your rate is 8 percent, enter **.08/12** in the Rate field. You should also multiply the number of payments in a year by the number of years of payments. If payments are monthly for five years, multiply 5 by 12 to get 60 and enter **60** in the Nper field.

When you are working with the PV function, negative numbers are *cash outflows* and positive numbers are *cash inflows*. Enter a negative number when you are making a payment. Enter a positive number when you are receiving cash.

With an annuity, you can make payments at the end of the period or at the beginning of the period. When you are calculating present value, if you make payments at the beginning of the period, enter a **1** as the Type argument; otherwise leave the argument blank.

Calculate Loan Payments

You can use Excel's PMT function (PMT is short for payment) when buying a house or car. This function enables you to compare loan terms and make an objective decision based on such factors as the amount of the monthly payment.

You can calculate loan payments in many ways when using Excel, but the PMT function may be the simplest method because you merely enter the arguments into the Function Wizard. To make your job even easier, enter this information into your worksheet before launching the wizard. Then by clicking in a cell, you can enter the value of the cell into the wizard. You can create a loan calculator that shows how varying arguments affect the results. Place the labels Principal, Interest, and Number of Months in a column. Type their respective values into adjacent cells to the right. For example, you can calculate the

payment amount at 5 percent, 5⅛ percent, and 5¼ percent to see the effect of changing the annual interest.

The PMT function takes three required arguments. To calculate the periodic rate, you enter an annual interest rate such as 5 percent and then type .05 divided by the number of payments you make per year. For example, if you pay monthly, enter .05/12 as the Rate argument. For Nper, enter the number of loan periods for the loan you are seeking. For example, if your loan is for 15 years and you will make payments monthly, multiply 15 years by 12 months to get 180 periods and then type **180** in the Nper field. For PV enter the amount of the loan. The PMT function calculates the amount of each payment. The payment amount appears surrounded by parentheses, signifying that the number is negative, and a cash outflow.

Calculate Loan Payments

① Type the principal — PV —, the interest rate, and the number of periods.

② Click in the cell in which you want the result to appear.

③ Click the Insert Function button.

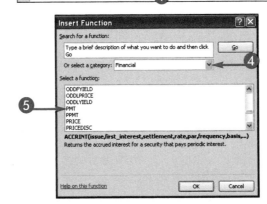

The Insert Function dialog box appears.

④ Click here and select Financial.

⑤ Double-click PMT.

The PMT Function Arguments dialog box appears.

6 Click to select the cell with the interest rate.

7 Divide the interest rate by the number of periods per year; for example, type **/12**.

8 Click to select the cell with the number of periods.

9 Click to select the cell with the principal.

10 Click OK.

● The result appears in the cell.

Note: *The result shows the amount of a single loan payment.*

Note: *You can repeat Steps 1 to 10 for other combinations of the three variables.*

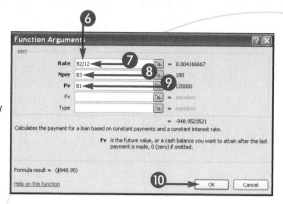

Function Arguments		? X
PMT		
Rate	B2/12	= 0.004166667
Nper	B3	= 180
Pv	B1	= 120000
Fv		= number
Type		= number
		= -948.9523521

Calculates the payment for a loan based on constant payments and a constant interest rate.

Fv is the future value, or a cash balance you want to attain after the last payment is made, 0 (zero) if omitted.

Formula result = ($948.95)

Help on this function

OK   Cancel

B4		*fx*	=PMT(B2/12,B3,B1)

	A	B
1	Principal	120000
2	Interest	0.05
3	Number of Months	180
4	Monthly Payments	($948.95)

Extra

Use the Type field in the payment function to specify whether payments are due at the beginning of the period or the end of the period. For example, if payments are due at the beginning of the month, enter a **1** in the Type field. If payments are due at the end of the month, leave the field blank or enter a **0**.

The PMT function returns both principal and interest. If you want to calculate the amount of interest paid in a period, use the IPMT function. If you want to calculate the amount of principal paid in a period, use the PPMT function. See the next task, "Calculate Principal or Interest," to learn more.

Excel's Goal Seek feature enables you to calculate payments. With Goal Seek, you can specify a goal, such as payments less than $1,100 per month, and have Excel vary a single value to reach the goal. The limitation is that you can vary only one value at a time. See Chapter 10 for more information.

Calculate Principal or Interest

When you use the PMT function to calculate a monthly loan payment, Excel calculates the total of the principal and the interest. See the previous task, "Calculate Loan Payments," to learn more about using the PMT function. If you need to know the principal or the interest portion of a payment, you can use the PPMT function or the IPMT function.

An *annuity* is a series of payments where each payment is the same amount, the period between payments is the same, the interest rate for each period is constant, and the interest is compounded. The PPMT function finds the principal portion of a loan payment when the loan is an annuity. The PPMT function takes six arguments: the interest rate, the number of the loan period for which you

want to obtain the principal, the total number of payments, the loan amount, the future value amount, and a number that indicates if payments are due at the end of the period or the beginning of the period.

The IPMT function finds the interest portion of a loan payment when the loan is an annuity. The IPMT function also takes six arguments: the interest rate, the number of the loan period for which you want to obtain the principal, the total number of payments, the loan amount, the future value amount, and a number that indicates if payments are due at the end of the period or the beginning of the period. For each period, the principal portion and the interest portion of a loan should equal the payment amount.

Calculate Principal or Interest

CALCULATE PRINCIPAL

1 Click the cell in which you want to place the principal.

2 Type **=PPMT(**.

Alternatively, select PPMT from the AutoComplete list that appears after you begin typing.

3 Click the Insert Function button.

4 In the PPMT Function Arguments dialog box, type the interest rate.

Note: *If you make payments more than once annually, divide the interest rate by the number of payments per year.*

5 Enter the period for which you want to obtain the principal.

6 Enter the number of periods for which you will make payments.

Note: *If you make payments more than once annually, multiply the number of years by the number of payments per year.*

7 Enter the loan amount.

8 Click OK.

● Excel calculates the principal.

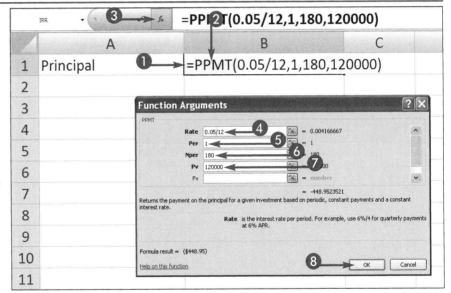

CALCULATE THE INTEREST

1. Click the cell in which you want to place the interest.
2. Type **=IPMT(**.

   Alternatively, select IPMT from the AutoComplete list that appears after you begin typing.
3. Click the Insert Function button.
4. In the IPMT Function Arguments dialog box, enter the interest rate.
5. Enter the period for which you want to find the interest.
6. Enter the number of periods for which you will make payments.
7. Enter the loan amount.
8. Click OK.

- Excel calculates the interest.

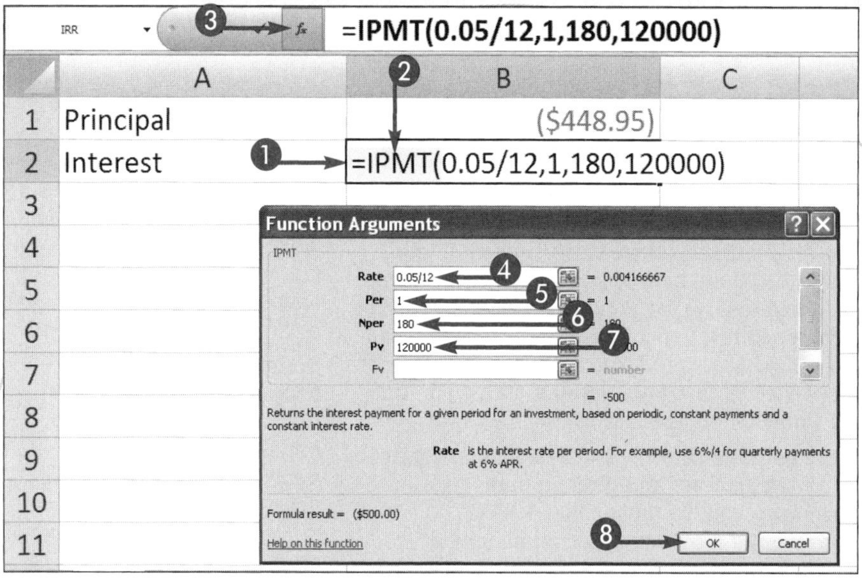

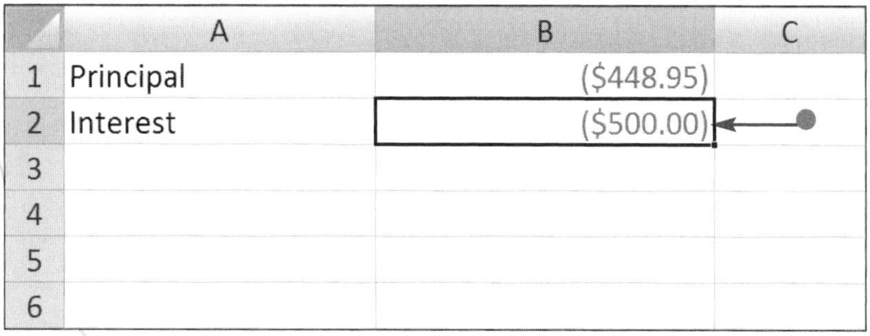

Apply It

If you need to find out how much principal or interest has accrued between two periods, you can use the `CUMPRINC` or the `CUMIPMT` function. Both of these functions take the same six arguments: `Rate`, the interest rate; `Nper`, the number of periods; `Pv`, the loan amount; `Start_period`, the first period in which you want to begin your calculation; `End_period`, the period in which you want to end your calculation; and `Type`, indicating when payments are due. Enter **0** as the `Type` argument if the payment is at the end of the period, or enter **1** if the payment is at the beginning of the period.

If you want to find the cumulative principal for periods 1 and 2 for a $120,000 loan at 5 percent per year for 180 periods, paid at the end of the period, you would enter the following formula: `=CUMPRINC(.05/12,180,120000,1, 2,0)`. The formula returns –899.78. For an illustration of `CUMPRINC` and `CUMIPMT`, see Sheet3 of Principal and Interest.xlsx, which you can find on the Web site for this book.

Calculate the Interest Rate

You can use Excel's RATE function to calculate the rate associated with an annuity. An annuity is a series of payments where each payment is the same amount, the period between payments is the same, the interest rate for each time period is constant, and the interest is compounded. Generally speaking, a bank loan is an annuity. If you receive a bank loan for $120,000 and you pay $948.95 monthly for 180 months, you can use the RATE function to calculate the interest rate.

When you are working with the RATE function, negative numbers are *cash outflows* and positive numbers are *cash inflows*. Your monthly payment of $948.95 is a cash outflow, so you enter it as a negative number. Your loan of $120,000 is a cash inflow, so you enter it as a positive number.

Excel's RATE function takes six arguments: Nper, the number of payment periods; Pmt, the amount of each payment; Pv, the amount of the loan; Fv, the future value you want to attain; and Type, a number indicating when payments are due. If you make your payments at the beginning of the period, enter 1 as the Type argument.

Optionally, you can provide an additional argument, your best-guess estimate as to the rate of return. Calculating the rate is an iterative process where Excel starts with an initial guess for the rate and attempts to refine that guess to obtain the sought answer. The default value, if you do not provide an estimate, is .10, representing a 10 percent rate of return. Your estimate gives Excel a starting point at which to calculate the RATE. If after 20 tries Excel cannot return a value, it returns a #NUM! error. You should enter a value in the Guess field and try again.

Calculate the Interest Rate

1. Click in the cell in which you want the result to appear.

2. Type **=RATE(**.

   Alternatively, select RATE from the AutoComplete list that appears after you begin typing.

3. Click the Insert Function button.

4. In the RATE Function Arguments dialog box, click a cell to select the number of periods, or type the number of periods.

5. Click a cell to select the payment, or type the payment.

6. Click a cell to select the loan amount, or type the loan amount.

Note: Optionally, you can provide an estimated rate of return just to get Excel started.

7. Click OK.

- The result appears in the cell.

Note: In this example, payments are made monthly, so the monthly rate appears in the cell. To obtain the annual rate, you must multiply the monthly rate by 12.

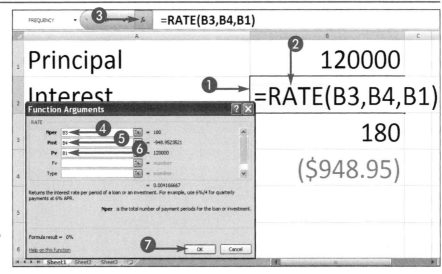

8 Press F2.

9 Type *** 12**.

10 Press Enter.

● The annual rate appears.

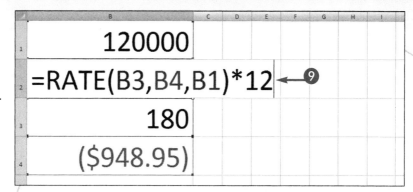

Principal 120000

Interest →5%

Number of Months 180

Monthly Payments ($948.95)

Apply It

If you know the amount of a loan, the interest rate associated with the loan, and the periodic payment, you can calculate the number of periods by using the NPER function. The NPER function takes the following arguments: Rate, the interest rate; Pmt, the payment made each period; Pv, the loan amount; Fv, the future value; and Type, a number indicating when payments are due. Enter **0** or leave the Type argument blank if the payment is at the end of the period; enter **1** if the payment is at the beginning of the period.

If you want to find the number of periods for a $120,000 loan at 5 percent annually with monthly payments of $948.95, enter the following formula: =NPER(.05/12,-948.95,120000). The function returns 180. To see an example of this function, see Sheet2 of Interest Rate.xlsx, which you can find on the Web site for this book.

Calculate the Internal Rate of Return

You can use Excel's IRR function to calculate the rate of return on an investment. When you are using the IRR function, the cash flows do not have to be equal, but they must occur at regular intervals. As an example, you make a loan of $6,607 on January 1, year 1. You receive payments every January 1 for four succeeding years. You can use the IRR function to determine the interest rate you receive on the loan.

Your loan of $6,607 is a cash outflow, so you enter it as a negative number. Each payment is a cash inflow, so you enter them as a positive numbers. When using the IRR function, you must enter at least one positive and one negative number.

Optionally, you can provide an additional argument, your best-guess estimate as to the rate of return. Calculating

the rate is an iterative process where Excel starts with an initial guess for the rate and attempts to refine that guess to obtain the sought answer. The default value, if you do not provide an estimate, is .10, representing a 10 percent rate of return. Your estimate gives Excel a starting point at which to calculate the RATE. If after 20 tries Excel cannot return a value, it returns a #NUM! error. You should enter a value in the Guess field and try again.

Excel's IRR function has strict assumptions. Cash flows must be regularly timed and take place at the same point within each payment period. IRR may perform less reliably for inconsistently timed payments and variable interest rates. Excel uses the order of the values to interpret the cash flows, so enter your values in the proper sequence.

Calculate the Internal Rate of Return

① Type the series of projected cash flows into a worksheet.

② Click in the cell in which the result appears.

③ Click the Insert Function button.

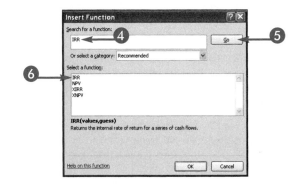

The Insert Function dialog box appears.

④ Type **IRR**.

⑤ Click Go.

⑥ Double-click IRR.

The IRR Function Arguments dialog box appears.

⑦ Click and drag to select the cash-flow values you entered in Step 1 or type the range.

● Optionally, you can provide an estimated rate of return just to get Excel started.

⑧ Click OK.

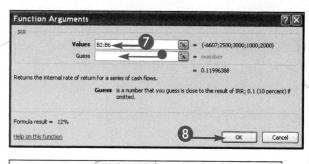

● The cell with the formula displays the results of the calculations as a percent with no decimal places.

Repeat Steps 1 to 7 for each set of anticipated future cash flows.

B7		f_x	=IRR(B2:B6)

	A	B	C	D	E
1	Year	Cash Flows			
2	1	-6607			
3	2	2500			
4	3	3000			
5	4	1000			
6	5	2000			
7		12%			
8					

Apply It

The IRR function is related to the NPV function, which calculates the net present value of future cash flows. See the task "Calculate Present Value" to learn more about the concept of present value. Whereas IRR returns a percentage — the rate of return on the initial investment — NPV returns the amount that must be invested to achieve the specified rate of return.

The NPV function takes two basic types of arguments: Rate, which is the rate of return, and Values, which are the series of inflows and outflows. The NPV function can hold up to 254 value arguments. An array is a list of values enclosed in curly braces. You can enter an array into a Value field. Excel interprets the order of the cash flows as occurring in the order in which you enter them into the Value fields. To see an example of the NPV function, refer to the file IRR.xls, Sheet2.

The NPV function differs from the PV function in the following ways: when you are using the NPV function, the amount of each cash flow does not have to be the same and payments can begin only at the end of the period.

Calculate Straight-Line Depreciation

Buildings, cars, trucks, and equipment are all examples of depreciable assets. Accountants consider an asset depreciable if it has a useful life of more than one year but does not last indefinitely. Because accountants want to match the cost of an asset with the revenue produced from using the asset, they allocate the cost of a depreciable asset over the life of the asset. Accountants use several depreciation methods to allocate cost.

The straight-line method of depreciation allocates depreciation evenly over the useful life of the asset. Salvage value is the value of an asset once its useful life has expired. To calculate straight-line depreciation, you take the cost of the asset, subtract any salvage value, and then divide by the useful life of the asset. The result

is the amount of depreciation allocated to each period. For example, you purchase a piece of equipment on January 1 for $8,500, the equipment has a useful life of four years, and it can be sold for $500 at the end of four years. To calculate the annual depreciation, you use the formula $= (8500-500)/4$. The result, 2,000, is the annual depreciation.

You can use Excel's SLN function to calculate straight-line depreciation. The SLN function takes three arguments: Cost, the initial cost of the asset; Salvage, the salvage value of the asset; and Life, the life of the asset in periods. If you purchase an asset mid-year, you may want to calculate depreciation in months. When calculating depreciation in months, enter the number of months that make up the useful life of the asset as the Life argument.

Calculate Straight-Line Depreciation

① Click in the cell in which you want the results to appear.

② Click the Insert Function button.

The Insert Function dialog box appears.

③ Type **SLN**.

④ Click Go.

⑤ Double-click SLN.

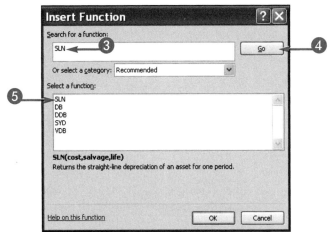

The SLN Function Arguments dialog box appears.

⑥ Click to select the cell with the cost, or type the cost.

⑦ Click to select the cell with the salvage value, or type the salvage value.

⑧ Click to select the cell with the useful life, or type the useful life.

⑨ Click OK.

● Excel calculates depreciation for one period.

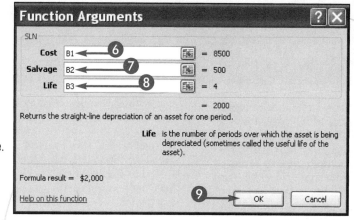

Function Arguments ? X

SLN

Cost	B1 ← ⑥	🔢 = 8500
Salvage	B2 ← ⑦	🔢 = 500
Life	B3 ← ⑧	🔢 = 4

= 2000

Returns the straight-line depreciation of an asset for one period.

Life is the number of periods over which the asset is being depreciated (sometimes called the useful life of the asset).

Formula result = $2,000

Help on this function

⑨ → OK   Cancel

| B4 | | f_x | =SLN(B1,B2,B3) |

	A	B	C
1	Cost	$8,500	
2	Salvage Value	$500	
3	Useful Life	4	
4	Annual Depreciation	$2,000 ← ●	
5			

Extra

The carrying value is the cost of an asset minus the total depreciation taken to date. The depreciation for an asset with a cost of $8,500, a salvage value of $500, and a useful life of four years would be allocated as follows:

	ANNUAL DEPRECIATION EXPENSE	ACCUMULATED DEPRECIATION	CARRYING VALUE
Beginning Year 1			$8,500
End Year 1	$2,000	$2,000	$6,500
End Year 2	$2,000	$4,000	$4,500
End Year 3	$2,000	$6,000	$2,500
End Year 4	$2,000	$8,000	$500

Calculate Declining Balance Depreciation

When calculating depreciation, accountants try to match the cost of an asset with the revenue it produces. Some assets produce more in earlier years than they do in later years. For those assets, accountants use accelerated methods of depreciation. Accelerated methods of depreciation take more depreciation in the earlier years than they do in the later years. Declining balance is an accelerated method of depreciation. You can use Excel's DB function to calculate declining balance depreciation.

The carrying value is the cost of an asset minus the total depreciation taken to date. When you use the declining balance depreciation method, you calculate a rate. The rate could be 50 percent, for example. You apply the rate to the carrying value to get the annual depreciation. Because the carrying value goes down each year, your depreciation is higher in earlier years than it is in later years. Excel uses the following formula to calculate the rate: `rate = 1- ((salvage/cost)^(1/life))`, rounded to three decimal places. After Excel calculates the rate, it uses the following formula to calculate depreciation: `depreciation = (cost-depreciation from prior periods)* rate`. The first and last periods are special. The formula for the first period is `cost*rate month/12`. The formula for the last period is `((cost-total depreciation for prior periods)*rate*12-month))/12`.

The DB function takes five arguments: the cost of the asset, the salvage value, the useful life, the period for which you are calculating depreciation, and the number of months in the first year. If you leave the `Month` argument blank, Excel assumes the number of months in the first year to be 12.

Calculate Declining Balance Depreciation

① Click in the cell in which you want the results to appear.

② Click the Insert Function button.

	A	B	C
1	Cost	$8,500	
2	Salvage Value	$500	
3	Useful Life	4	
4			
5	Equipment		
6	Year	Depreciation	
7	1		
8	2	$2,124	
9	3	$1,045	
10	4	$512 *Adjusted*	
11			

B7

The Insert Function dialog box appears.

③ Type **DB**.

④ Click Go.

⑤ Double-click DB.

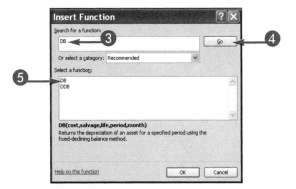

Insert Function

Search for a function:

DB

Go

Or select a category: Recommended

Select a function:

DB
DDB

DB(cost,salvage,life,period,month)
Returns the depreciation of an asset for a specified period using the fixed-declining balance method.

Help on this function

OK   Cancel

The DB Function Arguments dialog box appears.

6 Click to select the cell with the cost, or type the cost.

7 Click to select the cell with the salvage value, or type the salvage value.

8 Click to select the cell with the useful life, or type the useful life.

9 Click to select the cell with the period, or type the period.

10 Click to select the cell with the number of months in the first year, or type the months.

11 Click OK.

● Excel calculates the depreciation for one period.

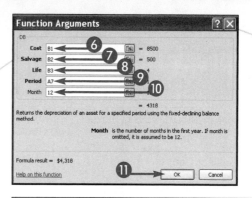

	A	B	C
		B7	fx =DB(B1,B2,B3,A7,12)
1	Cost	$8,500	
2	Salvage Value	$500	
3	Useful Life	4	
4			
5	Equipment		
6	Year	Depreciation	
7	1	$4,318	
8	2	$2,124	
9	3	$1,045	
10	4	$512	*Adjusted*
11			

Extra

The declining balance method of depreciation depreciates an asset with a cost of $8,500, a salvage value of $500, and a useful life of four years as follows:

	ANNUAL DEPRECIATION EXPENSE	ACCUMULATED DEPRECIATION	CARRYING VALUE
Beginning of Year 1			$8,500
End Year 1	$4,318	$4,318	$4,182
End Year 2	$2,124	$6,442	$2,058
End Year 3	$1,045	$7,488	$1,012
End Year 4	$512*	$8,000	$500

*Amount adjusted for rounding error.

Calculate Double-Declining Balance Depreciation

ike the declining balance method discussed in the previous task, double-declining balance is an accelerated depreciation method. The carrying value is the cost of an asset minus the amount of depreciation taken to date. Salvage value is the amount you can sell an asset for after its useful life. Double-declining balance takes the rate you would apply by using straight-line depreciation, doubles it, and then applies the doubled rate to the carrying value of the asset. For example, under the straight-line method of depreciation, if you purchase an asset that has a useful life of four years, you would take depreciation at a rate of 1/4th per year or 25 percent. Under the double-declining balance method, you double the 25 percent and take 50 percent of the carrying value as the annual depreciation; however, you do not depreciate the asset below the salvage value. You can use the DDB function to calculate double-declining balance

depreciation. The DDB function uses the following formula to calculate double-declining balance depreciation:

=MIN((cost-depreciation taken to date)*
(rate),(cost-salvage value-depreciation taken to date))

You must supply the DDB function with the following information: Cost, the cost of the asset; Salvage, the amount you can sell the asset for after its useful life; Life, the useful life in periods; Period, the period for which you are calculating depreciation; and Factor, the rate at which the balance declines. If you are doubling the straight-line rate, enter 2 as the Factor or leave the Factor argument blank. If you want to use a rate other than twice the straight-line rate, enter the factor you want to use. For example, enter 1.5 if you want to use a rate of 150 percent.

Calculate Double-Declining Balance Depreciation

① Click in the cell in which you want the results to appear.

② Click the Insert Function button.

	A	B	C
	B7	② f_x	
1	Cost	$8,500	
2	Salvage Value	$1,500	
3	Useful Life	4	
4			
5	Equipment		
6	Year	Depreciation	
7	1		①
8	2	$2,125	
9	3	$625	
10	4	$0	
11			

The Insert Function dialog box appears.

③ Type **DDB**.

④ Click Go.

⑤ Double-click DDB.

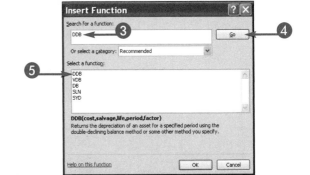

The DDB Function Arguments dialog box appears.

6 Click to select the cell with the cost, or type the cost.

7 Click to select the cell with the salvage value, or type the salvage value.

8 Click to select the cell with the useful life, or type the useful life.

9 Click to select the cell with the period, or type the period for which you want to calculate depreciation.

10 Click to select the cell with the factor, or type the factor.

11 Click OK.

● Excel calculates depreciation for one period.

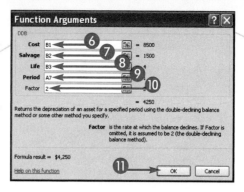

B7		f_x	=DDB(B1,B2,B3,A7,2)

	A		B	C
1	Cost		$8,500	
2	Salvage Value		$1,500	
3	Useful Life		4	
4				
5	Equipment			
6		Year	Depreciation	
7		1	$4,250	
8		2	$2,125	
9		3	$625	
10		4	$0	
11				

Extra

The declining balance method of depreciation depreciates an asset with a cost of $8,500, a salvage value of $1,500, and a useful life of four years as follows:

	ANNUAL DEPRECIATION EXPENSE	ACCUMULATED DEPRECIATION	CARRYING VALUE
Beginning of Year			$8,500
End Year 1	$4,250	$4,250	$4,250
End Year 2	$2,125	$6,375	$2,125
End Year 3	$625*	$7,000	$1,500
End Year 4	$0*	$7,500	$1,500

*The DDB function will not depreciate the asset below the salvage value.

Calculate Sum-of-the-Years-Digits Depreciation

When calculating depreciation, accountants try to match the cost of an asset with the revenue it produces. Some assets produce more in earlier years than they do in later years. For those assets, accountants use accelerated methods of depreciation. Sum-of-the-years-digits is an accelerated depreciation method. When you calculate sum-of-the-years-digits depreciation manually, you use a fraction to calculate annual depreciation. The numerator of the fraction is the remaining years of useful life. The denominator is the sum of the digits that make up the useful life. For example, if you want to calculate depreciation for the first year of an asset with a useful life of four years, cost of 8,500, and a salvage value of 500, the numerator is 4 and the denominator is 10, the sum of 1+2+3+4. You multiply the fraction by the cost of

the asset minus the salvage value. The calculation for the first year is 4/10*8000, or 3,200; the calculation for the second year is 3/10*8000, or 2,400; the calculation for the third year is 2/10*8000; or 1,600. The calculation for the fourth year is 1/10*8000, or 800. You can use the SYD function to calculate sum-of-the-years-digits depreciation in Excel. The SYD function uses the following formula:

SYD = ((cost-salvage)*(life-per+1)*2)/
((life)*(life+1))

You must supply the SYD function with the following information: Cost, the cost of the asset; Salvage, the amount you can sell the asset for after its useful life; Life, the useful life in periods; and Per, the period for which you are calculating depreciation.

Calculate Sum-of-the-Years-Digits Depreciation

① Click in the cell in which you want the results to appear.

② Click the Insert Function button.

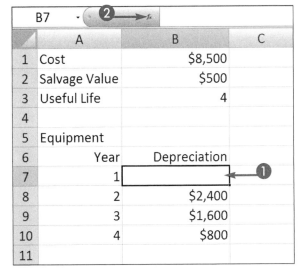

The Insert Function dialog box appears.

③ Type **SYD**.

④ Click Go.

⑤ Double-click SYD.

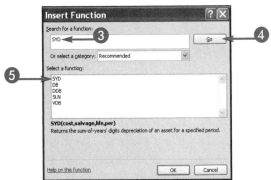

The SYD Function Arguments dialog box appears.

6 Click to select the cell with the cost, or type the cost.

7 Click to select the cell with the salvage value, or type the salvage value.

8 Click to select the cell with the useful life, or type the useful life.

9 Click to select the cell with the period for which you want to calculate depreciation, or type the period.

10 Click OK.

● Excel calculates depreciation for one period.

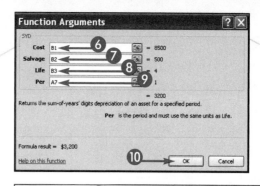

	Function Arguments	? X
SYD		
Cost	B1	= 8500
Salvage	B2	= 500
Life	B3	4
Per	A7	1

= 3200

Returns the sum-of-years' digits depreciation of an asset for a specified period.

Per is the period and must use the same units as Life.

Formula result = $3,200

Help on this function   **10**   OK   Cancel

B7 f_x =SYD(B1,B2,B3,A7)

	A	B	C
1	Cost	$8,500	
2	Salvage Value	$500	
3	Useful Life	4	
4			
5	Equipment		
6	Year	Depreciation	
7	1	$3,200	
8	2	$2,400	
9	3	$1,600	
10	4	$800	
11			

Extra

The sum-of-the-years-digits method of depreciation depreciates an asset with a cost of $8,500, a salvage value of $500, and a useful life of four years as follows:

	ANNUAL DEPRECIATION EXPENSE	ACCUMULATED DEPRECIATION	CARRYING VALUE
Beginning of Year 1			$8,500
End Year 1	$3,200	$3,200	$5,300
End Year 2	$2,400	$5,600	$2,900
End Year 3	$1,600	$7,200	$1,300
End Year 4	$800	$8,000	$500

Calculate an Average

A n average is the sum of two or more values divided by the total number of values. With Excel, you can use the AVERAGE function to compute an average. Using the AVERAGE function is very easy — you can find out how to use the AVERAGE function in the Apply It section of this task. Excel also has functions that are more complex that you can use to compute an average. You can use the AVERAGEIF function to compute an average for data that meets the criteria you specify. For example, if you have a list that contains scores for several teams, you can use the AVERAGEIF function to compute the average score for the players on each individual team.

AVERAGEIF takes three arguments: Range, the range of values you want to examine by using the criteria you specify in the Criteria argument; Criteria, the criteria you want to apply to the range; and Average_range, the range of cells you want to average. The third argument, Average_range, is optional. If you do not include it, Excel averages the range you specify in the Range argument. When using AVERAGEIF, you can use a comparison operator to specify your criteria. For example, you can use 1 or "=1" to select all values that are equal to one, you can use ">50" to find all values greater than 50, or you can use "Jones" or "=Jones" to find all values equal to Jones.

In addition, you can use the question mark (?) and asterisk (*) wildcards when creating your condition. A ? will match a single character, and an * will match any series of characters. For example, 123?98 will match any value that starts with 123 and ends with 98, such as 123X98, 123-98, or 123A98. The criteria *son will match any value that ends with son, such as Johnson or Jackson.

Calculate an Average

① Create a list of values to average conditionally.

Note: *Excel tests each value to see whether it meets a condition. If it does, Excel uses it to calculate the average.*

② Click the cell in which you want the results to appear.

③ Click the Insert Function button.

● The Insert Function dialog box appears.

④ Click here and select Statistical.

⑤ Double-click AVERAGEIF.

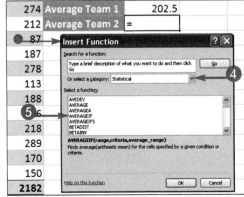

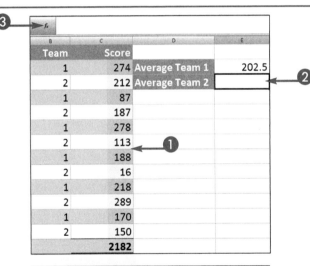

- The Function Arguments dialog box appears.

6 Click and drag to select the range you want to evaluate, or type the range name for the series.

7 Type your criteria.

You can use a comparison operator and a condition.

8 Click and drag to select the range or type the range name you want to average if your condition is met.

9 Click OK.

- The result appears in the cell with the formula.

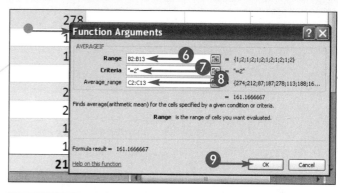

		B	C	D	E
		Team	**Score**		
		1	274	**Average Team 1**	202.5
		2	212	**Average Team 2**	161.2
		1	87		
		2	187		
		1	278		
		2	113		
		1	188		
		2	16		
		1	218		
		2	289		
		1	170		
		2	150		
			2182		

Apply It

You can use the AVERAGE function to calculate an average. This function takes one type of argument: Number1 through Number255. An array is a list of values enclosed in curly braces. For example {20, 25, 25, 30} is an array. In each Number argument, you can enter a number, a range that contains numbers, a range name, or an array. The AVERAGE function sums each value you enter and divides by the total number of values.

If A1 is equal to 20, A2 is equal to 25, A3 is equal to 25, A4 is equal to 30, and the range of cells A1 to A4 is named MyValues, all of the following are valid functions:

FORMULA	RESULT
=AVERAGE(10,20,30)	20
=AVERAGE(A1:A4)	25
=Average(MyValues)	25
=AVERAGE(A1:A4,40,30,20,10)	25
=AVERAGE({20,25,25,30})	25

Calculate the Median or the Mode

When analyzing data, you may need to find the median. The *median* is the midpoint in a series of numbers, the point at which half the values are greater than the others and half the values are less than the others when you arrange the values in numerical order. If you are analyzing the scores students receive on a test and the median score is 75, half the students received a score greater than 75 and half the students received a score less than 75. When finding the median, if the number of items in the series is even, the median is the average of the two middle values. For example, in the series 1, 9, 17, 19, 21, 25, 27, the median is the number 19 because three numbers are greater than 19 and three numbers are less than 19. In the series 1, 9, 17, 19, 21, 25, 27, 29, the median is 20 — the average of 19 and 21. You can use Excel's MEDIAN function to calculate the median.

The *mode* is the most common value in a list of values. For example, if your list of values is 1, 2, 3, 3, 2, 3, 1, the mode is 3 because it is the value that occurs most often. You can use Excel's MODE function to find the mode.

Both the MEDIAN and MODE functions take one type of argument, Number1 through Number255. An array is a list of values enclosed in curly braces. For example {20, 25, 25, 30} is an array. In each Number argument, you can enter a number, a range that contains numbers, a range name, or an array.

Calculate the Median or the Mode

CALCULATE THE MEDIAN

1. Click in the cell in which you want to calculate the median value.

2. Type **=MEDIAN(**.

   Alternatively, select MEDIAN from the AutoComplete list that appears after you begin typing.

3. Click the Insert Function button.

   ● The Function Arguments dialog box appears.

4. Type the range, range name, or values for which you want to find the median.

5. Click OK.

   ● Excel calculates the median.

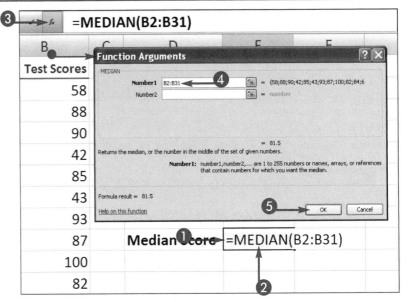

CALCULATE THE MODE

1 Click in the cell in which you want to calculate the mode.

2 Type **=MODE(**.

Alternatively, select MODE from the AutoComplete list that appears after you begin typing.

3 Click the Insert Function button.

● The Function Arguments dialog box appears.

4 Type the range, range name, or values for which you want to find the mode.

5 Click OK.

● Excel calculates the mode.

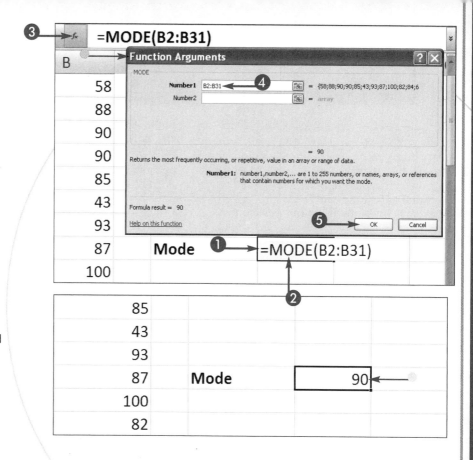

Extra

Excel interprets the logical value TRUE to be 1 and the logical value FALSE to be 0. If you type the logical values into MEDIAN or MODE functions, you can use logical values when calculating the median or mode. If an array or a range of cells contains a logical value, the MEDIAN and MODE functions do not include the logical value in the calculation of the median or mode.

Statisticians refer to an average as the *mean*. *Central tendency* is defined as a typical value in a distribution or a value that represents the majority of cases. The most commonly used measures of central tendency are mean, mode, and median.

The Data Analysis Toolpak is an Excel add-in. Included in the Data Analysis Toolpak is a wizard you can use to calculate descriptive statistics. Among the statistics you can calculate are the mean, the mode, and the median. See the task "Calculate Descriptive Statistics" to learn more.

Calculate Rank

S ometimes you want to find how one thing ranks in relation to others. For example, you might want to find out how a particular student's test score ranks in relation to all other students: Did the student receive the highest score, the second highest score, and so on? The RANK function ranks a number relative to other numbers in a list. If you sort a list in numerical order, the rank is equal to the position where the number would fall in the list. You can tell the RANK function whether the list on which you want to base the rank should be sorted in ascending order or descending order.

If two numbers have the same value, the RANK function gives them the same rank. For example, in the list 100, 95, 90, 85, 85, 80, 60, the RANK function ranks the

number 85 fourth. If two or more numbers have the same rank, subsequent numbers are affected. In the preceding list, the RANK function ranks 80 sixth.

The RANK function takes three arguments: Number, the number for which you want to find the rank; Ref, the array or cell range you want to evaluate; and Order, the order in which you want to sort the list. Type a 0 or omit the Order argument if you want to sort the list in descending order. Type a nonzero value if you want to sort the list in ascending order. When using the RANK function, if you reference nonnumeric values, the RANK function ignores them.

Calculate Rank

① Click the cell in which you want the results to appear.

② Click the Insert Function button.

● The Insert Function dialog box appears.

③ Click here and select Statistical.

④ Double-click RANK.

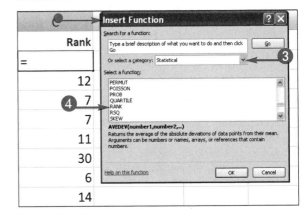

- The Function Arguments dialog box appears.

⑤ Click to select the cell or type the number for which you want the rank.

⑥ Type the range or the array you want to evaluate your number against.

⑦ Type **0** for descending order or any nonzero value for ascending order.

⑧ Click OK.

○ The result appears in the cell in which you placed the formula.

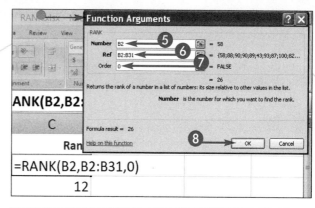

=RANK(B2,B2:B31,0)

12

| C2 | | f_x | =RANK(B2,B2:B31,0) |

	A	B	C
1	Student #	Test Scores	Rank
2	570013	58	26
3	580312	88	12
4	931107	90	7
5	932758	90	7
6	729584	89	11
7	396617	43	30
8	906749	93	6
9	604930	87	14
10	299802	100	1

Extra

You can use the PERCENTRANK function to determine the rank of a value as a percentage of all the values in your data set. The PERCENTRANK function takes three arguments: Array, the array or range you want to use to determine the percent rank; X, the value you want to rank; and Significance, the number of significant digits in which you want your results returned. The default is three digits. If you leave this argument blank, the PERCENTRANK function uses the default.

The PERCENTRANK function uses the following formula: pr=a/(b+c). In the formula, pr equals the percent rank, a equals the number of values smaller than the value for which you are looking, b equals the number of values smaller than or equal to the value for which you are looking, and c equals the number of values larger than the value for which you are looking.

The PERCENTRANK function gives equal values the same rank. If you want to format the value returned as a percentage, select the cell, click the Home tab, and then click the Percent Style button (%).

Calculate Frequency

When you collect large amounts of data, organizing your data can help you see patterns. Usually, you start by sorting your data so you can see the range of values. The next step might be to do a simple frequency distribution so you can see how often each value occurs. To understand your data further, you might create a grouped frequency distribution. Grouping your data makes it easy for you to compare categories of data.

You can use Excel's FREQUENCY function to group your data into categories. For example, you can use the FREQUENCY function to display student test scores. The first group might be scores less than or equal to 50, representing scores 50 percent or lower; your second group might be 51 to 60; the next group 61 to 70, and so on, up to scores of 90 percent or higher. Excel counts the number of occurrences in each group.

You must supply the FREQUENCY function with two arguments: the Data_array and the Bins_array. The Data_array is the list of values you want to group. The Bins_array is the list of groupings you want to use. To use the FREQUENCY function, you must select the cells into which you want to place your results. If you have five groups, select six cells — one more cell than the number of groups you have. Type the function or enter it into the Function Arguments dialog box. Frequency is an array function; curly braces must surround your function. If you use the Function Arguments dialog box, press Ctrl+Shift+Enter after you enter your arguments. Excel will place curly braces around your function. If curly braces do not surround your function, your function will not calculate.

Calculate Frequency

① Select the cells in which you want the results to appear.

② Click the Insert Function button.

● The Insert Function dialog box appears.

③ Click here and select Statistical.

④ Double-click FREQUENCY.

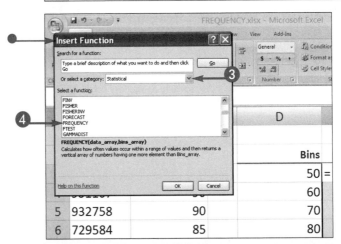

- The Function Arguments dialog box appears.

5 Select the range, type the range name, or type the array you want to evaluate.

6 Select the grouping you want to use.

7 Press Ctrl+Shift+Enter.

Do not click OK. Clicking OK will not place curly braces around your formula.

- The results appear in the cells you selected.

Function Arguments

FREQUENCY

| Data_array | B2:B31 | {58;88;90;90;85;43;93;87;100;82;84;6 |
| Bins_array | D3:D7 | {50;60;70;80;90} |

= {1;5;3;2;13;6}

Calculates how often values occur within a range of values and then returns a vertical array of numbers having one more element than Bins_array.

Data_array is an array of or reference to a set of values for which you want to count frequencies (blanks and text are ignored).

Formula result = 1

Help on this function   OK   Cancel

		F
		uency
3	88	50 =FREQUENCY(B2:
4	90	60	5
5	90	70	3
6	85	80	2
7	43	90	13
8	93		6
9	87		

E3   fx {=FREQUENCY(B2:B31,D3:D7)}

	B	C	D	E	F
2	58			Bins	Frequency
3	88		50	1
4	90		60	5
5	90		70	3
6	85		80	2
7	43		90	13
8	93			6
9	87			
10	100			

Extra

When you create your frequency distribution, keep the following rules in mind:

- Keep the number of groups reasonable, between five and ten is good. If you have too few or too many groups, you can lose your ability to convey information easily. Too few intervals can hide trends and too many intervals can mask details.

- Keep your intervals simple. Intervals of 5, 10, or 20 are good because they are easy to understand.

- Start your interval with a value that is divisible by the interval size. That will make your frequency distribution easy to read.

- All intervals should have the same number of values. Again, this makes your frequency distribution easy to understand.

You can use Excel's chart tools to chart your frequency distribution. Use a Column chart. Place your groupings on the horizontal axis and your frequencies on the vertical axis.

Calculate Variance and Standard Deviation

Statisticians refer to the average of a group of values as the *mean*. When you have a list of numbers, you can use the variance and standard deviation to show how much a group of numbers varies from the mean — the larger the variance, the more the values vary from the mean. You can use standard deviation to do things such as compare the risk involved in purchasing stock. Simply put, the higher the standard deviation, the riskier the stock.

When manually calculating variance, you start by calculating the mean of all the values in your list, and then you subtract each value in the list from the mean value. This tells you how much each value deviates from the mean. You then square each deviation, sum the squared deviations, and then divide the sum by the number of values minus 1 to obtain the variance.

Instead of performing this complex calculation to calculate the variance, you can use the VAR function to obtain the variance. The VAR function takes one type of argument, Number1 through Number255. An array is a list of values enclosed in curly braces. For example {20, 25, 25, 30} is an array. In each Number argument, you can enter a number, a range that contains numbers, a range name, or an array.

Finding the variance is often useful, but because the variance is a squared value, it is difficult to interpret the variance in relation to the mean. Therefore, statisticians often calculate the square root of the variance. They call the resulting value the *standard deviation*. You can use Excel's STDEV function to calculate the standard deviation. The STDEV function takes the same type of argument as the VAR function and works in much the same way.

Calculate Variance and Standard Deviation

CALCULATE VARIANCE

1. Click in the cell in which you want to calculate the variance.

2. Type **=VAR(**.

   Alternatively, select VAR from the AutoComplete list that appears after you begin typing.

3. Click the Insert Function button.

   • The Function Arguments dialog box appears.

4. Type the range, range name, or values for which you want to find the variance.

5. Click OK.

   • Excel calculates the variance.

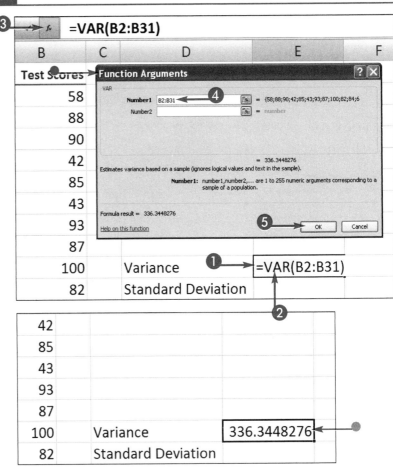

CALCULATE THE STANDARD DEVIATION

1. Click in the cell in which you want to calculate the standard deviation.

2. Type **=STDEV(**.

   Alternatively, select STDEV from the AutoComplete list that appears after you begin typing.

3. Click the Insert Function button.

   ● The Function Arguments dialog box appears.

4. Type the range, range name, or values for which you want to find the standard deviation.

5. Click OK.

   ● Excel calculates the standard deviation.

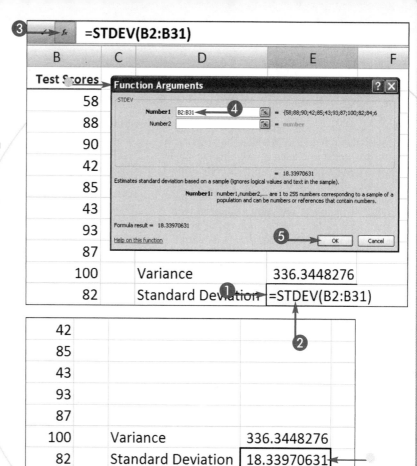

Extra

When calculating and using standard deviation, keep the following in mind:

- The standard deviation is always a positive number.
- A single outlier can distort the standard deviation.
- If every value in a data set is the same, the standard deviation is zero.
- If two sets of data have approximately the same mean, the higher the standard deviation the more variability there is in the data.
- If your data is distributed normally, about 68 percent of your data lies between one standard deviation from both sides of the mean, approximately 95 percent of your data lies between two standard deviations from both sides of the mean, and approximately 99 percent of your data lies between three standard deviations from both sides of the mean.

Find the Correlation

With the CORREL function, you can measure the relationship between two variables. You can explore questions such as whether baseball players hit fewer home runs as they age. A correlation does not prove one thing causes another. The most you can say is that one number varies with the other. Their variation may be the result of how you measured your numbers or the result of some factor underlying both variables. When you use correlations, you start with a theory that two things are related. If there is a correlation, you must then gather evidence and develop plausible reasons for the correlation.

Use the CORREL function to determine a correlation. CORREL takes two arguments: array1 and array2 — the two lists of numbers. The result of the function is a

number, r, between –1 and 1. The closer r gets to –1 or 1, the stronger the relationship. If r is close to or equal to 0, that means that there is little to no correlation between the variables. If r is negative, the relationship is an inverse relationship — for example, as age increases, batting averages decrease. A positive result suggests that as one variable increases, so does the other. For example, as age increases, batting average increases.

When using CORREL, if a reference cell contains text, logical values, or empty cells, Excel ignores those values. However, reference cells that have a value of 0 are included in the calculation. If the number of data points in array1 and array2 are not equal, Excel returns the error message #N/A.

Find the Correlation

① Click the cell in which you want to place your answer.

② Type **=CORREL(**.

Alternatively, select CORREL from the AutoComplete list that appears after you begin typing.

	A	B	C	D
	Sales Representative	2007 Sales ($)	Years Employed	
1				
2	Johnson	200,415	4	
3	Smith	300,125	3	
4	Jones	142,569	3	
5	Jefferson	509,268	1	
6	Kinkade	205,916	4	
7	Richardson	452,361	4	
8	Allen	321,210	7	
9	Briget	423,156	8	
10	Paulson	215,467	3	
11	Morris	234,567	4	
12	Total	3,005,054		
13	Correlation Between Sales and Years Employed	=CORREL(		
14		CORREL(**array1**, array2)		
15				

③ Click the Insert Function button.

NETWORKDAYS f_x =CORREL(

	A	B	C	D
	Sales Representative	2007 Sales ($)	Years Employed	
1				
2	Johnson	200,415	4	
3	Smith	300,125	3	
4	Jones	142,569	3	
5	Jefferson	509,268	1	
6	Kinkade	205,916	4	
7	Richardson	452,361	4	
8	Allen	321,210	7	
9	Briget	423,156	8	
10	Paulson	215,467	3	
11	Morris	234,567	4	
12	Total	3,005,054		
13	Correlation Between Sales and Years Employed	=CORREL(		
14		CORREL(**array1**, array2)		
15				

The Function Arguments dialog box appears.

④ Click and drag to select the first series of numbers, or type the cell range.

⑤ Click and drag to select the second series of numbers, or type the cell range.

Note: *You can select a subset of a list, but make sure the same subset is selected for each list.*

⑥ Click OK.

● The correlation coefficient appears.

Note: *The sign suggests whether the relationship is positive (+) or negative (−).*

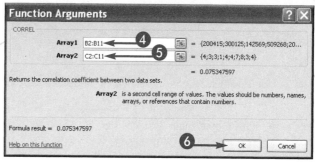

B13		f_x	=CORREL(B2:B11,C2:C11)	
	A		B	C	D
			2007 Sales	**Years**	
1	**Sales Representative**		**($)**	**Employed**	
2	Johnson		200,415	4	
3	Smith		300,125	3	
4	Jones		142,569	3	
5	Jefferson		509,268	1	
6	Kinkade		205,916	4	
7	Richardson		452,361	4	
8	Allen		321,210	7	
9	Briget		423,156	8	
10	Paulson		215,467	3	
11	Morris		234,567	4	
12	**Total**		**3,005,054**		
	Correlation Between Sales				
13	**and Years Employed**		0.0753476		
14					

Extra

An *add-in* is software that adds one or more features to Excel. To learn how to install add-ins, see the next task, "Install Excel Add-Ins." The Analysis Toolpak is an add-In that contains a number of statistical tools, including the Correlation tool, which you can use to calculate correlations. Correlations calculated by using the Correlation tool do not automatically update as you update your worksheet.

Squaring the value of r makes the value easier to understand. The square of r tells you how the percent of the variation in one value relates to the other value. To find the percent of variation, you square r and then drop the decimal point. For example, if r is equal to .5, the square of r is 25 percent. The 25 percent value tells you that 25 percent of the variation is related.

Install Excel Add-Ins

nstalling add-ins gives you additional Excel features not available in the Ribbon by default. An *add-in* is software that adds one or more features to Excel. Bundled add-in software is included with Excel but is not automatically installed when you install Excel. The following are among the add-ins that come standard with Excel:

- The Conditional Sum Wizard enables you to create a formula that only sums the values that meet the criteria you specify.

- The Euro Currency Tools add-in enables you to calculate exchange rates between the Euro and other currencies.

- The Data Analysis Toolpak provides you with a number of tools you can use for statistical analysis.

The remainder of the chapter introduces a few of the statistical add-ins in the Data Analysis Toolpak.

You install the bundled add-ins by using the Excel Options dialog box. You can find them in the Add-Ins section. Once installed, the add-ins are available right away. In many cases, they are on the Add-Ins tab. However, the Data Analysis Toolpak appears on the Data tab.

Removing an add-in is easy. Click the Office button, click Excel Options, click Add-ins, click the add-in you want to remove, and then click Go. The Add-Ins dialog box appears. Click to deselect the add-in you want to remove and then click OK. Excel removes the add-in.

You can take advantage of third-party add-ins. This type of software adds functionality in support of advanced work in chemistry, risk analysis, modeling, project management, statistics, and other fields. Third-party add-ins usually have their own installation and usage procedures. Consult the developer of these programs for documentation.

Install Excel Add-Ins

1. Click the Office button.

   A menu appears.

2. Click Excel Options.

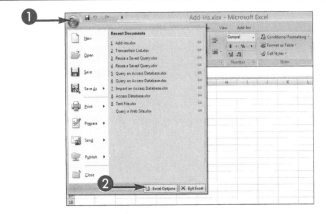

   The Excel Options dialog box appears.

3. Click Add-Ins.

- The View and Manage Microsoft Office Add-ins screen appears.

4. Click an add-in.

   The example uses the Analysis Toolpak.

5. Click Go.

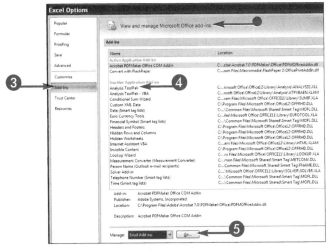

- The Add-Ins dialog box appears and provides access to several options.

6 Click to select an add-in (☐ changes to ☑).

7 Click OK.

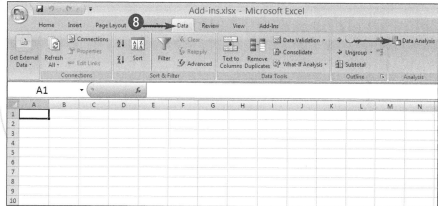

8 Click the Data tab.

- Excel places the Add-in in the Ribbon.

Extra

You can download additional Excel add-ins from the Microsoft download site. For example, for Excel 2007, Microsoft has an add-in that adds a Get Started tab to the Excel 2007 Ribbon. The commands on this tab give you quick access to free online content to help you learn Excel 2007 quickly.

Microsoft has a set of SQL Server 2005 Data Mining Add-ins for Office 2007 that allows you to take advantage of SQL Server 2005's predictive analytics in Excel 2007. The add-ins are Table Analysis Tools for Excel and Data Mining Client for Excel.

To learn about special-purpose Excel add-ins in your field, you can perform a Google search by going to www.google.com. Your search terms should include Excel, the field of knowledge — for example, chemistry — and other information you might have, such as vendor name. Third-party vendors are responsible for supporting their own products.

Calculate a Moving Average

The Moving Average tool projects values based on the average value over a specified period. Using a moving average can reveal trends that are masked when you use a simple average because a simple average gives equal weight to each value. A moving average weighs recent values equally and ignores older values, thereby allowing you to spot trends. You can use a moving average to forecast sales, stock prices, or other trends.

You specify the number of values, or *intervals*, Excel should use to calculate the moving average. If you do not supply an interval, Excel uses the default value of 3, which means that the moving average is calculated by averaging the last three values.

Unlike other tools available for Data Analysis, the Moving Average tool can only output the values to the current worksheet. You need to specify the first cell you

want to use for the results. If the first row contains a label, your data should start in the second row. In addition to a forecast, you can elect to have Excel compute the standard error. If you select this option, Excel creates an additional column that contains the standard error. The standard error is a measure of the relative accuracy of the predictions.

You can also create a chart that shows the relationship between the actual values in the data set and the forecasted moving average. If you select this option, Excel places the chart on the same worksheet as the moving average values.

Excel provides the Moving Average tool as part of the Data Analysis Toolpak. See the previous task, "Install Excel Add-Ins," to learn how to install the Data Analysis Toolpak.

Calculate a Moving Average

① Create the range of data to use to predict the moving average.

② Click the Data tab.

③ Click Data Analysis.

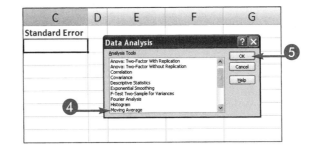

The Data Analysis dialog box appears.

④ Click Moving Average.

⑤ Click OK.

The Moving Average dialog box appears.

6 Click and drag, enter a range name, or type the values you want to analyze.

7 If the first row contains labels, click Labels in First Row (☐ changes to ☑).

8 Specify an integer value for the interval.

Note: *If the integer value is omitted, Excel uses a default value of 3.*

9 Specify the output cell reference.

● You can click Chart Output (☐ changes to ☑) to chart the values.

10 Click Standard Errors (☐ changes to ☑) to create Standard Error values.

11 Click OK.

● Excel computes the moving average and standard error.

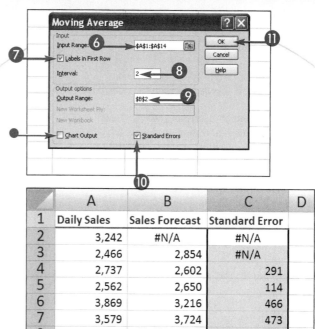

	A	B	C	D
1	Daily Sales	Sales Forecast	Standard Error	
2	3,242	#N/A	#N/A	
3	2,466	2,854	#N/A	
4	2,737	2,602	291	
5	2,562	2,650	114	
6	3,869	3,216	466	
7	3,579	3,724	473	
8	2,977	3,278	236	
9	3,729	3,353	341	
10	2,533	3,131	499	
11	3,187	2,860	482	
12	2,276	2,732	396	
13	2,686	2,481	353	
14	3,083	2,885	202	
15				

Extra

When you use the Moving Average tool, Excel calculates an average to determine each moving average value. The first few values in the column will contain the value #N/A. The number of cells that contain #N/A is one less than the integer value specified for the Interval value. For example, if the specified interval is 3, the first two cells in the Moving Average column contain the value #N/A because you do not have three values to average.

When you create a chart for the Moving Average, Excel automatically uses default labels for each data series, the axes, and the chart title. You can use the chart options to change the text of each label.

Compare Variances

You can use an F-test to determine whether two variances are equal. *Variance* is a measurement of how much a group of values varies from the group's mean value. For example, if you have two plants producing the same product, one in Indiana and one in Texas, and both have efficiency levels of 95 percent, but you want to know which plant remained consistently more efficient throughout the year, you can perform an F-test. If you find that the Indiana plant has a lower variance than the Texas plant, you know that the Indiana plant performed more efficiently.

When you use an F-test analysis, Excel compares the ratio of the variance between the two groups of data. Excel calculates an F statistic (F) for the two sets of data, which is the ratio of the Mean Standard Square Error

(MS) between the groups to the MS within the groups. If the F statistic is less than the F critical value, you cannot reject the null hypothesis that the variances of the two groups are the same. An F statistic close to 1 indicates that two groups have equal variances.

To perform this test, you must provide Excel with the ranges of both data groups as well as an Alpha level, or the statistical confidence level you expect. The Alpha field is the probability of the null hypothesis being true. You specify a value between 0 and 1 for the confidence level. The default level of .05 is equivalent to a 95-percent confidence level. To make your table easily identifiable, you can let Excel know that you have labels in the first row of your worksheet.

Compare Variances

① Create data for which you want to calculate the F-test.

② Click the Data tab.

③ Click Data Analysis.

● The Data Analysis dialog box appears.

④ Click F-Test Two-Sample for Variances.

⑤ Click OK.

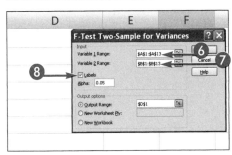

The F-Test Two-Sample for Variances dialog box displays.

⑥ Select the first range of cells to analyze.

⑦ Select the second range of cells to analyze.

⑧ If your data range has labels, click Labels (☐ changes to ☑).

9 Type a value between 0 and 1 for the significance level.

10 Specify the output location (○ changes to ◉).

11 Click OK.

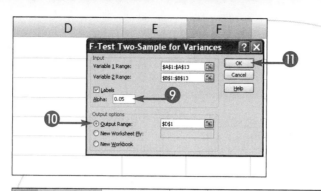

● Excel compares the variances between the two groups.

	A	B	C	D	E	F
1	**Indiana**	**Texas**		F-Test Two-Sample for Variances		
2	979	884				
3	985	723			*Indiana*	*Texas*
4	955	913		Mean	879.6667	859.75
5	924	965		Variance	6960.97	6119.114
6	890	875		Observations	12	12
7	756	930		df	11	11
8	790	886		F	1.137578	
9	850	751		P(F<=f) one-tail	0.417266	
10	930	785		F Critical one-tail	2.81793	
11	777	810				

Extra

When you use the F-test analysis tool, Excel calculates several values, as described in the following table.

STATISTIC	DESCRIPTION
Mean	The average value, or center of the distribution, of the data group.
Variance	A measurement of the spread or dispersion of the data. The average squared distance between each datum and the mean.
Observations	Indicates the number of values in each list.
df	Indicates the Degrees of Freedom, or the number of values that are free to vary after a statistic has been computed from a set of data.
F	The ratio of the variance of the individual groups to the entire range of values. The F statistic is the ratio of the mean square between the data sets over the mean square within the data sets.
P(F<=f) one-tail	A value between 0 and 1 that indicates the probability of observing a test statistic at least as extreme as the one observed. The closer the value is to 1, the higher the probability.
F critical one-tail	The critical value of the F distribution. It is dependent on both the level and the degrees of freedom. It is the standard against which the F statistic is compared.

Using the Data Analysis Toolpak to Determine Rank and Percentile

I f you want to rank a series of values in a list, you can use the Rank and Percentile tool. With this tool, Excel takes a list of numeric values and ranks them from highest to lowest by both a numeric and a percentage value. It also calculates a percentile for your value. For example, you may want to rank the sales from different salespeople within the organization to show not only which person had the highest sales but also to determine the salesperson's percentile when compared to the entire sales team. This feature is perfect for ranking the top-selling item, the most efficient facility within a company, or the machine or team that produces the highest level of output.

You can only rank one row or column of values at a time. Excel allows you to select multiple rows or columns as the input range, but Excel only analyzes the first row or column. You can only have a label in the first row of a column. If the specified range contains any other text, an error message displays.

You can output the results of the Rank and Percentile tool to a specific range of cells within the current worksheet, a new worksheet, or a new workbook. If you select New Worksheet, you can specify the worksheet name or allow Excel to assign a default name.

Excel provides the Rank and Percentile tool as part of the Data Analysis Toolpak. See the task "Install Excel Add-Ins" to learn how to install the Data Analysis Toolpak.

Using the Data Analysis Toolpak to Determine Rank and Percentile

1 Create the data you want to analyze.

2 Click the Data tab.

3 Click Data Analysis.

• The Data Analysis dialog box appears.

4 Click Rank and Percentile.

5 Click OK.

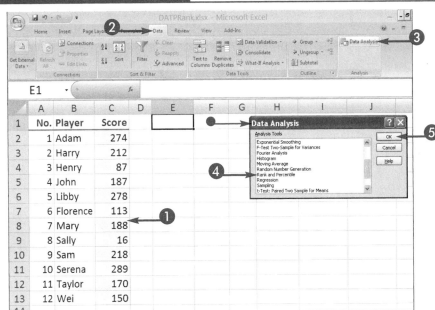

The Rank and Percentile dialog box appears.

6 Specify the range of cells to analyze.

7 Specify whether data values are rows or columns (○ changes to ◉).

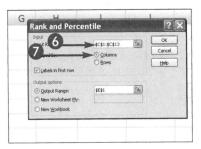

8 If the first row contains labels, click Labels in First Row (☐ changes to ☑).

9 Specify the output location (○ changes to ⦿).

10 Click OK.

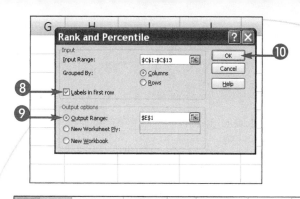

● Excel ranks the specified range of data.

	A	B	C	D	E	F	G	H
1	No.	Player	Score		Point	Score	Rank	Percent
2	1	Adam	274		10	289	1	100.00%
3	2	Harry	212		5	278	2	90.90%
4	3	Henry	87		1	274	3	81.80%
5	4	John	187		9	218	4	72.70%
6	5	Libby	278		2	212	5	63.60%
7	6	Florence	113		7	188	6	54.50%
8	7	Mary	188		4	187	7	45.40%
9	8	Sally	16		11	170	8	36.30%
10	9	Sam	218		12	150	9	27.20%
11	10	Serena	289		6	113	10	18.10%
12	11	Taylor	170		3	87	11	9.00%
13	12	Wei	150		8	16	12	0.00%
14								

Extra

Excel creates a four-column table containing ranking information for the specified values, as outlined in the following table.

COLUMN	DESCRIPTION
Point	The location of the data value within the specified input range. For example, if the value was originally the third numeric value in the input data, the point value is 3.
Input	Contains the input values sorted based upon the ranking.
Rank	The numeric ranking of each value with 1 being the highest ranking value in the list.
Percent	A percentage ranking for the input values. The percentage indicates the percentage of values that are below the specified value.

Calculate Descriptive Statistics

Y ou can have Excel quickly calculate 16 different statistical measurements and summarize them in a list using the Descriptive Statistics tool. For an analyst, this feature is perfect for calculating statistical information on large databases or worksheets. When you use this tool, Excel produces a table containing standard statistical calculations for each group of data values in your list, including the mean, standard error, median, mode, standard deviation, sample variance, kurtosis, skewness, range, minimum, maximum, sum, count, largest value, smallest value, and confidence level. For example, if you use it to compare a list containing sales amounts for different regions, Excel produces a table containing the statistical values related to each region.

With the Descriptive Statistics tool, you must specify the range of cells containing the sets of data. You also must indicate whether you have your data sets grouped in rows or in columns. Each row or column must contain a different set of data. You can make the output easier to identify by labeling your data.

You can use the last four options in the Descriptive Statistics dialog box to specify which descriptive statistic values Excel calculates. Use the Summary Statistics option to calculate all of the common descriptive statistic values. If you want to calculate the confidence level of the mean, you specify the confidence level. For example, 90% indicates a significance of 10%. Kth Largest and Kth Smallest allow you to find specific values in the group, such as the second smallest or third largest number. If you specify a value of 1, you receive the same values Excel gives you for the Minimum and Maximum values.

Calculate Descriptive Statistics

① Click the Data tab.

② Click Data Analysis.

● The Data Analysis dialog box appears.

③ Click Descriptive Statistics.

④ Click OK.

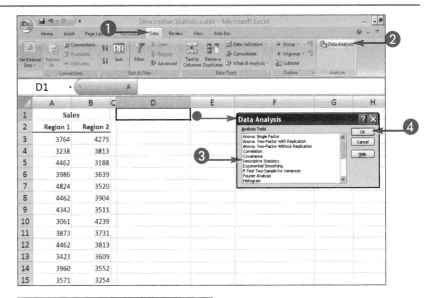

The Descriptive Statistics dialog box appears.

⑤ Specify the range of cells to analyze.

⑥ Specify whether data values are in rows or columns.

⑦ Click if you have labels in your first row or column (☐ changes to ☑).

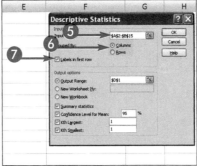

8 Specify the output location (○ changes to ◉).

9 Click Summary Statistics (☐ changes to ☑) to produce a table with all 16 of Excel's statistical measurements.

10 Click Confidence Level for Mean (☐ changes to ☑) to show the confidence level.

11 Type a Confidence Level.

12 You can click Kth Largest and Kth Smallest (☐ changes to ☑) to display specific values in each group.

13 Click OK.

● Excel analyzes the data and produces descriptive statistics for each group of values.

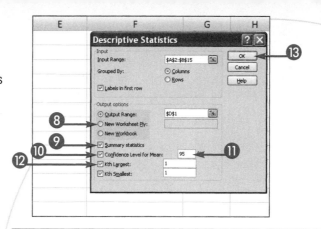

	A	B	C	D	E	F	G
1	Sales			Region 1		Region 2	
2	Region 1	Region 2					
3	3764	4275		Mean	3956	Mean	3696
4	3238	3813		Standard Error	149.0151429	Standard Error	89.59095078
5	4462	3188		Median	3960	Median	3639
6	3986	3639		Mode	4462	Mode	3813
7	4824	3520		Standard Deviation	537.2817386	Standard Deviation	323.0247669
8	4462	3904		Sample Variance	288671.6667	Sample Variance	104345
9	4342	3511		Kurtosis	-0.952326355	Kurtosis	-0.014711934
10	3061	4239		Skewness	-0.128917837	Skewness	0.389755268
11	3873	3731		Range	1763	Range	1087
12	4462	3813		Minimum	3061	Minimum	3188
13	3423	3609		Maximum	4824	Maximum	4275
14	3960	3552		Sum	51428	Sum	48048
15	3571	3254		Count	13	Count	13
16				Largest(1)	4824	Largest(1)	4275
17				Smallest(1)	3061	Smallest(1)	3188
18				Confidence Level(95.0%)	324.6761048	Confidence Level(95.0%)	195.2019128
19							

Extra

When you use the Descriptive Statistics tool, Excel calculates several values:

STATISTIC	DESCRIPTION
Mean	The average value, or center of the distribution, of the data group.
Standard Error	The square root of the sample size (n) divided into the standard deviation over the square root of the sample size (n).
Median	The middle value in the group of data.
Mode	The most common value in the group of data.
Standard Deviation	The dispersion of the group of data values around the mean.
Sample Variance	The standard deviation squared, or the measure of the dispersion of the data.
Kurtosis	The measure of how concentrated data is to the center of the distribution.
Skewness	The degree of symmetry in distribution around a central axis.
Range	The difference between the largest and smallest values.
Minimum/Maximum	The smallest and largest values in the group.
Sum	The total when you add all of the values in the group.
Count	The number of values in the group.
Largest(N)/Smallest(N)	The largest and smallest values in the group, where N is a specified integer.
Confidence Level	How much your value deviates from the mean.

Enter Data with a Form

A *list* is a worksheet structured as a set of columns and rows. Each column represents a single type of data. In Excel, you can use a form to simplify entering data into a list. A form speeds up your data entry by providing a blank field for each column in your list. Place labels in the first row of your list. Your form will use these labels as field names. You type your data into your form and use the Tab key to move from field to field. After you complete each set of fields, you click the Next button to enter the record into a row in your list and then you type in a new record. You can move backward and forward through your list to view or modify your data.

Your form also doubles as a search box. You can use your form to search for and edit your data. With the list

and form displayed, click your form's Criteria button. In a blank field, type an operator, such as = or >, and a value in one or more fields. If the value you are looking for is text, place quotes around the value; for example, ="Jones". If the value is numerical, do not use quotes; for example, >50000. If several records match your criteria, you can display the additional records by clicking the Find Prev (Previous) and Find Next buttons, as appropriate.

You must add the Form button to the Quick Access toolbar before you can use forms. Refer to the Extra section of the task "Assign a Macro to the Quick Access Toolbar" in Chapter 12 to learn how to add a button to the Quick Access toolbar.

Enter Data with a Form

① Type your column labels.

② Click and drag to select your column heads.

③ Click the Form button.

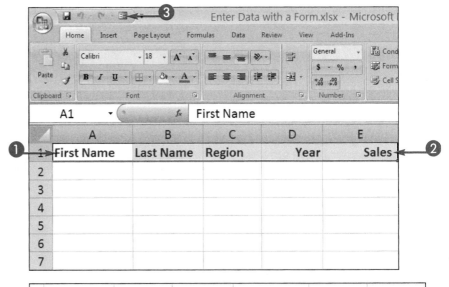

A warning appears.

④ Read the warning and then click OK.

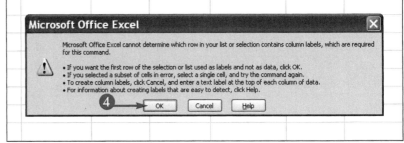

- The data form appears, consisting of one field for each column label you created.

5 Type the requested information into the first field.

6 Press Tab to move to the next field.

7 Repeat Steps 5 and 6 to complete the remaining fields.

8 After completing the first set of fields, click New to start a new record.

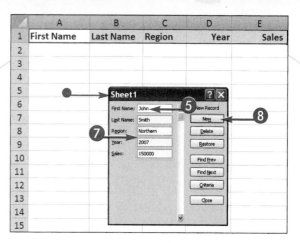

- The data fills the worksheet and the form fields clear, ready for another record.

9 Repeat Steps 5 to 8 for each new record.

10 Click Close after entering all your data.

A list of your records appears in the worksheet.

Apply It

Using the sample file Form.xlsx, Sheet2, which is on the Web site for this book, you can find all records for Jones. Click in cell A2 and then click the Form button in the Quick Access toolbar. Your data appears in the form. Click the Criteria button, type **Jones** in the Last Name field, and then click Find Next and/or Find Prev to find the records that meet your criteria. Alternatively, you can find all records with sales greater than 50,000 dollars. Click the Criteria button in the Sales field and type **>50000**.

While you are editing a record through a form, you can click the Restore button at any time to bring back the original contents of the field. You can click the Delete button to delete a record. However, if you use the Delete button, Excel permanently deletes the record. You cannot bring back the record with the Undo command. You cannot use a form to edit values returned by a formula.

Filter Duplicate Records

Excel provides many tools for managing long lists. With such lists, you may need to identify and display unique records. A store manager, for example, might want to have a unique list of customers in a particular state so she can mail the customers information about a sale. Alternatively, a baseball-card collector might want to find the number of unique players represented in his collection so he can create a catalog.

Excel provides tools for displaying unique records that meet certain criteria. You start with a worksheet formatted as a list, in which some of the records are duplicates, meaning the values in two or more rows are the same. Use Excel's advanced filtering tool to identify and filter the duplicates. You must specify the criteria by which you want to filter your data. Your criteria consist of a least two rows, one

with one or more labels and the other with criteria. Because Excel hides the duplicate rows, the best placement for your criteria is above, not beside, your list. Place at least one blank row between your criteria range and your list.

You have two options when you create a filtered list using Excel's advanced filtering tool. You can have your filtered list appear in place — under the column heads of your unfiltered list — thereby temporarily replacing your unfiltered list. Alternatively, if you want to keep your unfiltered list in your worksheet, you can place your filtered list in another location. Use the Copy To field in the Advanced Filter dialog box to specify the location. If you copy your list to another location, you can specify which fields you want to copy by typing the column labels into the area you specify in the Copy To field.

Filter Duplicate Records

1. Setup:
   - Your list
   - Criteria range, with criteria
   - Copy to location

2. Click a cell in your list.

3. Click the Data tab.

4. Click Advanced in the Sort & Filter group.

5. In the Advanced Filter dialog box, click Copy To Another Location (○ changes to ◉).

6. Click and drag to select your entire list, or type the cell range.

7. Click and drag to select your criteria range, or type the cell range.

8. Click and drag to select the labels for your Copy To range.

9. Click Unique Records Only (☐ changes to ☑).

10. Click OK.

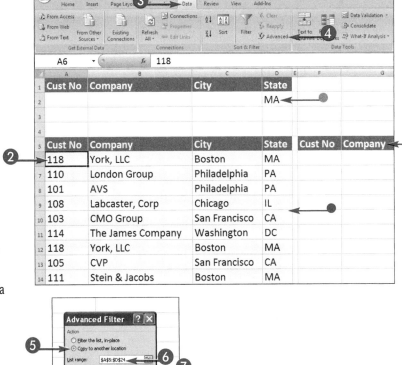

- The unique records appear under the labels.

  In this example, Excel returns a unique list of customers in Massachusetts (MA).

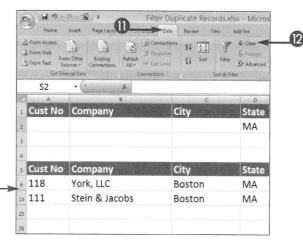

- If you chose Filter the List, In-place in Step 5, your screen will look similar to the one shown here.

⑪ Click the Data tab.

⑫ Click Clear.

  Excel displays all the records

Extra

You can use Excel's advanced filtering feature to display a unique list — a list with just one copy of rows in which every field in every column is the same. Click the Data tab. Click Advanced in the Sort & Filter group. The Advanced Filter dialog box appears. Select whether you want to filter your list in place or to another location (○ changes to ◉). Complete the List Range field. Do not enter a Criteria Range. Enter a Copy To location, if Excel is filtering in place. Click Unique Records Only (☐ changes to ☑), and then click OK. Excel displays unique records. For a demonstration, see Sheet3 of Filter Duplicate Records.xlsx, which is on the Web site for this book.

Filtering duplicate records temporarily removes them from view. If you want to delete duplicate records permanently, select your list, and click the Data tab. Then, in the Data tools group, click Remove Duplicates. The Remove Duplicates dialog box appears. If your list has headers, click My Data has Headers (☐ changes to ☑). Select the columns you want to check for duplicates and then click OK. Excel deletes the duplicate records.

Perform Simple Sorts and Filters

Sorting and filtering your lists offers different views of your data. When you sort, you rearrange your data in ascending or descending order. The meaning of these terms depends on the kind of data you have. Customer data arranged by the date in ascending order shows the earliest record first; descending order shows the latest record first. When you sort by customer name, the names appear in ascending (A to Z) or descending (Z to A) order. When you sort numeric data in ascending order, the numbers sort from the lowest number to the highest. In descending order, numbers sort from highest to lowest. When you arrange a list in a familiar order, you can easily find data, group data, and present it meaningfully to others.

Filtering works like a sieve through which you pass your data, displaying only data that meets your criteria. In a

customer survey, for example, you can choose to view only customers who live in a certain state or city or are of a certain age or gender.

When you click Filter in the Sort & Filter group on the Data tab, Excel places down arrows next to each of the fields in your table. You can use the down arrows to display a menu with options that enable you to sort and filter your data. You can apply multiple filters to the same list.

If you have added, deleted, or modified your data, based your data on dynamic filters such as Today, This Week, or Year to Date, or if values returned by formulas have changed, you may need to refresh your filter. To refresh, click Reapply on the Data tab in the Sort & Filter group.

Perform Simple Sorts and Filters

SORT A LIST

1. Click a cell in a list.

2. Click the Data tab.

3. Click a sort direction.

   Click A to Z to sort from lowest to highest — ascending order.

   Click Z to A to sort from highest to lowest — descending order.

● Excel sorts your list by the column you selected.

FILTER A LIST

1. Click a cell in your table.

2. Click the Data tab.

3. Click Filter in the Sort & Filter group.

- Down arrows appear next to your field headers.

④ Click a down arrow.

The Sort & Filter dialog box appears.

⑤ Click to deselect the items you do not want
(☑ changes to ☐).

⑥ Click OK.

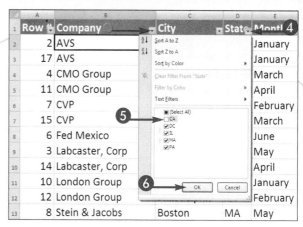

- Excel filters your list.

In the example, records from California (CA)
do not appear.

Extra

When you perform a filter, Excel places down arrows (▾) next to your field headers. Fields you have filtered have a filter on the down arrow button (▾). Fields you have sorted in ascending order have an up-arrow on the down-arrow button (▴). Fields you have sorted in descending order have a down-arrow on the down-arrow button (▾).

To clear all filters, click Clear in the Sort & Filter group on the Data tab. To remove the down arrows next to your field names, click Filter. To bring the down arrows back, click Filter, again. Filter toggles the Sort & Filter feature on and off.

Excel defines different sorts as follows: For numbers, ascending order goes from the smallest number to the largest. For text that includes numerals, as in U2 and K12, ascending order places numerals before symbols and symbols before letters. Case does not matter unless you click Options in the Sort dialog box and then click the Case Sensitive check box (☐ changes to ☑). To open the Sort dialog box, click Sort in the Sort & Filter group on the Data tab.

Perform Complex Sorts

Sorting a list by one criterion, such as sales, arranges your records for easy scanning. You can also sort by multiple criteria — a sort within a sort.

Data is either discrete or continuous. Discrete data assumes only a few values; for example, region, quarter, and gender are discrete. Quarter is discrete because it has only four possible values: Quarter 1, Quarter 2, Quarter 3, and Quarter 4. Gender is discrete because it has only two possible values: male and female. Continuous data can have a wide variety, if not an infinite number, of values; examples are incomes and names. Sorting discrete data groups like values so you can compare one category to another. Sorting continuous data imposes order by alphabetizing it or ranking it numerically.

When possible, sort first by a discrete category such as quarter, region, or gender. That way, subsequent sorts apply to the multiple values contained within each category. For example, after sorting your sales records by quarter, you could sort them by region to make it easy to compare sales by quarter and within each quarter by region. With your data sorted in this way, you can create subtotals, averages, and counts at every break in a category — that is, for all sales in a quarter and for each region.

You define complex sorts by using the Sort dialog box. Ascending and descending are not your only options. When using the Sort dialog box, you can click Options to specify a custom order. For example, you can order months chronologically from January to December instead of alphabetically from April to November. You can even create your own custom sort order.

Perform Complex Sorts

1. Click a cell in your list.

2. Click the Data tab.

3. Click Sort in the Sort & Filter group.

The Sort dialog box appears.

4. Click here and select the column by which you want to sort.

5. Click here and select Values.

6. Click here and select a sort order.

7. Click the Add Level button.

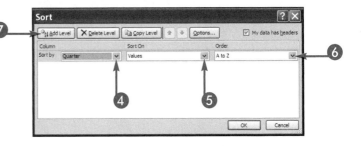

8. Repeat Steps 4 and 5 to sort by an additional criterion.

9. Click here and select Custom List.

● The Custom Lists dialog box appears.

10. Click to sort by days of the week or months of the year.

This example sorts by months of the year.

11. Click OK to close the Custom Lists dialog box.

12. Click OK to close the Sort dialog box.

● Your list sorts according to the order specified.

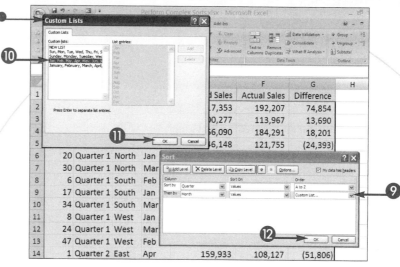

	A	B	C	D	E
1	Rec No	Quarter	Region	Month	Budgeted Sales	Act
2	42	Quarter 1	East	Jan	166,090
3	20	Quarter 1	North	Jan	193,124
4	17	Quarter 1	South	Jan	148,012
5	8	Quarter 1	West	Jan	125,091
6	12	Quarter 1	East	Feb	100,277
7	14	Quarter 1	North	Feb	146,148
8	6	Quarter 1	South	Feb	119,700
9	47	Quarter 1	West	Feb	152,771
10	9	Quarter 1	East	Mar	117,353
11	30	Quarter 1	North	Mar	167,757
12	34	Quarter 1	South	Mar	184,879
13	24	Quarter 1	West	Mar	176,231
14	1	Quarter 2	East	Apr	159,933

Extra

If you have a data series you use often, you can create a custom list and use it to sort. For example, say you collect data by region and you always list the data in the following order: Northeast, Southeast, North Central, South Central, Northwest, and Southwest. You can create a custom list that will enable you to sort based on this sort order.

To create a custom list, type the list you want to sort by into a vertical range of cells and then click the Office button. A menu appears. Click Excel Options. The Excel Options dialog box appears. Click Popular. In the Change the Most Popular Options in Excel pane, click the Edit Custom Lists button. The Custom Lists dialog box appears. In the Import Lists from Cells field, type the range for the list you created and then click Import. Alternatively, you can type your list in the List Entries field. Click OK. Your custom list is now ready for you to use in sorts. Just select Custom List in the Sort dialog box.

Sort by Cell Color, Font Color, or Icon

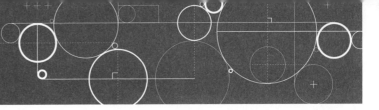

You can use conditional formatting to set criteria and then format your data based on that criteria. For example, you can have the highest ten values in a list appear in a particular color or font, or with an icon. You can have values that meet other criteria appear in another color or font, or with another icon. You can then sort your data based on the cell color, font, or icon you assigned.

You can also use conditional formatting to monitor conditions. For example, if your company offers a bonus whenever sales exceed $150,000, you can have Excel highlight cells containing sales figures whenever the value is more than $150,000. Changes affect conditionally formatted data. If, after a change, a cell no longer meets the condition, Excel removes the

highlighting. Conversely, if, after a change, a cell meets the condition, Excel adds highlighting. You determine exactly what the condition is and what should happen if a cell meets the condition. To learn more about conditional formatting, see Chapter 10.

You can manually assign cells a font color or cell color. Then you can sort cells by these colors. Select a single column and then use the Sort dialog box to sort your data. If you want to nest your sorts, you must format your data as a list. In the Sort dialog box, you select the font color or cell color you want to sort by and then tell Excel whether you want to send items of that type to the top or the bottom of the list. You can create sorts within sorts by sorting on different columns.

Sort by Cell Color, Font Color, or Icon

① Format your data with a color, font, or icon.

② Select the data you want to sort.

Note: *If you have formatted your data as a table, click any cell in the table. See the task "Define Data as a Table" later in this chapter.*

③ Click the Data tab.

④ Click Sort in the Sort & Filter group.

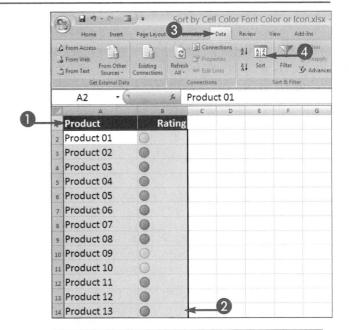

The Sort dialog box appears.

⑤ Click here and select the column by which you want to sort.

⑥ Click here and select whether you want to sort by a value, cell color, font color, or cell icon.

● If you select Cell Color, Font Color, or Cell Icon, an Order field appears.

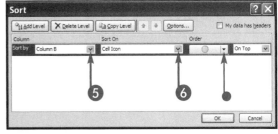

⑦ Click here and select a color or icon.

⑧ Click here and select On Top or On Bottom.

Click On Top to send the items that match the criteria to the top of the list.

Click On Bottom to send the items that match the criteria to the bottom of the list.

⑨ Click the Add Level button to add another level of sort.

⑩ Repeat Steps 5 to 9 to create additional sorts.

⑪ Click OK when you have finished.

● Excel sorts your data by font, color, or icon.

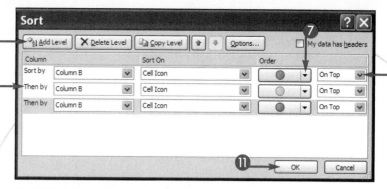

Extra

In the Sort dialog box, click Delete Level to delete a level of sort. Click Copy Level to copy a level of sort. Click 🔼 to move a sort level up. Click 🔽 to move a sort level down.

An alternative way to sort by cell color, font color, or icon is to right-click any cell that has the cell color, font color, or icon by which you want to sort. A menu appears. Click Sort. Another menu appears. Click to choose from Put Selected Cell Color on Top, Put Selected Font Color on Top, or Put Selected Icon on Top.

By default, Excel sorts from top to bottom. If you want to sort from left to right, click Sort on the Data tab in the Sort & Filter group. The Sort dialog box appears. Click the Options button in the Sort dialog box. The Sort Options dialog box appears. Click Sort Left to Right (◯ changes to ◉).

By default, sorts are not case sensitive. If you want to make them case sensitive, click Case Sensitive (☐ changes to ☑) in the Sort Options dialog box. Excel orders lowercase letters before uppercase letters.

Perform Complex Filters

W hereas sorting rearranges all records in ascending or descending order, filtering enables you to see only the records that match your criteria, hiding the rest. When filtering records, you can use the Custom AutoFilter dialog box to create complex filters. For example, you could use the following criteria: Age is greater than 65 and State equals Missouri, where Age and State are the names of column heads and you want to return all people in Missouri over 65.

When you filter a list, down arrows appear to the right of every column head. Click a column's down arrow to open the Custom AutoFilter dialog box, where you can select criteria. By applying a filter, you can display only those records that contain the values you specify — for example, all customers in Missouri. Using a custom AutoFilter, you

can create multiple filters in a single column by using and or or. Use and if you want to return records when both criteria are true — for example, all records that begin with SW and end with –04. Use or when you want to return records when either condition is true — for example, all records in Philadelphia or Chicago.

With Excel, you can combine filters, applying different criteria to different columns. By applying several filters, you can quickly narrow a long list to the few records of interest to you. If you apply too narrow a range of values, however, the criteria might not return any records. To filter a list by multiple criteria, start with a worksheet formatted as a list. See the task "Enter Data with a Form" to learn more about lists.

Perform Complex Filters

① Click a cell in your list.

② Click the Data tab.

③ Click Filter in the Sort & Filter group.

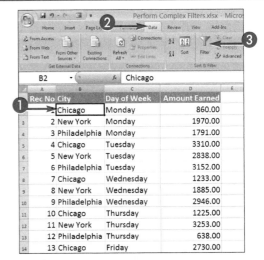

● Down arrows appear next to all of your column heads.

④ Click the down arrow next to the field you want to filter.

⑤ Click Number Filters if you chose a number field.

   Alternatively, click Text Filters if you chose a text field or Date Filters if you chose a date field.

⑥ Click Custom Filter.

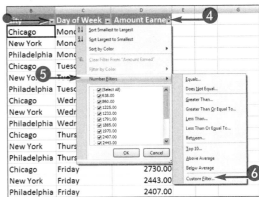

The Custom AutoFilter dialog box appears.

7 Click here and select an operator.

8 Type a value or select a value.

- You can repeat Steps 7 and 8 if you want to create a second criterion. Choose And (○ changes to ●) if you want both criteria to be met. Choose Or (○ changes to ●) if you want either criterion to be met.

9 Click OK.

- The list displays records matching your criteria.

Click the Data tab and then click Clear in the Sort & Filter group to clear your filter.

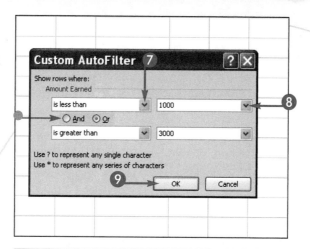

	A	B	C	D	E
1	Rec N	City	Day of Week	Amount Earne	
2	1	Chicago	Monday	860.00	
5	4	Chicago	Tuesday	3310.00	
7	6	Philadelphia	Tuesday	3152.00	
12	11	New York	Thursday	3253.00	
13	12	Philadelphia	Thursday	638.00	
17					
18					

Apply It

You can use a numeric filter to return all values that are above or below average. Click the down arrow next to the numeric field you want to filter. A menu appears. Click Number Filters and then click either Above Average or Below Average, based on your preference. Excel filters your list and the appropriate values appear.

You can also use a numeric filter to view the top or bottom N values in a list, where N stands for the number of values you want to view. Click the down arrow next to the numeric field you want to filter. A menu appears. Click Number Filters and then click Top Ten. The Top 10 AutoFilter dialog box appears. Select Top if you want to view the top N values. Click Bottom if you want to view the bottom N values. Type the number of values you want to view and then select whether you want Excel to return results based on a number or a percentage. Click OK. Excel returns the results you requested.

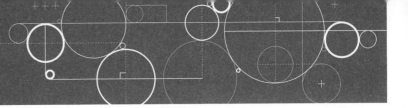

Enter Criteria to Find Records

Once you have created a list of data, you may want to retrieve specific information from the list. Using Excel's Advanced Filter, you can set up complex filters and use them to limit the data you retrieve.

When using Excel's Advanced Filter, you must identify an area called the *criteria range*. In the criteria range, you tell Excel exactly what you are looking for. For example, you can tell Excel you want to retrieve all males with an income of $100,000 or more.

Types of Criteria

You can use two types of criteria to find records: comparison criteria and computed criteria.

With comparison criteria, you enter your criteria underneath a field label. For example, if you want to find all people with an income greater than $100,000, you would enter **>100000** under the field labeled Income as shown in the table.

Criteria:

LAST_NAME	FIRST_NAME	PROPERTY_TAX	INCOME_TAX	STATE	INCOME
					>100000

List:

LAST_NAME	FIRST_NAME	PROPERTY_TAX	INCOME_TAX	STATE	INCOME
Mayfield	Adam	4,143	23,487	MA	117,436
Jones	Libby	4,230	14,537	MA	146,621
Jacs	Henry	3,875	12,844	MA	64,220
Mathews	John	3,933	25,174	MA	125,871

With computed criteria, you use a formula to find the records for which you are looking. Use computed criteria when your list does not have a field with the information for which you are looking. For example, if you want to extract all records from the list in the illustration where the property tax plus the income tax is greater than $20,000, you could use the formula =Property_Tax+Income_Tax>20000 as your criteria.

When you use computed criteria, at least one variable in the formula must be a field in your list. However, the criteria label cannot be one of field labels used by your list. When using the example, you could create a new label called Total_Tax and place your formula under that label. Excel interprets all criterion that use field labels from your list as comparison criteria.

Setting Up Your Criteria Range

You can place your criteria range anywhere in your workbook, but the best places are above your list or on a separate worksheet. You should create one row that lists your field labels. You do not have to include all of your labels but you must include every label for which you are going to enter comparison criteria. You should also place the labels that you are going to use for computed criteria on this row. You need at least one additional row. You will place your criteria on the additional rows.

Entering Comparison Criteria

You can use comparison criteria to find text, numbers, dates, and logical values. If you want to match a series of characters, place the characters under the field label. For example, if you want to find all records for people with the last name Jones, type **Jones** under the field label `Last_Name` in the criteria range.

Wildcards are available for you to use. Use a question mark (?) to match any single character. For example, `J?ne` will find `Jane` and `June`. Use an asterisk (*) to match any series of characters. For example, `*son` will find `Jackson` and `Johnson`. If you need to find a question mark or an asterisk, place a tilde (~) in front of the asterisk or question mark. Excel assumes that there is an asterisk after every search entry. Therefore, if you type **John** under the `Last_Name` field label, Excel will find everyone whose last name begins with John. If you want to find an exact match for a text value, enter your criteria in the format `="=text"`. For example, if you want to find John, but not Johnson, type **="=John"**.

You can also use comparison operators. To learn more about comparison operators see Chapter 2. Type the comparison operator followed by the value you are trying to find. For example, to find all records where the income is equal to or greater than $100,000, type **>=100000** under the Income field label. To find all last names that are alphabetically greater than Jacs, you type **>Jacs** under the `Last_Name` field label. Comparison criteria are not case sensitive. To find all blank fields, type an equal sign with nothing after it. To find all nonblank fields, type the unequal operator (**<>**) with nothing after it.

Entering Computed Criteria

When you enter computed criteria, you must use a formula that evaluates to the logical value `TRUE` or the logical value `FALSE`, based on whether your criteria match records in your list, and your formula must include a reference to at least one field label from your list. If you use computed criteria, your field labels must conform to the rules for naming a range. To learn more about naming ranges, see Chapter 2.

You create your formula by using a relative cell reference to the first data row in your list. For example, `=C8+D8>20000` is a valid formula, if the first data row in your formula is row 8. If you name the data fields in the first row of your data list, you can use range names in your formula. For example, if you name C8 `Property_Tax` and D8 `Income_Tax`, you can use the formula `=Property_Tax+Income_Tax>20000`.

You create a new label and place your formula under that label in the criteria range. The cell will display either the word `TRUE` or the word `FALSE`.

Using Multiple Criteria

You can use a criteria range to specify multiple criteria. For example, you can find all people with the last name Jones whose incomes are more than $50,000. You can also find all people whose property tax is more than $4,000 or whose income tax is more than $20,000. If you want both criteria to be met, place your criteria on the same row. If you want either criterion to be met, place your criteria on separate rows.

Meet both criteria:

LAST_NAME	FIRST_NAME	PROPERTY_TAX	INCOME_TAX	STATE	INCOME
Jones					>50000

Meet either criteria:

LAST_NAME	FIRST_NAME	PROPERTY_TAX	INCOME_TAX	STATE	INCOME
		>4000			
			>20000		

Filter by Multiple Criteria

With advanced filtering, you can go beyond the limitations of the AutoFilter command. You can use advanced filtering to create two or more filters and easily coordinate a set of filters between columns. For example, you can filter a survey to find people age 35 or younger who are male and people age 60 or older who are female.

Advanced filtering requires a bit of work, even when you are using the Advanced Filter menu command. You must find a block of cells on your worksheet and create a criteria range. Use one or more column heads from a list. In the cell below each label, type criteria by which to filter each column, such as <=35 to find people 35 and under and = "=M" to find all males. See the previous task, "Enter Criteria to Find Records," for detailed instructions.

You have two options when you create any type of filtered list. You can have your filtered list appear in place — under the column heads of your unfiltered list — thereby hiding the unfiltered list. Or, you can have your filtered list appear in another location, thereby allowing you to keep your original list in your worksheet. If you want to filter your list in place, in the Advanced Filter dialog box, click Filter the List, In-place. If you want to keep your unfiltered list in your worksheet, in the Advanced Filter dialog box, click Copy To Another Location and then enter the location where you want to place your filtered list in the Copy To field.

Make sure your Copy To range has enough room below it to include all the values that may return in the filtered list. If you place the Copy To range above your original list, the results may overwrite the list and disrupt the filtering. Placing the copy to the side of the list or below it protects your original list.

Filter by Multiple Criteria

1 On the worksheet with your list, type the column head names of the columns you want to filter.

2 Type the criteria by which you want to filter values.

Note: *Use operators to define criteria and place text in quotes. For example, to find all males, type = "=M". Excel will display =M.*

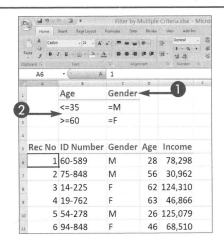

3 Click the Data tab.

4 Click Advanced.

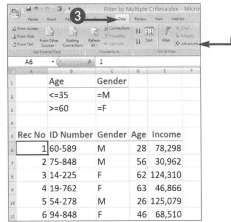

- The Advanced Filter dialog box appears.

5 Click to indicate where to place the filtered list (○ changes to ◉).

You can click Copy To Another Location to copy the list to another location and retain the original list.

6 Click and drag to select, or type the range for the entire list including labels.

7 Click and drag to select, or type the range for the criteria defined in Step 2.

8 If you chose to copy the filtered list in Step 5, click the first cell for the filter.

9 Click OK.

- The filtered list appears.

- Click Clear on the Data tab in the Sort & Filter group to clear your filter.

	Age	Gender
	<=35	=M
	>=60	=F

ID Number	Gender	Age	Income
60-589	M	28	78,298
75-848	M	56	30,962
14-225	F	62	124,310
19-762	F	63	46,866

Advanced Filter

Action
- ◉ Filter the list, in-place
- ○ Copy to another location

List range: $A$5:$E$100
Criteria range: Sheet1!$B$1:$C$3
Copy to:

☐ Unique records only

OK   Cancel

Filter by Multiple Criteria.xlsx - Micro

A6   1

Rec No	ID Number	Gender	Age	Income
1	60-589	M	28	78,298
3	14-225	F		62 124,310
4	19-762	F		63 46,866
5	54-278	M		26 125,079
7	77-909	M		23 29,940
8	28-016	F		61 115,827
9	31-423	M		23 117,466
11	44-548	M		22 33,514
12	54-978	M		33 94,559
23	40-263	F		61 144,108
29	15-911	M		32 72,806

Apply It

By default, the criteria you enter are not case sensitive. Excel views "10-611-ab" to be the same as "10-611-AB." You can, however, use the EXACT function to create criteria that are case sensitive. To start, create a column label in your criteria range and name it Exact Match. In the field below the Exact Match column label, type the EXACT function. For example, type =EXACT(B6,10-611-ab). B6 refers to the column you want to filter, B, and the first row under the label of the list range, 6.

Now, click the Data tab. Click Advanced in the Sort & Filter group. The Advanced Filter dialog box appears. Click to choose from Filter the List, In-place and Copy To Another Location (○ changes to ◉). Type the list range into the List Range field. Type the criteria range into the Criteria Range field. Enter a copy-to location if necessary and then click OK. Excel filters your list, finding only exact matches. If you name your list range Database, your criteria range Criteria, and your copy-to range Extract, Excel automatically places these values into the Advanced Filter dialog box. You can find this example in the file Filter by Multiple Criteria.xlsx in Sheet2 on the Web site that accompanies this book.

Subtotal Sorted Data

After you sort and group your data into categories such as quarter and region, you can perform a calculation on each category. Excel provides the tools for performing simple calculations to compare one category with another. With a sort defined for at least one column, you can find the average, sum, min, max, number of items, and much more for that column or another column. Excel calls this feature *subtotaling*, even though you can use it to do more than subtotal.

Subtotaling uses outlining to hide data so you can compare rows or columns. When you calculate the average, sum, or other calculation for a sorted list, outlining enables you to view only the results of the calculation.

You can create several levels of subtotals for a single sorted list. You start by using the Subtotal dialog box to create the highest-level subtotal. Then you open the Subtotal dialog box again to create the next-level subtotal. You can create up to eight levels. Make sure you have not checked the Replace Current Subtotals check box in the Subtotal dialog box as you create each level.

You can create subtotals on columns other than the one defining the sort. For example, if you sort by quarter, you can sum sales or some other column. With subtotals, you can do a count on a column with text entries. Under other circumstances, the Count function works only with numbers.

You can remove outlining by clicking the Data tab and then, in the Outline group, clicking Ungroup, Clear Outline.

Subtotal Sorted Data

1. Click a cell in your sorted list.

2. Click the Data tab.

3. Click Subtotal in the Outline group.

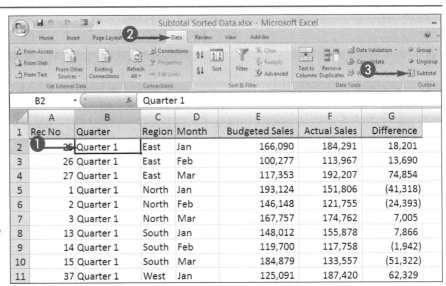

The Subtotal dialog box appears.

4. Click here and select the category by which you want to subtotal.

5. Click here and select the type of calculation you want to perform.

6. Click one or more columns to subtotal (☐ changes to ☑).

7. Click OK.

8. Repeat Steps 4 to 7 to create additional groups.

- Make sure the Replace Current Subtotals box is not checked (☑ changes to ☐).

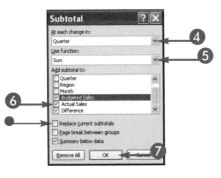

The list appears with the outlining controls that enable you to compare the results.

⑨ To compare results in different rows, click the minus signs (–).

	A	B	C	D	E
1	Rec No	Quarter	Region	Month	Budgeted Sales
2	25	Quarter 1	East	Jan	166,090
3	26	Quarter 1	East	Feb	100,277
4	27	Quarter 1	East	Mar	117,353
5			East Total		383,720
6	1	Quarter 1	North	Jan	193,124
7	2	Quarter 1	North	Feb	146,148
8	3	Quarter 1	North	Mar	167,757
9			North Total		507,029
10	13	Quarter 1	South	Jan	148,012
11	14	Quarter 1	South	Feb	119,700
12	15	Quarter 1	South	Mar	184,879
13			South Total		452,591
14	37	Quarter 1	West	Jan	125,091
15	38	Quarter 1	West	Feb	152,771

Only the result rows appear.

⑩ To redisplay all results, click the plus signs (+).

Excel displays all results.

	B	C	D	E	F
1	Quarter	Region	Month	Budgeted Sales	Actual Sales
18	Quarter 1 Total			1,797,433	1,857,435
35	Quarter 2 Total			1,697,270	1,796,732
39		East Total		513,778	481,139
43		North Total		456,796	397,351
47		South Total		530,095	488,448
51		West Total		503,157	507,413
52	Quarter 3 Total			2,003,826	1,874,351
56		East Total		389,048	467,418
60		North Total		461,880	485,422
64		South Total		467,591	479,990
68		West Total		430,601	402,118
69	Quarter 4 Total			1,749,120	1,834,948
70	Grand Total			7,247,649	7,363,466
71					

Apply It

If you organize your data by columns, you may want to group it by columns. For example, if column heads in your worksheet are the months of the year, you can manually create columns that summarize the year and each quarter. For example, you can find the yearly and quarterly totals and averages. You can then manually create a first-level group for the year and then create second-level groups for the quarters.

You start by creating your worksheet. After each quarter, create a column for the quarterly summary and then manually enter the formulas needed to calculate the quarterly summary. Next, create a column for the yearly summary and then manually enter the formulas needed to calculate the yearly summary.

You are now ready to group your data by column. Select all of your data except your row labels and the column for your yearly total. Click the Data tab and then click Group. The Group dialog box appears. Click Columns and then click OK. Excel groups your yearly data. Select the columns for your first quarter. Click the Data tab and then click Group. The Group dialog box appears. Click Columns and then click OK. Excel groups your first quarter. Continue grouping quarters. You can find this example in the file Subtotal Sorted Data.xlsx on Sheet2 on the Web site for this book.

Count Filtered Records

ike standard worksheet functions, database functions enable you to perform calculations and summarize data patterns. Database functions are meant for lists and are especially good at summarizing the subsets you create by filtering your list. Most database functions combine two tasks: they filter a group of records based on values in a single column, and then they count the records or perform another simple operation on the filtered data.

DCOUNT is a database function that counts the number of cells containing a number. DCOUNT takes three arguments. The first argument, Database, identifies the cell range for the entire list. The second argument, Field, identifies the cell range for the column from which you want to extract data. You can enter the column

label enclosed in quotes; for example, "Age". Or you can enter the column number. The first column in the list is 1, the second is 2, and so on. In the third argument, Criteria, you provide Excel with the range location of your criteria for extracting information. For example, your criteria could be Age >50, where Age is the column label. You build the criteria manually, copying column labels and defining the conditions in the cells below them. You then place the range in your formula. You can use any range as long as the range includes at least one column label and one cell below it. If you want to count every record in the list, leave the cells in your criteria range below your label blank. If your criteria is text, enter it in the format = " = Text Value" . If you do not, Excel may calculate improperly.

Count Filtered Records

① Insert several rows above your table to hold the criteria range.

② Type the column heads for which you want to count records.

③ Type the criterion for counting records.

④ Click a cell to hold your formula.

C3		f_x			
	A	B	C	D	E	F
1			Age ← ②		
2		③ →	> 50		
3		Result:		← ④	
4					
5	Rec No	ID Numb	Gender	Age	Income
6	1	60-589	M	28	78,298
7	2	75-848	M	56	30,962
8	3	14-225	F	62	124,310
9	4	19-762	F	63	46,866
10	5	54-278	M	26	125,079
11	6	94-848	F	46	68,510
12	7	77-909	M	23	29,940
13	8	28-016	F	61	115,827
14	9	31-423	M	23	117,466
15	10	66-833	M	55	99,951

⑤ Type **=DCOUNT(.**

Alternatively, click the function on the AutoComplete list.

⑥ Click the Insert Function button.

RANDBETWEEN	⑥ →	f_x	=DCOUNT(		
	A	B	C	D	E	F
1			Age		
2			> 50		
3		Result:	=DCOUNT(	← ⑤	
4			DCOUNT(**database**, field, criteria)		
5	Rec No	ID Numb	Gender	Age	Income
6	1	60-589	M	28	78,298
7	2	75-848	M	56	30,962
8	3	14-225	F	62	124,310
9	4	19-762	F	63	46,866
10	5	54-278	M	26	125,079
11	6	94-848	F	46	68,510
12	7	77-909	M	23	29,940
13	8	28-016	F	61	115,827
14	9	31-423	M	23	117,466

The Function Arguments dialog box appears.

7 Click and drag to select all the cells in your list, or type the cell range.

8 Type the column name within quotation marks.

Or type the column's number or the column's range.

9 Click and drag to select the cells or type the cell range from Steps 2 and 3.

10 Click OK.

● The result appears.

Click Clear on the Data tab in the Sort & Filter group to clear your filter.

Note: *The* DCOUNT *function counts only cells containing numbers. For non-numeric data, use the* DCOUNTA *function.*

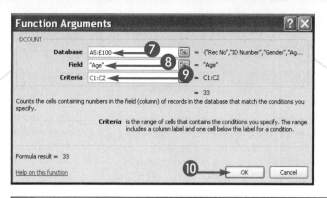

	A	B	C	D	E	F
1			**Age**			
2			> 50			
3		Result:	33			
4						
5	**Rec No**	**ID Num**	**Gender**	**Ag**	**Incom**	
6	1	60-589	M	28	78,298	
7	2	75-848	M	56	30,962	
8	3	14-225	F	62	124,310	
9	4	19-762	F	63	46,866	
10	5	54-278	M	26	125,079	
11	6	94-848	F	46	68,510	
12	7	77-909	M	23	29,940	
13	8	28-016	F	61	115,827	
14	9	31-423	M	23	117,466	

Extra

The names of database functions begin with a D to distinguish them from worksheet functions. As with worksheet functions, you can use the Function Wizard to build database functions. Type the function into a cell — for example, =DCOUNT() — and click the Insert Function button.

Excel offers several database functions. They all take the same arguments: Database, Field, and Criteria. The table that follows lists a few:

FUNCTION	DESCRIPTION
DCOUNTA	Counts nonblank cells that match the criteria you specify
DGET	Extracts the one record that meets the criteria you specify
DMAX	Returns the largest number that meets the criteria you specify
DMIN	Returns the smallest number that meets the criteria you specify
DAVERAGE	Returns the average of the numbers that meet the criteria you specify
DSUM	Returns the sum of the numbers that meet the criteria you specify

Define Data as a Table

In Excel, a table is a special type of list. Like all lists, a table is a set of columns and rows where each column represents a single type of data. To create a table, you simply define a list as a table. When you define a list as a table, Excel adds sort and filter down arrows to each column label, enabling you to readily sort and filter your data. To learn how to use these down arrows, see earlier tasks in this chapter.

Tables have a unique quality. When you enter a formula into a table column that does not have any data in it, it becomes a calculated column. Calculated columns automatically calculate when you create a new row. However, if you type a formula in a table column that already contains data, Excel does not automatically create a calculated column. You, however, can turn the column into a calculated column by clicking the Create Calculated Column button that appears after you type your formula.

By selecting Total Row on the Design tab, you can easily add totals to your Excel table. Totals allow you to find the sum, count, max, min, or other value based on a column. You can calculate a different value for each column in your table.

You can create a new table row by pressing the Tab key while in the last field in the last row of your table. To create a new table column, type the label name next to the last label in the last column of the table.

Define Data as a Table

1 Click and drag to select the data you want to define as a table.

Include column labels.

2 Click the Insert tab.

3 Click Table in the Tables group.

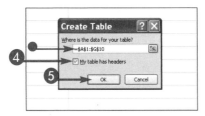

The Create Table dialog box appears.

● The data range you selected appears here.

4 Click here if your table has column labels (☐ changes to ☑).

5 Click OK.

Excel converts your data to a table.

- The Table tools become available.

- Each column has a down arrow. Click the arrow to sort and filter.

Note: Refer to the earlier tasks of this chapter to learn how to sort and filter.

6 Click the Design tab.

7 Click Total Row (☐ changes to ☑).

- Excel places a total at the end of your table.

8 Click a field in the Total row.

A down arrow appears next to the field.

9 Click the down arrow and select how you want to total the column.

Excel creates a total.

In this example, Excel averages the column.

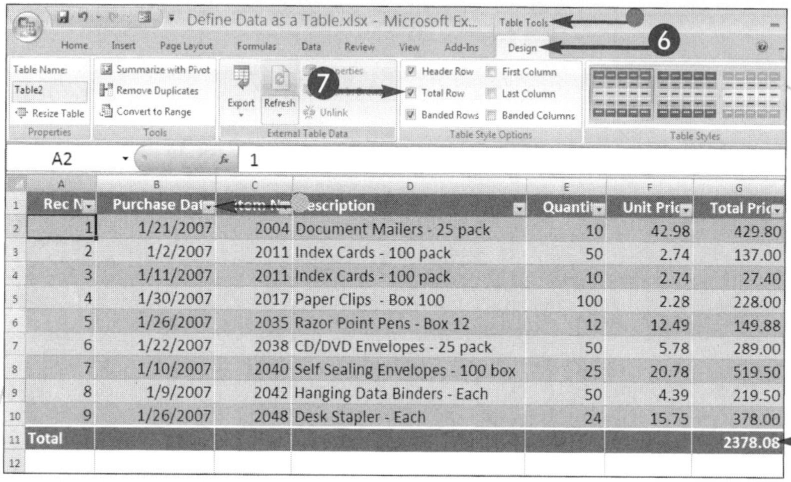

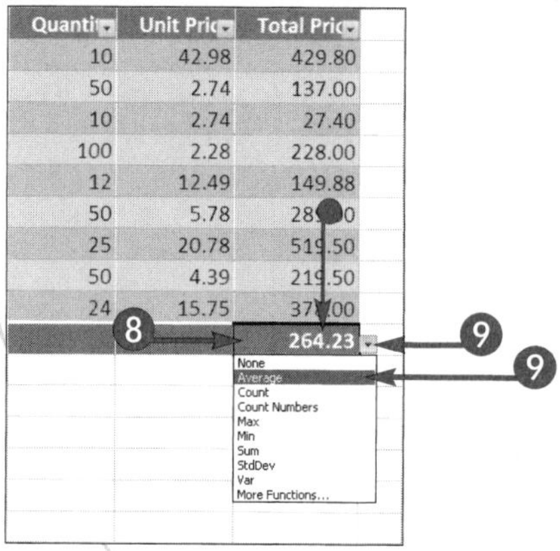

Rec N	Purchase Date	Item N	Description	Quantity	Unit Price	Total Price
1	1/21/2007	2004	Document Mailers - 25 pack	10	42.98	429.80
2	1/2/2007	2011	Index Cards - 100 pack	50	2.74	137.00
3	1/11/2007	2011	Index Cards - 100 pack	10	2.74	27.40
4	1/30/2007	2017	Paper Clips - Box 100	100	2.28	228.00
5	1/26/2007	2035	Razor Point Pens - Box 12	12	12.49	149.88
6	1/22/2007	2038	CD/DVD Envelopes - 25 pack	50	5.78	289.00
7	1/10/2007	2040	Self Sealing Envelopes - 100 box	25	20.78	519.50
8	1/9/2007	2042	Hanging Data Binders - Each	50	4.39	219.50
9	1/26/2007	2048	Desk Stapler - Each	24	15.75	378.00
Total						2378.08

Quantity	Unit Price	Total Price
10	42.98	429.80
50	2.74	137.00
10	2.74	27.40
100	2.28	228.00
12	12.49	149.88
50	5.78	289.00
25	20.78	519.50
50	4.39	219.50
24	15.75	378.00
		264.23

None
Average
Count
Count Numbers
Max
Min
Sum
StdDev
Var
More Functions…

Extra

If you add a formula to your table but you do not want it to be a calculated column, click Undo Calculated Column on the AutoCorrect Options menu that automatically appears when you complete the entry of your formula.

If you do not want Excel to create calculated fields automatically, click the Office button. A menu appears. Click Excel Options. Click Proofing. Click the AutoCorrect Options button. The AutoCorrect dialog box appears. Click the AutoFormat as You Type tab. Deselect Fill Formulas in Tables to create calculated columns.

Calculated columns can have exceptions. Create an exception by typing an alternate value or formula into a cell in the column.

You can use the Insert and Delete options on the Home tab in the Cells group to insert and delete rows and columns from your table. To insert rows or columns, click anywhere in your table. Click the Home tab. Click the down arrow next to Insert in the Cells group and then click Insert Table Rows Above or Insert Table Columns to Left.

To delete rows or columns, click anywhere in your table. Click the Home tab. Click the down arrow next to Delete in the Cells group and then click Delete Table Rows or Delete Table Columns.

Modify a Table Style

Table styles format the rows and columns of your table to make your table easier to read. When you create a table, Excel applies the default style. You can easily change or remove any style applied to your table. Excel provides you with a large gallery of styles from which to choose. As you move your mouse pointer over each style in the gallery, Excel gives you a quick preview of how that style will appear when applied. You can remove a style by clicking Clear at the bottom of the Style gallery.

Excel also provides a number of table-style options you can use to modify your table style. By choosing banded rows or banded columns, you can have every other row or every other column appear in a different color. You can also apply special formatting to the last column or the first column in your table if you want the titles, totals, or information in those columns to stand out.

Table styles make your table more attractive and user friendly. If you have a favorite style, you can set that style to be the default. Then whenever you define a list to be a table, Excel will apply that style.

You can convert a table back to a regular range of cells. Click anywhere in your table, click the Design tab, and then click Convert a Range in the Tools group. At the prompt, click Yes. Excel converts the table to a normal range and removes the down arrows.

You can also use your table as a basis for a PivotTable. Click anywhere in your table, click the Design tab, and then click Summarize with Pivot. The Create PivotTable dialog box appears. Use it to create your PivotTable. To learn more about PivotTables, see Chapter 7.

Modify a Table Style

1. Click any cell in your table.

● The Table tools become available.

2. Click the Design tab.

3. Click the down arrow in the Table Styles group.

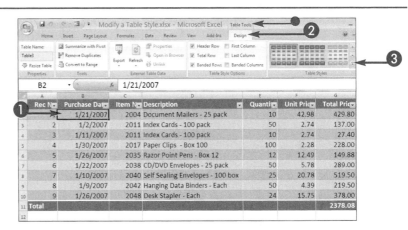

● A gallery of styles becomes available.

4. Click a style to apply it to your table.

5. Click Clear to remove a style from your table.

6. Right-click a style.

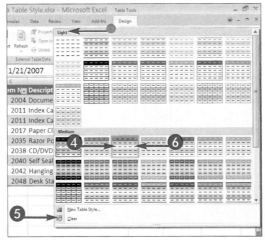

A menu appears.

7 Click Set As Default.

Excel makes the style the default style.

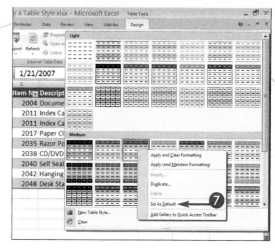

8 Click to remove banded rows (☑ changes to ☐).

9 Click to add banded columns (☐ changes to ☑).

10 Click to apply special formatting to the first column (☐ changes to ☑).

11 Click to apply special formatting to the last column (☐ changes to ☑).

● Excel formats your table.

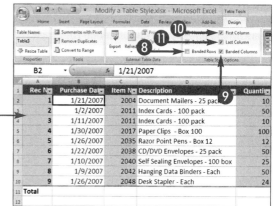

Extra

You can easily add columns your table. Click any cell in your table. The Table tools become available. Click the Design tab and then click Resize Table in the Properties group. The Resize Table dialog box appears. Click and drag to select the new range, or type the range in the Select the New Data Range for Your Table field and then click OK. You can also resize your table by clicking and dragging the bottom-right corner of your table.

You can create your own table style by modifying an existing style. Click any cell in your table. Click the Design tab. Click the down arrow in the Table Styles group. A gallery of styles appears. Click the style you want to modify and then right-click. A menu appears. Click Duplicate. The Modify Table Quick Style dialog box appears. Use it to modify your style. Type a name in the Name field. In the Table Elements box, click the element you want to modify and then click Format. The Format Cells dialog box appears. Use it to change the existing formatting.

Create a PivotTable

Excel offers you much more than a way of keeping track of your data and doing calculations. It also provides tools to analyze your data and thus understand it better so you can make more effective decisions.

One of the most useful tools, the PivotTable, is also one of the least understood. Similar to cross-tabulation in statistics, a PivotTable shows how data is distributed across categories. For example, you can analyze data and display how different products sell by region and by quarter. Alternatively, you can analyze income distribution or consumer preferences by gender and age bracket. PivotTables help you answer questions about your data.

You base PivotTables on lists. Lists are made up of rows and columns. You can use a worksheet list or you can connect to a list from another data source, such as Access. For more information on lists, see Chapter 6. For more information on external data sources, see Chapter 9.

The row and column labels of a PivotTable usually have discrete information, meaning the values fall into categories. For example, gender is a discrete category because all values are either male or female. Quarter is another discrete category because all values fall into one of four quarters: Quarter 1, Quarter 2, Quarter 3, or Quarter 4. Salary and weight are not discrete (they are continuous) because a wide range of values is possible for each.

The body of a PivotTable — the data area — usually has continuous data and shows how the data are distributed across rows and columns. For example, you could show how the number of units sold is distributed among sales regions in different quarters.

Create a PivotTable

① Click and drag to select the data you want to include in your PivotTable.

Note: *Make sure to include the row and column headings.*

If you are going to use an external data source, skip this step.

② Click the Insert tab.

③ Click PivotTable in the Tables group.

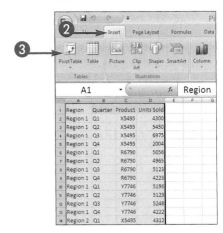

128

The Create PivotTable dialog box appears.

④ Click a data source (○ changes to ◉).

● If you selected a range in the current workbook, the range appears here.

● If you are going to use an external data source, click here and then click the Choose Connection button and choose the database to which you want to connect.

⑤ Click to select where to place the report.

● If you want to place the PivotTable on the existing worksheet, click the cell in which you want to place the PivotTable, or type a location.

⑥ Click OK.

● Excel opens the PivotTable Field List.

● The PivotTable tools become available.

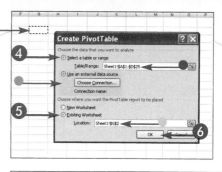

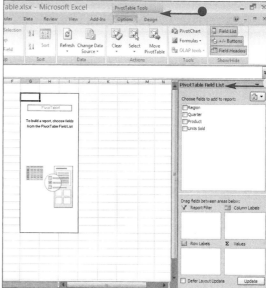

Extra

If you want the clear a PivotTable, click anywhere in your PivotTable. The PivotTable tools become available. Click the Options tab. Click Clear in the Actions group. A menu appears. Click Clear All. Excel removes all formatting, filters, labels, and values from your report. You can rebuild your report by using the PivotTable Field List.

If you want to remove a PivotTable from your worksheet, click anywhere in the PivotTable. The PivotTable tools become available. Click the Options tab. Click Select in the Actions group. A menu appears. Click Entire Table. Excel selects the entire table. Press the Delete key. Excel deletes your PivotTable.

When you create a PivotTable, you must base it on data structured as a list. Your list should include column headings in the first row. Tables are structured as lists. You can base your PivotTable on a table. To learn more about lists and tables, see Chapter 6. When creating a PivotTable, do not use a worksheet list with blank columns or rows. If you do, Excel may not create the PivotTable correctly.

continued →

The PivotTable layout consists of several elements: report filters, data, columns, and rows. Use the PivotTable Field List to organize the elements. When working with a PivotTable, you can bring the Field List into view by clicking anywhere in the PivotTable, clicking the Options tab, and then clicking Field List in the Show/Hide group.

To construct a PivotTable, choose the fields you want to include in your report and then drag fields from the PivotTable Field List into the Report Filter, Column Labels, Row Labels, and Sum (Σ) Values boxes. You can click and drag more than one field into an area. By using Report Filter fields, you can filter the data that appears in your report. Row Label fields appear as row labels down the left side of your PivotTable, and Column Label fields appear as column labels across the top of your PivotTable.

Place your continuous data fields in the Σ Values box. Fields placed in the Σ Values box make up the data area. You can sort and filter your PivotTable column and row data, and you can arrange and rearrange field layouts.

Fields and column and row labels display in the order you place them in the Column and Row Labels boxes. You can change the display order by clicking and dragging the fields within the box.

When you create a PivotTable, you can place it on a new worksheet or on the existing worksheet. If you choose New Worksheet in the Create PivotTable dialog box, Excel creates and moves you to a new worksheet in your workbook and opens the PivotTable Field List. If you choose Existing Worksheet, Excel opens the PivotTable Field List so you create your PivotTable on the current worksheet.

Create a PivotTable (continued)

⑦ Click to select the fields you want to include in your PivotTable (☐ changes to ☑).

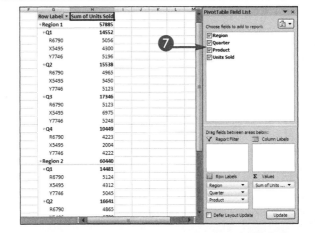

⑧ Click and drag fields among the Report Filter, Column Labels, Row Labels, and Σ Values boxes.

● If you want to filter what displays in a PivotTable page, click and drag the field by which you want to filter to the Report Filter box.

● Click and drag fields you want to display as columns to the Column Labels box.

● Click and drag fields you want to display as rows to the Row Labels box.

● Click and drag fields you want to display as data to the Σ Values box.

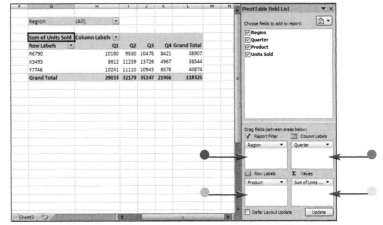

- As you build the PivotTable, your changes instantly appear.

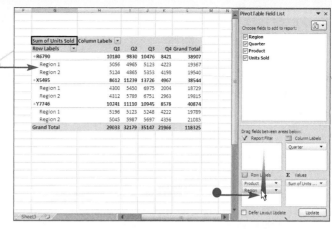

(9) Click the field header and then choose your sort and filter options.

Note: *For more information on sorting and filtering, see Chapter 6.*

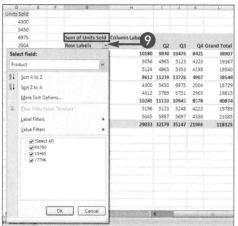

Extra

Excel has divided the PivotTable Field List into two sections: Field and Areas. The Field section lists all the fields available for you to use when creating your PivotTable. The Areas section gives you the ability to design your report.

To change the way the PivotTable Field List displays, click the Field List button (🔳▾) located in the upper-right corner of the PivotTable Field List box. A menu appears. Choose from the following options: Fields Section and Areas Section Stacked, Fields Section and Areas Section Side by Side, Fields Section Only, Areas Section Only (2 by 2), and Areas Section Only (1 by 4). The Fields Section and Areas Section Stacked option places the Field section at the top of the PivotTable Field List box and the Area section directly below it. The Fields Section and Areas Section Side by Side option places the Field section on the left side of the PivotTable Field List box and the Area section to the right of it. The Fields Section Only option only displays the Fields section and the Areas Section Only option only displays the Area section, in either a two-by-two or one-by-four format.

Modify PivotTable Data and Layout

PivotTables help you answer essential questions about your data. To extend the value of PivotTables, Excel allows you to change the data on which you base PivotTables and the manner in which you lay them out. PivotTables can easily get quite complex. Fortunately, you need not regenerate and re-edit a PivotTable every time the underlying data changes. Instead, you can refresh a table by clicking Refresh in the Data group.

You can easily change the layout of a PivotTable by clicking the Design tab and choosing the PivotTable style and layout you want. Excel 2007 has many pre-designed styles from which to choose. When you create a PivotTable, Excel applies the default style. You can easily change or remove any style applied to your PivotTable.

As you roll your cursor over each style in the gallery, Excel gives you a quick preview of how that style will appear when you apply it. If you do not want a style applied to your PivotTable, click Clear, which is located at the bottom of the Style gallery.

Excel also provides a number of table-style options you can use to modify your PivotTable style. By choosing banded rows or banded columns, you can have every other row or every other column appear in a different color. You can also apply special formatting to your row and column labels by selecting Row Header and/or Column Header in the PivotTable Style Options dialog box.

Excel 2007 also lets you display your table in a compact, tabular, or outline form. Try each form to determine which one displays your data best.

Modify PivotTable Data and Layout

REFRESH DATA

① Make changes to your data.

● The data changed here.

● There is no change here.

② Click any cell in your PivotTable.

○ The PivotTable tools become available.

③ Click the Options tab.

④ Click Refresh in the Data group.

○ Numbers and calculations reflect changes in the data.

First PivotTable (top):

Units Sold						
7000	Sum of Units Sold		Quarter			
5000	Region	Product	Q1	Q2	Q3	Q4
4000	Region 1					
6000		R6790	9525	5000	4000	6000
4300		X5495	4300	5450	6975	2004
5450		Y7746	5196	5123	5248	4222
6975	Region 2					
2004		R6790	5124	4865	5353	4198
5196		X5495	4312	5789	6751	2963
5123		Y7746	5045	5987	5697	4356
5248	Grand Total		33502	32214	34024	23743
4222						

Second PivotTable (bottom):

Modify Pivot Table.xlsx - Microsoft Ex... PivotTable Tools

Page Layout Formulas Data Review Options Design

Field: Group Selection PivotChart Field List
Units Sold Ungroup Formulas +/- Buttons
Field Settings Group Field Sort Refresh Change Data Source Clear Select Move PivotTable OLAP tools Field Headers
Active Field Group Sort Data Actions Tools Show/Hide

f_x 7000

ts Sold							
7000	Sum of Units Sold		Quarter				
5000	Region	Product	Q1	Q2	Q3	Q4	Grand Total
4000	Region 1						
6000		R6790	7000	5000	4000	6000	22000
4300		X5495	4300	5450	6975	2004	18729
5450		Y7746	5196	5123	5248	4222	19789
6975	Region 2						
2004		R6790	5124	4865	5353	4198	19540
5196		X5495	4312	5789	6751	2963	19815
5123		Y7746	5045	5987	5697	4356	21085
5248	Grand Total		30977	32214	34024	23743	120958
4222							

CHANGE LAYOUT

1. Click any cell in the PivotTable.

● The PivotTable tools become available.

2. Click the Design tab.

3. Click here and select the style you want.

● Excel applies the style.

4. Click to select Pivot Style options (☐ changes to ☑).

Row Headers adds special formatting to the row heads.

Column Headers adds special formatting to the column heads.

Banded Rows adds formatting to every other row.

Banded Columns adds formatting to every other column.

5. Click Report Layout in the Layout group.

A menu of layouts appears.

6. Click a layout.

● Excel changes your report layout.

Extra

By default, Excel creates or modifies your PivotTable as you click and drag fields among the Report Filter, Column Labels, Row Labels, and Sum Values fields. If you do not want your PivotTable created or modified dynamically, click the Defer Layout Update box (☐ changes to ☑) at the bottom of the PivotTable Field List and then click the Update button when you are ready to create or modify your PivotTable.

If you choose the Design tab and then click Blank Rows in the Layout group, you can click a menu item to insert or remove a blank line after each group.

While in an PivotTable field, when you click the Design tab and then choose Report Layout in the Layout group, a menu appears. If you choose Show in Compact Form, you can indent your row labels. To specify how much you want to indent by, click anywhere in your PivotTable. The PivotTable tools become available. Click the Options tab and then click Options in the PivotTable group. The PivotTable Options dialog box appears. Click the Layout and Format tab. In the When in Compact Form Indent Row Labels field, type the number of characters you want to indent. You can enter any value between 0 and 127.

Compute Subtotals and Grand Totals

You can use PivotTables to compare and contrast the distribution of data across categories. You may need a variety of statistics to examine differences between categories. To aid you, PivotTables can automatically calculate subtotals and grand totals for the columns and rows in your list. When calculating subtotals or grand totals, you have a choice of calculations, including sum, average, count, standard deviation, minimum, and maximum.

Use the Field Settings dialog box to tell Excel how to subtotal row and column labels. You have three choices: Automatic, None, and Custom. The default function is Sum for numeric fields and Count for text fields. Automatic uses the default function for the field. None displays without a subtotal. Custom allows you to select the types of subtotals you want to create. If you are using an Online Analytical Processing (OLAP) data source, you cannot use Custom.

Use the Value Field Settings dialog box to tell Excel how to total Σ Values. Changing the type of calculation used to generate values in a row or column can result in improperly formatted data. To remedy this, use the Number Format button in the Value Field Settings box to access the number-formatting capabilities of the Format Cells dialog box. You may, for example, want to add a thousands separator so you see 7,236,273 instead of 7236273.

You can use the Design tab to control the display of grand totals. Use the Grand Totals option in the Layout group to tell Excel whether you want to show grand totals for rows and columns, just for rows, or just for columns. The Design Tabs Layout group also has options to control the display of subtotals. Use the Subtotal option to tell Excel whether you want to show subtotals and whether the subtotals should appear at the top or the bottom of the group.

Compute Subtotals and Grand Totals

SUBTOTAL ROW AND COLUMN LABELS

1 Click any field in your PivotTable.

● If the PivotTable Field List does not appear, click the Options tab and then click Field List.

2 Click the row or column label field for which you want a subtotal.

A menu of options appears.

3 Click Field Settings.

● The Field Settings dialog box appears.

4 Click the type of calculation you want to use to summarize your data (○ changes to ◉).

Click Automatic to use the default.

Click None for no subtotal.

Click Custom to select the type of subtotals you want.

5 If you select Custom, click your options.

6 Click OK.

○ Excel adds subtotals to your PivotTable.

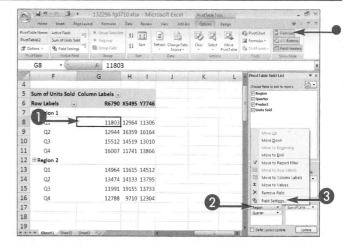

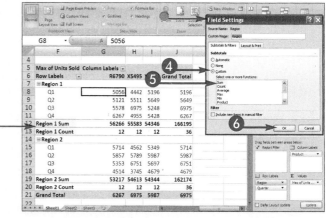

TOTAL Σ VALUES

① Click a Σ value field.

A menu appears.

② Click Value Field Settings.

⊚ The Value Field Settings dialog box appears.

③ Click the option you want to use to summarize your data.

● You can click Number Format to change the format of the number in your PivotTable.

④ Click OK.

● Excel totals to your PivotTable, using the function you selected.

⊚ Click the Design tab and then click Grand Totals in the Layout group. Make sure Excel is set to display grand totals.

This example uses MAX to summarize the data.

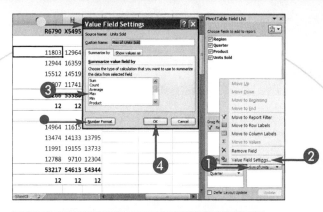

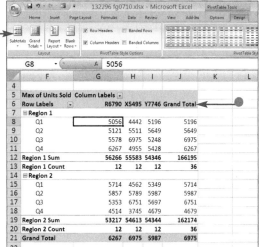

Extra

You can access a variety of calculation options on the Show Values As tab of the Value Field Settings dialog box. The following table describes the calculations available:

OPTION	DESCRIPTION
Difference From	Calculates the difference between two PivotTable cells
% Of	Determines the percentage of the current PivotTable cell to the selected base value
% Difference From	Determines the percentage difference between two cell values
Running Total In	Shows the running total in each cell
% of Row	Finds the percentage of the cell value to the total row
% of Column	Finds the percentage of the cell value to the total column
% of Total	Finds the percentage of the cell value to the grand total value
Index	Calculates by using the following formula: `((value in cell) x (Grand Total of Grand Totals))/((Grand Row Total) x (Grand Column Total))`

Create a PivotTable Calculated Field

ithin a PivotTable, you can create new fields, called *calculated fields,* that you can base on the values in existing fields. You create a calculated field by creating a formula. Your formula can include functions; operators such as +, −, *, and /; and existing fields, including other calculated fields. For example, you could enter the following formula:

`= SUM(Units Sold, 100) * 1.10`

Your formula cannot use cell references.

You usually use calculated fields with continuous data such as incomes, prices, miles, and sales. For example, you can multiply each value in a field called `Price` by a sales tax rate to create a calculated field called `Tax`.

Use the Insert Calculated Field dialog box to name your calculated field and create the formula you want to use. You can also use this dialog box to modify existing calculated fields or delete fields you no longer want to use. Once created, your calculated fields are available in the PivotTable Field List for use in your PivotTable. You cannot place calculated fields in report filters, column labels, or row labels. You can only place calculated fields in the data area, so place your calculated field in Σ Values.

If you want to see a list of all the formulas used by your PivotTable, you can use the List Formulas option under Formulas on the Options tab to list all the formulas in your worksheet and their names.

Create a PivotTable Calculated Field

① Click any field in your PivotTable.

● The PivotTable tools become available.

● If the Field List does not appear, click the Options tab and then click Field List.

② Click Formulas in the Tools group.

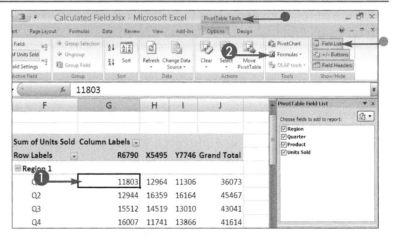

A menu appears.

③ Click Calculated Field.

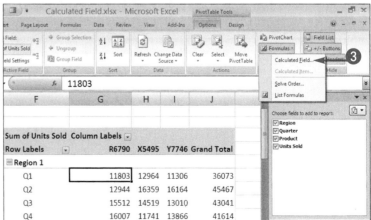

The Insert Calculated Field dialog box appears.

④ Type a name for the new field.

⑤ Double-click an existing field to use in defining the field.

⑥ Type an operator and the value, such as **+2000**.

⑦ Click OK.

● The calculated field appears at the end of the Field List.

● You can place the calculated field in the Σ values box.

● Values for the calculated field fill the data area.

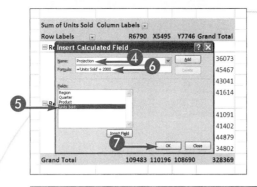

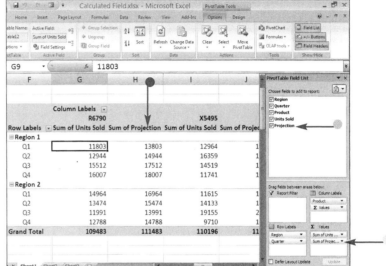

Hide Rows or Columns in a PivotTable

Grouping allows you to compare groups of data. For example, if your PivotTable shows each week as a column, you can group the weeks, so that you can compare months. When you group columns or rows, Excel totals the data, creates a field header, and creates a field with a drill-down button that displays either a plus or a minus sign. You can click the button to either collapse or expand the data. If you do not want to display the button, you can click Buttons in the Show/Hide group on the Options tab to toggle the display of buttons to off. If after grouping your data, you want to ungroup it, you can.

Hide Rows or Columns in a PivotTable

① Click and drag the row or column labels to select the rows or columns you want to hide.

② Click the Options tab.

③ Click Group Selection in the Group group.

● A new cell appears, with a minus button.

④ Click the minus button.

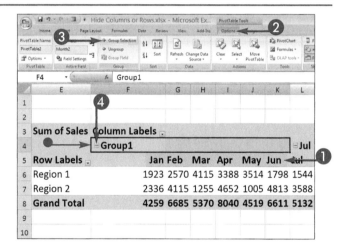

● Excel hides the details of the rows or columns and displays the total.

● The minus sign on the button turns into a plus sign.

Note: *You can click the plus button to see the hidden cells again.*

⑤ Click the cell that contains the group header.

⑥ Click Ungroup in the Group group.

Excel removes the grouping.

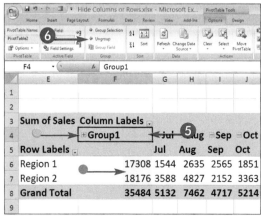

Sort a PivotTable

When you sort, you can see patterns in your data. You can sort PivotTables by field labels or by data values. When you sort by field labels, the corresponding data values are sorted as well. The opposite is also true: sorting the data values rearranges the field labels.

You can sort your PivotTable in either ascending or descending order. You can also specify the sort direction: top to bottom or left to right. This can get a bit confusing, so the Sort By Value dialog box provides an explanation of the results of your sort selection.

You can manually rearrange column and row labels by clicking and dragging them to a new location. As you move your mouse pointer over the border of a cell, a four-sided arrow indicates that you can click and drag the cell.

Extra

You can click the down arrow next to the field header to sort and filter your PivotTable data. For example, to sort by row or column label, click the down arrow and then select a sort option from the menu. Click More Sort Options to open the Sort dialog box. In the Sort dialog box, click the More Options button. If you do not want your row or column heading sorted every time you update your report, deselect (☑ changes to ☐) that option. For more information on sorting and filtering with field headings, see Chapter 6. You can also open the Sort dialog box by clicking a row or column label and then clicking Sort in the Sort group of the Options tab.

Sort a PivotTable

SORT FIELD LABELS

① Click any field in your PivotTable.

● The PivotTable tools become available.

② Click the Options tab.

③ Click and drag to select the field labels you want to sort.

④ Click the ascending or descending button in the Sort group.

● Excel sorts your field labels.

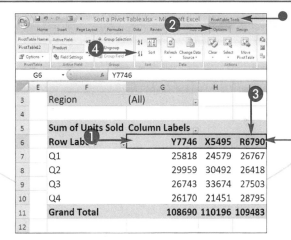

SORT DATA FIELDS

① Click and drag to select the data you want to sort.

② Click Sort in the Sort group.

The Sort By Value dialog box appears.

③ Click a Sort option (○ changes to ◉).

④ Click a Sort direction (○ changes to ◉).

● The Sort By Value dialog box provides an explanation of what will result from your sort selection.

⑤ Click OK.

● Excel sorts your data fields.

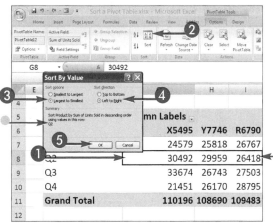

Retrieve Values from a PivotTable

When you create a PivotTable, down arrows appear. You can use these down arrows for filtering. Filtering allows you to view only the data that is relevant to you. For example, if your data consists of Regions One through Four and you want to focus on Region Four, you can filter your PivotTable so only Region Four appears on-screen. To learn more about filtering, see Chapter 6. As you filter your data, Excel changes the cell in which the data is located. If you use cell references to retrieve data from your PivotTable, filtering can cause you to retrieve the wrong data. To avoid this problem, use the GETPIVOTDATA function to retrieve summary data from your PivotTable.

When creating a GETPIVOTDATA function, use the Data_field to specify in quotes the name of the data field that contains the data you want to retrieve. For example, if you are retrieving data from the units sold, type "**Units sold**".

Use the Pivot_table field to reference any cell or cell range in the PivotTable. If your PivotTable is on another worksheet, be sure to include the worksheet name. Excel uses this information to determine which PivotTable contains the information you want.

Excel gives you up to 126 optional field and item pairs you can use to describe your data. For example, if you are retrieving data from the Region field, type "**Region**" in Field and **Region 4** in Item and then continue describing your data.

If the field you are attempting to retrieve is not visible on-screen, you will receive an error message.

This task explains how to create your function by using the Function Arguments dialog box to create your function; however, there is an easier way. Type an equal sign (=) and then click the cell whose value you want to retrieve.

Retrieve Values from a PivotTable

① Click the cell into which you want to place the retrieved value.

② Type **=GETPIVOTDATA(**.

As you begin to type, the AutoComplete list appears. You can select the value from here.

③ Click the Insert Function button (fx).

The Function Arguments dialog box appears.

④ Type the data field that contains the results you want to retrieve.

⑤ Type the cell address of any cell in your PivotTable.

⑥ Type the field and item pairs that describe the data you want to retrieve.

⑦ Continue typing field and item pairs.

⑧ Click OK.

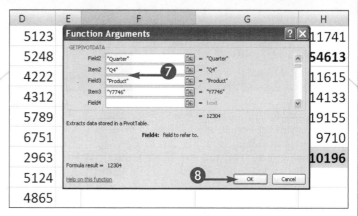

	D	E	F	G
	5123			11741
	5248			54613
	4222			11615
	4312			14133
	5789			19155
	6751			9710
	2963			10196
	5124			
	4865			

Excel retrieves the value you entered into your function.

If the cell location changes because of filtering, Excel is still able to retrieve the value.

Note: Excel cannot retrieve a value that does not appear on-screen.

	D	E	F	G
11	5123		Q4	13866
12	5248		**⊟Region 2**	**54344**
13	4222		Q1	14512
14	4312		Q2	13795
15	5789		Q3	13733
16	6751		Q4	12304
17	2963		**Grand Total**	**108690**
18	5124			
19	4865			
20	5353		12304	
21	4198			

Extra

A cell in a PivotTable may summarize several rows of information. To view the underlying data for a cell, double-click the cell. The rows appear in a new worksheet. Changes you make to the new worksheet have no effect on the original data.

You can move a PivotTable. Click anywhere in the PivotTable. The PivotTable tools become available. Click the Options tab. Click Move PivotTable in the Actions group. The Move PivotTable dialog box appears. Click to select whether you want to move the PivotTable to a new worksheet or to another location on the existing worksheet (○ changes to ◉). If you click New Worksheet and then click OK, Excel creates a new worksheet and places your PivotTable on it. If you click Existing Worksheet, type the cell address of the new location and then click OK. Excel moves your PivotTable.

Create a Chart

Excel gives you tools for quickly generating a chart or visual representation of the numbers in your worksheet. Charts clarify patterns that can get lost in columns of numbers and text, and they make your data more accessible to people who are not familiar with, or do not want to delve into, the details. Charts can make a greater impression than rows and columns of numbers because the mind perceives, processes, and recalls visual information more quickly than textual or numerical information. In addition, shapes and colors have real impact.

With Excel 2007, you can create charts with dramatic visual appeal quickly and easily. Simply select the data you want to chart and then choose a chart type from the Insert tab's Chart group. Excel provides several chart types from which to choose, including column, line, pie, bar, area, and scatter charts. In addition, each chart type has a number of subtype options.

After you create your chart, Excel makes Chart tools available to you through the Design, Layout, and Format contextual tabs. Using the Chart tools, you can choose a chart style and layout. You can change the color scheme of your chart with chart styles, and use layouts to add a chart title, axis labels, a legend, or a data table to your chart. A chart title summarizes chart content, axis labels explain each axis, a legend explains the colors used to represent data, and a data table displays the data presented in the chart. Chart tools make changing row data to column data, or vice versa, as simple as clicking a button.

Create a Chart

① Click and drag to select the worksheet data you want to chart. Include row and column headings.

② Click the Insert tab.

③ Click a chart type in the Charts group.

④ Click a chart subtype.

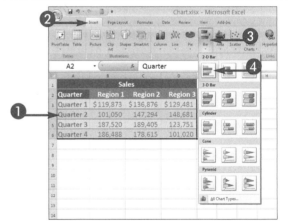

Excel creates a chart based on the data you selected.

● Row data.

● Column data.

● The Chart tools become available.

⑤ Click the Design tab.

⑥ Click here and select a chart style.

   Excel applies the style to your chart.

⑦ Click Quick Layout in the Chart Layouts group.

⑧ Click to select a chart layout.

   Excel applies the layout to your chart.

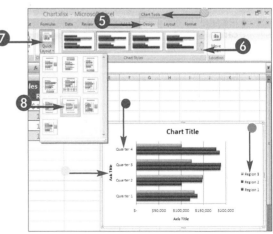

9 Right-click the chart title or an axis title.

A context menu appears.

10 Click Edit Text.

11 Type to change the title or axis label.

12 Click Switch Row/Column in the Data group.

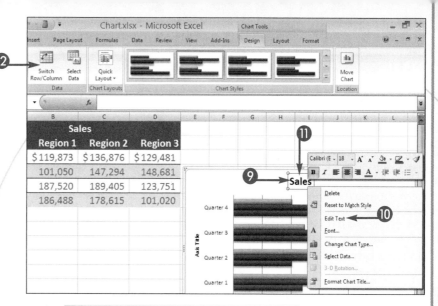

● Excel switches the row and column data.

Extra

Excel ships with the Column chart as the default chart type. You can change the default chart type by clicking the launcher in the Insert tab's Chart group to open the Insert Chart dialog box. Click a chart type and a subtype, and then click the Set as Default Chart button located at the bottom of the Insert Chart dialog box.

To create a chart quickly and easily using all of Excel's charting defaults, select the data you want to chart and then press F11. Excel creates a chart on a new chart sheet. You can modify the chart by using any of the Chart tools. If you want your chart embedded in your current worksheet instead of on a chart sheet, press Alt+F1.

You can manually change the placement of the various elements that make up your chart. For example, you can move the legend from the left side of your chart to the right side. Roll your mouse pointer over the element you want to move. When your mouse pointer turns into a four-sided arrow, click and drag the element to a new location.

Add Chart Details

After you create your chart in Excel, modifying it or adding details is easy. In fact, you can modify virtually all the elements of a chart. For example, when you create a chart, Excel places it on the same worksheet as the data from which you created it. You can move the chart to another worksheet or to a special chart sheet. If you choose to move your chart to a chart sheet, you must name the sheet. Excel creates the chart sheet and places the name you gave it on the tab.

Many chart types have a 3-D option. To make a 3-D chart easier to read, you can use the X and Y fields in the 3-D

Rotation pane to change the chart rotation. The X field rotates the horizontal axis of your chart and the Y field rotates the vertical axis of your chart. As you rotate your chart, Excel provides a live preview of your changes. If at any time you want to return to the default rotation, click the Default Rotation button near the bottom of the Format Chart Area dialog box. In addition to changing your chart's rotation, you may also want to change your chart's perspective. Changing the rotation and/or perspective is useful if the bars in the front of your bar chart hide bars in the back of your bar chart. Use the Perspective field in the 3-D Rotation dialog box to change the perspective.

Add Chart Details

CHANGE CHART LOCATION

1 Click your chart.

● The Chart tools become available.

2 Click the Design tab.

3 Click Move Chart in the Location group.

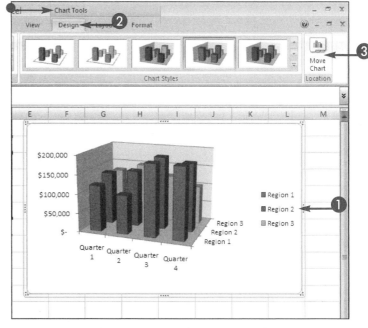

The Move Chart dialog box appears.

4 Click New Sheet (○ changes to ◉).

● Alternatively, click Object In (○ changes to ◉) to place the chart on another worksheet.

● If you click Object In, click here and select the sheet on which you want to place the chart.

5 Type a name for the sheet.

6 Click OK.

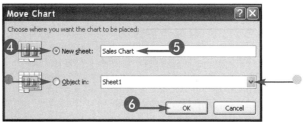

- Excel places the chart on a chart sheet.

CHANGE ROTATION AND PERSPECTIVE

1 Click the Layout tab.

2 Click 3-D Rotation in the Background group.

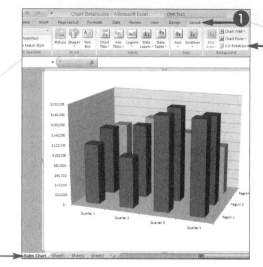

- The Format Chart Area dialog box appears.

3 Type a value to increase or decrease the X rotation.

4 Type a value to increase or decrease the Y rotation.

- Click here to return to the default rotation.

5 Type a value to increase or decrease the perspective.

6 Click Close.

- Excel rotates and changes the perspective of your chart.

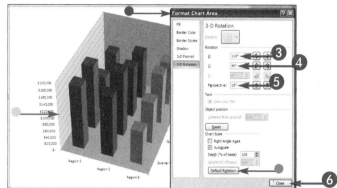

Extra

You can add, remove, or change the plot area's fill when working with two-dimensional charts. Just click your chart, click the Layout tab, and then click Plot Area in the Background group. A menu of options appears. From the menu, click More Plot Area Options. The Format Plot Area dialog box appears. Click Fill. Click Solid Fill to place solid color in the fill area. Use the color box to select the color you want.

Click Gradient Fill to place a gradient fill in the plot area. Use the Gradient Fill pane to set the colors, type, and direction of your gradient fill.

Click Picture or Texture Fill to fill your plot area with a picture or texture. You can select a texture from the menu or you can click the File button to locate a picture or texture you want to insert. Click the Clipboard button to fill the plot area with the item currently on the Clipboard. Click the Clip Art button and then double-click the clip-art item with which you want to fill the plot area. Regardless of what you fill the plot area with, you can adjust the transparency.

continued →

Add Chart
Details (continued)

To make your chart more readable, you may want to change some of the attributes of your chart. You can easily change the walls and floor of your three-dimensional charts. The walls are the side and back of your chart, and the floor is the bottom of your chart. You can choose to show the chart walls and/or floor, not show the walls and/or floor, or fill the chart walls and/or floor with a color, gradient, or picture. Choose Solid Fill in the appropriate format dialog box to fill with a color, choose Gradient Fill to fill with a gradient, or choose Picture or Texture Fill to fill with a picture or texture.

Excel bases axis values on the range of values in your data. Axis values encompass the range. For example, if the lowest value represented in your chart is 101,020 and the highest value represented in your chart is

189,405, your axis values might range from 0 to 200,000. Axis labels describe the data displayed on each axis. Excel provides several options for choosing whether to display axis values and how to display the axis values and labels on each axis, including the horizontal, vertical, and depth axis of a 3-D chart.

When you create a chart in Excel, Excel creates horizontal and vertical gridlines to mark major and minor intervals in your data series. If your axis values run from 0 to 200,000, major gridlines might be at 20,000, 40,000, 60,000, and so on. Minor gridlines might be at 2,000, 4,000, 6,000, and so on. You can remove the gridlines, display major gridlines only, display minor gridlines only, or display major and minor gridlines.

Add Chart Details *(continued)*

CHANGE THE WALL AND FLOOR

1 Click your chart.

● The Chart tools become available.

2 Click the Layout tab.

3 Click Chart Wall in the Background group.

4 Click More Wall Options.

● Alternatively, choose an option from the menu.

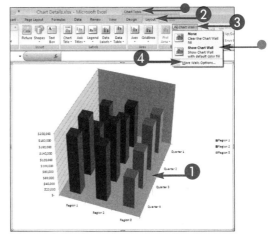

● The Format Walls dialog box appears.

5 Click Fill.

6 Click to choose a fill option (○ changes to ◉).

7 Click Close.

● Excel changes the fill of the chart wall.

● Click Chart Floor in the Background group and repeat Steps 4 to 6 to change the chart floor.

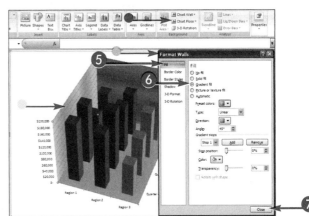

ADJUST THE AXIS

1. Click the Layout tab.

2. Click Axes in the Axes group.

3. Click Primary Horizontal Axis.

Note: *To change the vertical axis, click Primary Vertical Axis. To change the depth axis, click Depth Axis.*

4. Click a Primary Horizontal Axis option.

● Excel changes the display of your horizontal axis.

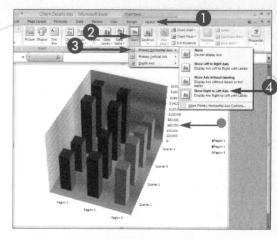

CHANGE THE GRIDLINES

1. Click the Layout tab.

2. Click Gridlines in the Axes group.

3. Click Primary Horizontal Gridlines.

Note: *To change the vertical gridlines, click Primary Vertical Gridlines and click a menu option. To change the depth gridlines, click Depth Gridlines and choose a menu option.*

4. Click a menu option.

Note: *None shows no gridlines, Major Gridlines shows major units, Minor Gridlines shows minor units, Major and Minor shows major and minor units.*

● Excel changes the display of your horizontal axis.

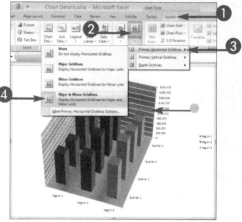

Extra

To resize your chart, click your chart. A border surrounds it, with dots on the sides and corners. Place the mouse pointer over the dots. When a double arrow appears, click and drag to resize your chart.

You can also resize your chart by using the Ribbon. Click your chart. The Chart tools become available. Click the Format tab. The Size group has two fields: Shape Height and Shape Width. Use the Shape Height field to adjust the height of your chart. Use the Shape Width field to adjust the width of your chart. Be careful when resizing, because it may skew the chart and distort the presentation of the content.

You can use the menu options that appear when you click one of the buttons in the Labels group on the Layout tab to tell Excel things such as whether, where, and how to display a chart title, axis titles, legend, data labels, or data tables. Click the More option at the bottom of the menu to open a dialog box in which you can format a chart title, a legend, axis titles, data labels, or data tables.

Change the Chart Type

Excel provides a variety of chart types and subtypes from which to choose. If you are not satisfied with the chart type you have chosen, you can easily make another choice.

You can use a column or bar chart to plot data arranged in rows and columns. Both types are useful when your data changes over time or when you want to compare data values. Use stacked bar or column charts to show the relationship of individual items to the whole. Use 3-D charts to show data on two axes. The cylinder, cone, and pyramid bar and column subtypes provide you with interesting ways to present your charts.

Area and line charts are also good for plotting data organized into columns and rows. Use an area chart to show how values change over time and how each part of the whole contributes to the change. Line charts are ideal for showing trends in your data; consider using a line chart to show changes measured at regular intervals.

Pie charts are useful when you want to display data arranged in one column or one row. Each data point in a pie chart represents a percentage of the whole pie. Like pie charts, each data point in a doughnut chart represents a percentage of the whole pie; however, a doughnut chart can display more than one column or row of data.

Excel stock charts display the high, low, and close; open, high, low, and, close; volume, high, low, and close; and volume, open, high, low, and close values of a stock. When creating a stock chart, you must arrange your columns of data with the date in the first column followed by the order given in the chart name; for example, date, high, low, close.

Change the Chart Type

① Click your chart.

● The Chart tools become available.

② Click the Design tab.

③ Click Change Chart Type in the Type group.

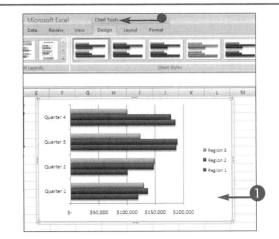

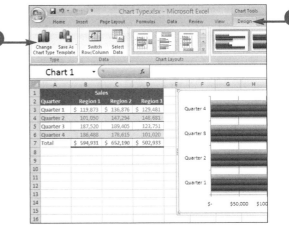

The Change Chart Type dialog box appears.

④ Click a new chart type.

⑤ Click a subtype.

⑥ Click OK.

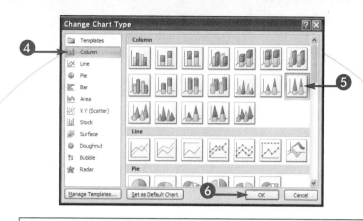

The chart appears, formatted in the new chart type and subtype.

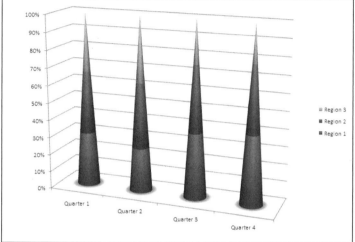

Extra

Once you have your chart designed exactly the way you want it, you can save your design as a template. By using templates, you can save your settings and apply them to other charts. To create a template, click your chart. The Chart tools become available. Click the Design tab. Click Save as Template in the Type group. The Save Chart Template dialog box appears. Make sure you are in the Charts folder; then type the name you want to give your template and click Save.

To use your template, select the data you want to chart, click the Insert tab, and then click the launcher in the Charts group. The Insert Charts dialog box appears. Click Templates, click your template, and then click OK. Excel creates a chart based on the settings in your template.

To apply your template to an existing chart, click your chart. The Chart tools become available. Click the Design tab. Click Change Chart Type in the Type group. The Change Chart Type dialog box appears. Click Templates, click your template, and then click OK. Excel applies your template to your chart.

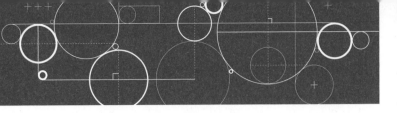

Add a Trendline

Trendlines help you see both the size and direction of changes in your data, and you can use them to forecast future or past values based on available data. A trendline is the line through your data series that is as close as possible to every point in your data series. You can add a trendline to any chart type except 3-D, stacked, radar, pie, surface, and doughnut charts. Excel superimposes the trendline over your chart.

Excel provides the following trendline types: linear, logarithmic, polynomial, power, exponential, and moving average. You choose a trendline type based on the type of data you have. Excel generates a statistic called R-squared. R-squared represents the fraction of the observed data that is explained by the fitted trendline/curve. The closer R-squared is to 1, the better the line fits your data. You can choose to have the R-squared value appear on your chart.

Use a linear trendline if your data increases or decreases at a steady rate. Use a logarithmic trendline when your data increases or decreases quickly and then levels out. Use a polynomial trendline when your data fluctuates up and down. Generally, you can estimate the order of a polynomial by the number of hills or valleys that occur. If your data has one hill or valley, it is usually somewhere around an order-2 polynomial. If it has two hills or valleys, it is usually somewhere around an order-3 polynomial, and so on. Use a power trendline to compare data that increases at a specific rate. Use a moving average trendline to smooth out your data so you can see fluctuations in your data. A moving average trendline averages groups of sequential points in your data and then creates a trendline. Use the Period field in the Format Trendline dialog box to tell Excel how many fields to average.

Add a Trendline

1 Click your chart.

● The Chart tools become available.

2 Click the Layout tab.

3 Click Trendline in the Analysis group.

A menu appears.

4 Click More Trendline Options.

● Alternatively, click a menu option to choose the type of trendline you want to apply.

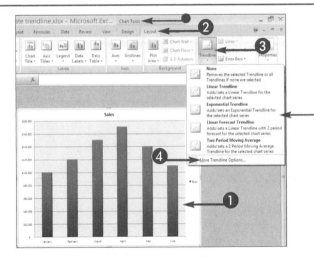

● The Format Trendline dialog box appears.

5 Click Trendline Options.

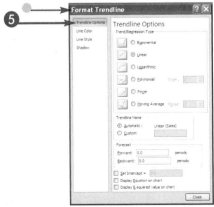

6 Click a regression type (○ changes to ⊙).

7 Set the number of periods to forecast.

8 Click Display R-squared Value on Chart (☐ changes to ☑).

R-squared gives you an idea of the accuracy of the line generated. The closer R-squared is to 1, the better the fit.

9 Click Close.

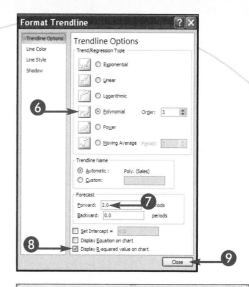

● The trendline appears on the chart. If selected in Step 8, the R-squared value appears on the chart.

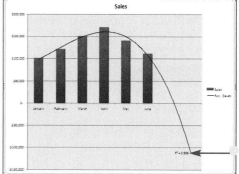

Extra

To create a linear series, you add the difference between the first value and the second value to the second value to create the next value. You then add the difference between the first and second values to each subsequent value. For example:

INITIAL VALUES	LINEAR SERIES
1,2	3,4,5
1,3	5,7,9
25,0	–25,–50,–75

If you want to project future values for a simple linear trend, you can use the fill handle. Select at least the last two rows of your data and then drag the fill handle. To learn more about the AutoFill feature and the fill handle, see Chapter 10.

To create a growth series, you divide the second value by the starting value. You then multiply the result by each subsequent value. For example:

INITIAL VALUES	GROWTH SERIES
3,6	12,24,48
2,5	12.5,31.25,78.125
2,3	4.5,6.75,10.125

You can also use the fill handle to predict a growth trend. Select at least the last two rows of your data, hold down the right mouse button, and then drag. Release the right mouse button and click Growth Trend on the shortcut menu that appears.

Add and Remove Chart Data

If you want to include new data in your chart or exclude data from your chart, you can use the Select Data Source dialog box to add and remove entire columns or rows of information or to change your data series entirely without changing your chart's type or other properties. Excel defines a data series as the related data points you plot in a chart. Excel gives each data series in your chart a unique color or pattern and provides a key to each data series in the chart legend. You can click the Switch Row/Column button in the Select Data Source dialog box to switch the plotted data from the rows in your worksheet to the columns in your worksheet or vice versa.

The Select Data Source dialog box Legend Entries (Series) box lists the names of your data series. You can

use this box to add, edit, or remove a data series. When you click the Add button, the Edit Series dialog box appears. You can use it to select new ranges to define your series name and your series values or you can type a name in the Series Name field and/or enter an array in the Series Values field. An array is a series of values, separated by commas. You must enclose arrays in curly braces; for example, {100000, 110000, 90000}. To edit, you must click the data series and then click the Edit button. To change the order of your data series, you click the series and then click the up and down arrow keys.

The Select Data Source dialog box Horizontal (Category) Axis Label box lists the labels on your horizontal axis. Click the Edit button to edit them.

Add and Remove Chart Data

CHANGE THE DATA AREA

If the chart is on the worksheet, position it so it does not overlap the data.

● Currently charted data.

① Click your chart.

● The Chart tools become available.

② Click the Design tab.

③ Click Select Data in the Data group.

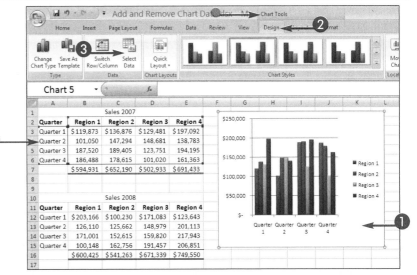

● The Select Data Source dialog box appears.

④ Click and drag to select the data you want to include in your chart, or type the cell range.

⑤ Click OK.

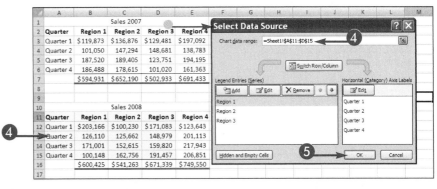

○ Excel redefines the data series area.

ADD A LEGEND ITEM

① Perform Steps 1 to 3 in the Change the Data Area section.

○ The Select Data Source dialog box appears.

② Click Add.

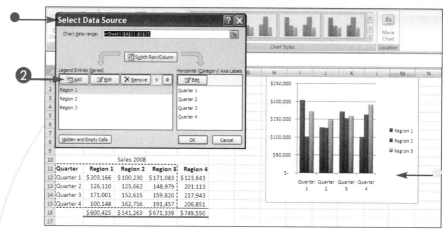

○ The Edit Series dialog box appears.

③ Click the cell with the name you want for your new data series, or type the cell address.

④ Click and drag to select the data series or type the range.

⑤ Click OK.

○ Excel adds the data series and legend name to your chart.

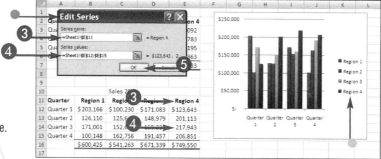

Extra

If you update the data on which you based your chart, you do not have to regenerate your chart. Excel charts automatically update to reflect changes you make to your data.

To delete data from your chart, click the data you want to delete in the Legend Entries (Series) box of the Select Data Source dialog box and then click Remove. Or, click the data series in the chart and then press the Delete key.

Here is a quick way to add data to a chart: Click and drag to select the data you want to include in the chart. Click the Copy button on the Home tab. Click the chart to select it and then click Paste on the Home tab. The chart reflects the added data series.

You can edit any element in your chart by clicking it and then right-clicking. A menu appears, sometimes with a mini-toolbar. Use the menu and mini-toolbar to delete elements, add elements, change the font, change the font size, change the alignment, or edit the data source.

Add Error Bars

With Excel, you can easily generate error bars to provide an estimate of the potential error in experimental or sampled data. In science, marketing, polling, and other fields, people make conclusions about populations by sampling the population or devising controlled experiments. When you sample data or generate data under laboratory conditions, the resulting numbers approximate the larger reality you are exploring. An error bar shows the range of possible values for these derived numbers.

With Excel, you can show the range of possible values in several ways, including as a fixed number, as a percentage of the data point, or in terms of standard deviation units. Use the Format Error Bars dialog box to make your choice. If you choose Fixed Value, you specify the constant value Excel displays as the error amount for each data point.

If you choose Percentage, Excel uses the percentage you specify in the Percentage box to calculate the possible error amount as a percentage of the value of the data point. If you choose Standard Deviation(s), Excel calculates the standard deviation, multiplies it by the number you enter into the Standard Deviation(s) box, and then uses the result. If you choose Standard Error, Excel calculates and uses the standard error. If you choose Custom, you can specify the error values Excel uses.

You can choose how Excel displays error bars. Choose Both if you want to display the actual data point plus and minus the error amount. Choose Minus if you want to display the actual data point minus the error amount. Choose Plus if you want to display the actual data point plus the error amount. You can display your error bar with or without caps on the ends.

Add Error Bars

1 Click your chart.

● The Chart tools become available.

2 Click the Layout tab.

3 Click Error Bars in the Analysis group.

A menu appears.

4 Click More Error Bars Options.

● Alternatively, click the appropriate menu option.

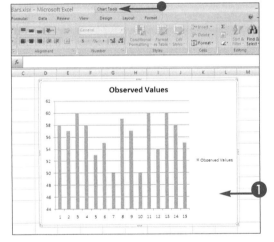

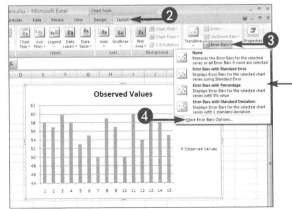

5 In the Format Error Bars dialog box, click Vertical Error Bars.

6 Click to choose a direction (○ changes to ◉).

Click Both if you want to show the possible error amount above and below the observed value.

Click Minus if you want to show the possible error amount below the observed value.

Click Plus if you want to show the possible error amount above the observed value.

7 Click to choose an end style (○ changes to ◉).

8 Click to choose an error amount type (○ changes to ◉).

9 Type a value if you chose Fixed Value, Percentage, or Standard Deviation(s) in Step 8.

10 Click Close.

● Your chart appears with error bars.

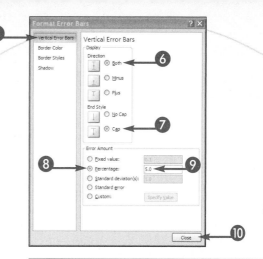

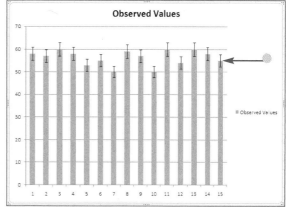

Extra

Standard deviation units indicate whether an experimental number is reasonably close to the population characteristic you are studying. For example, you can have a confidence level of 95 percent that the population mean falls within two standard deviation units of the sampled mean, which you know. Your confidence level in estimating population characteristics assumes that the sampled values are normally — or evenly — distributed around the mean, as in a bell curve.

Only certain chart types support error bars, including 2-D area, bar, column, line, and XY scatter charts. These types let you create error bars for the values measured by the y-axis. For the scatter chart, you can create both X and Y error bars.

You can add error bars and trendlines to a PivotChart. However, if you make changes to your PivotChart, Excel may remove the error bars or trendlines. Changes that may result in the loss of error bars or trendlines include changing the layout, removing fields, and hiding or displaying items.

You can use the Line Color, Line Style, and Shadow options in the Format Error Bars dialog box to change the line color or line style of your error bars or to add shadows to your error bars.

Create a Histogram

With Excel, you can use histograms to group a list of values into categories and compare the categories. Excel calls these categories *bins*. To display the test scores for a group of students, for example, your first bin might be <=60, representing scores lower than or equal to 60 percent, your second bin might be 70, and so on, up to a bin for test scores higher than 100 percent. Excel counts the number of occurrences in each bin.

When creating a histogram, you must provide three pieces of information. First, define the raw data you want to sort. Then define the bins. Finally, specify the cell in which you want the result to appear. Your bins must be in ascending order. The results can appear in the current worksheet, in a new worksheet, or in a new workbook. As you make

changes to your data, Excel does not automatically make changes to your histogram. You must regenerate your histogram when you make changes to your data.

Click the Chart Output option in the Histogram dialog box to create a histogram and a chart at the same time. You can modify the chart just as you would any other chart. Click the Cumulative Percentage option in the Histogram dialog box to create a histogram output table that includes cumulative percentages. Click the Pareto (sorted histogram) option to create a histogram output table that includes your data sorted from highest to lowest based on frequency.

The histogram tool is part of the Analysis Toolpak, which you may need to install as explained in the Extra section of this task.

Create a Histogram

① Type the values that define the bins.

Note: *The bins must be ordered from lowest to highest but need not be the same size.*

② Click the Data tab.

③ Click Data Analysis in the Analysis group.

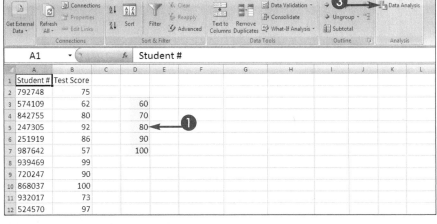

The Data Analysis dialog box appears.

④ Click Histogram.

⑤ Click OK.

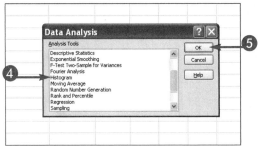

6 In the Histogram dialog box, click and drag to select the range of numbers to categorize, or type, the cell range.

7 Click and drag to select the range of bins created in Step 1, or type the cell range.

8 Click where you want to place your output (○ changes to ◉).

9 Click the cell where you want the results to start, or type the cell address.

10 Select another option, Chart Output in this example (☐ changes to ☑).

Note: Pareto sorts data from highest to lowest. Cumulative shows cumulative percentage.

11 Click OK.

The results appear on the same worksheet as the original data.

● Frequency means number of values per bin.

● More refers to the uncategorized values above the highest bin.

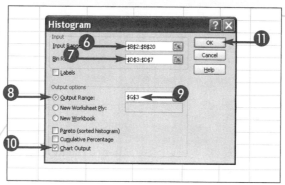

	A	B	C	D	E	F	G	H	I	J
1	Student #	Test Score								
2	792748	75								
3	574109	62		60			Bin	Frequency		
4	842755	80		70			60	2		
5	247305	92		80			70	4		
6	251919	86		90			80	5		
7	987642	57		100			90	3		
8	939469	99					100	5		
9	720247	90					More	0		
10	868037	100								
11	932017	73								
12	524570	97								
13	778992	86								
14	933913	65								
15	452047	57								
16	694470	71								
17	365890	100								
18	372234	76								
19	897246	67								
20	665187	61								

Extra

Before you create a histogram, you must install the Data Analysis Toolpak add-in. Click the Office button. A menu appears. Click Excel Options. The Excel Options dialog box appears. Click Add-Ins. In the View and Manage Microsoft Office Add-ins pane, click Analysis Toolpak and then click Go. The Add-Ins dialog box appears. Select Analysis Toolpak and then click OK. The Data Analysis Toolpak appears on the Data tab.

You can use the FREQUENCY function to create a histogram. You must supply the function with two arguments: Data_array and Bins_array. The Data_array argument is the list of data you want to place in bins. The Bins_array argument is the list of bins you want to use. To use the FREQUENCY function, you must select the cells into which you want to place your results. If you have five bins, select six cells — one more cell than the number of bins you have. Type the function or enter it into the Function Arguments dialog box. Frequency is an array function, so press Ctrl+Shift+Enter after you have entered your arguments instead of clicking OK. Refer to Sheet2 of Histogram.xlsx, which is on the Web site for this book, to see an example.

Chart Filtered Data

With Excel, you can quickly create a chart of the information in a worksheet. Charts show trends and anomalies that may be otherwise difficult to detect in columns of numbers. By choosing the appropriate type of chart and formatting the chart features, you can share your results with others and convey patterns in your data.

To create a chart, select the data you want to chart, click the Insert tab, and then click a chart type. Excel creates a chart. You can position your chart next to the data on which you base it, so when you change the data you can instantly observe the changes in the chart.

By using Excel's filtering features, you can filter your data. Filtering your data allows you to limit the data you

see. For example, if your worksheet has data for Quarter 1, Quarter 2, Quarter 3, and Quarter 4, you can filter your data so you see only Quarter 1 and Quarter 2. You can use the Filter option on the Data tab to filter your data, you can define your data as a table and use the table filtering options, or you can use functions to filter your data. To learn more about filtering, see Chapter 6.

By default, as you filter your data, Excel removes the filtered data from your chart. If you do not want Excel to remove filtered data, select the Show Data in Hidden Rows and Columns option in the Hidden and Empty Cell Settings dialog box. Excel displays all of your data in your chart.

Chart Filtered Data

① Create a chart.

② Filter the data on which the chart is based.

● A filter button on the down arrow indicates that you have filtered data.

By default, only the unfiltered data displays in the chart.

In this example, only Quarter 1 and Quarter 2 display.

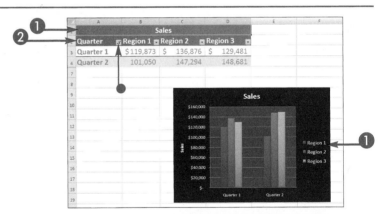

③ Click your chart.

● The Chart tools become available.

④ Click the Design tab.

⑤ Click Select Data in the Data group.

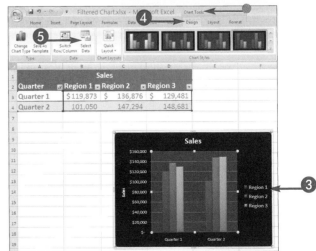

The Select Data Source dialog box appears.

6 Click the Hidden and Empty Cells button.

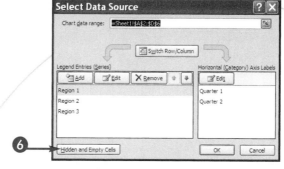

● The Hidden and Empty Cell Settings dialog box appears.

7 Click Show Data in Hidden Rows and Columns (☐ changes to ☑).

8 Click OK.

9 Click OK in the Select Data Source dialog box.

● Excel displays the hidden data in your chart.

Quarter 1, Quarter 2, Quarter 3, and Quarter 4 display.

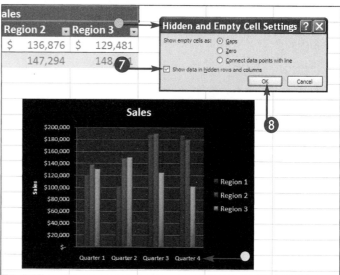

Extra

Sometimes you find yourself without a value for a period, transaction, or whatever you happen to be tracking. Perhaps the data was not recorded, was not validly recorded, or is just missing. The term *missing data* means a data series has *no* value for one or more cells. Excel makes it easy for you to show that data is missing.

The Hidden and Empty Cell Settings dialog box has three options for representing missing data: Gaps, Zero, and Connect Data Points with Line. You can only use Connect Data Points with Line when you are working with a line chart.

The default is Gaps. If you choose Gaps, Excel does not plot the missing data. This option makes it clear that data is missing, which is important when precision is important or not much data is missing. If you choose Zero, Excel treats the missing data as a zero, which can be misleading but may be desirable if you rely on functions that cannot handle a missing value. If you choose Connect Data Points with Line, Excel interpolates the data, constructing a data series based on the values of neighboring points.

Create a PivotChart

PivotTables reveal patterns in your data. PivotCharts, which you base on PivotTables, make patterns even more apparent. PivotCharts combine the dynamic cross-tabulation capabilities of a PivotTable with the visual appeal of a chart. Like all charts in Excel, PivotCharts have a chart type, axis, legend, and data, all of which you can modify to meet your needs. See the previous tasks in this chapter to learn more about working with charts.

When you create a chart from a PivotTable, you can base your chart on summary statistics, and you can easily adjust the row and column layout. When you change the layout of your PivotTable report, your PivotChart automatically changes. When you change the layout of your PivotChart, your PivotTable automatically changes.

After creating your chart, you can display the PivotTable Field List and thereby change the layout of your PivotTable. As you do, your PivotChart changes automatically. In addition, PivotCharts have options that are not readily available to other charts. PivotCharts have filter fields you can use to filter your axis field categories or your legend field series. When you use the PivotChart Filter pane to filter your chart, Excel also filters your PivotTable. As such, information you remove from the PivotChart is also removed from the PivotTable. PivotTables also have Σ Value fields. You can change the data in your report by changing the way Excel calculates Σ Value fields. A Σ Value field can calculate sum, average, count, min, max, product, and more. See Chapter 7 to learn more about PivotTables.

Create a PivotChart

① Click any cell in your PivotTable.

● The PivotTable tools become available.

② Click the Options tab.

③ Click PivotChart in the Tools group.

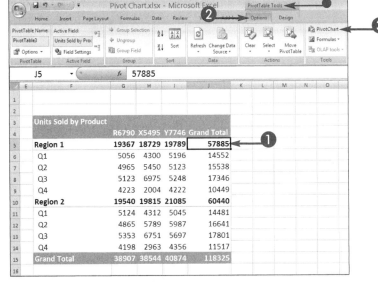

The Insert Chart dialog box appears.

④ Click to select a chart type.

⑤ Click to select a chart subtype.

⑥ Click OK.

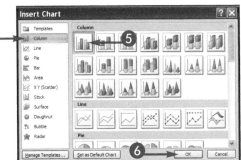

The PivotChart appears.

The PivotChart Filter pane appears.

7 Click here and then select the fields you want to appear in your chart.

8 Click here and then select the fields you want to appear in your legend.

Excel filters your chart.

9 Click the PivotTable Field List button.

The PivotTable Field List appears.

10 Modify your PivotTable layout.

● Excel changes the layout of your chart.

● Click here and then click Value Setting to change how your Σ Values calculate.

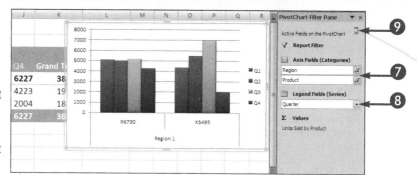

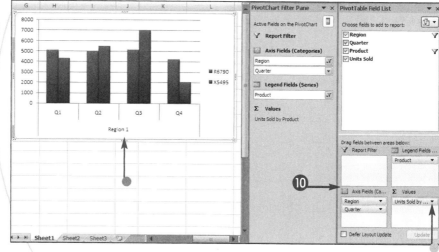

Extra

When you click a PivotChart, Excel makes the PivotChart tools available to you. You can use the Design, Layout, Format, and Analyze tabs to modify your PivotChart in much the same way you would modify any other chart.

To remove all the filters from your PivotChart, click your chart to activate the PivotChart tools. Click the Analyze tab, click Clear, and then click Clear Filters. To clear your PivotChart and your PivotTable, click the chart to activate the PivotChart tools, click the Analyze tab, click Clear, and then click Clear All.

By default, Excel embeds your PivotChart in the same worksheet in which your PivotTable is located. You can move your PivotChart. Click your chart. The PivotChart tools become available. Click the Design tab. Click Move Chart. The Move Chart dialog box appears. Click New Sheet and name the sheet to move your chart to a chart sheet. Click Object In and select the sheet if you want to move your chart to another worksheet. Click OK. Excel moves your chart.

Create a
Combination Chart

I f you show two or more data series in a single chart, you can change the chart type for one or more series and create a combination chart. Using different chart types can make it easier to distinguish different categories of data shown in the same chart. For example, you can create a combination chart that shows the number of homes sold as a line chart and the average sales price as a column chart.

When you plot two different types of data in the same chart, the range of values can vary wildly. For example, the range of values for homes sold might be between 9 and 15, while the range of values for the average sales price might be between 760,577 and 936,966. You can plot each of these data series on a different vertical axis

to make it easier for the user to see values for the associated series. In the example, you could plot average sales prices on one vertical axis and number of homes sold on the other vertical axis.

To create a combination chart, you first create a chart with both data series shown as the same chart type; if the data series' values vary wildly, you change the legend for one of the data series, and then you change the chart type for one of the data series.

The chart legend changes to reflect the changes you have made to your chart. For example, if a chart changes from a line chart to a bar chart, an appropriate colored bar displays in the legend.

Create a Combination Chart

① Select the data you want to chart.

② Click the Insert tab.

③ Select a chart type. Excel charts your data.

● The Homes Sold data series.

● The Average Sales Price data series.

CREATE A SECONDARY AXIS

① Click a data point in the series you want to place on a secondary axis.

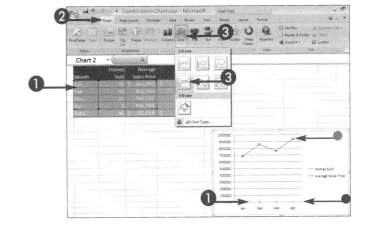

② The Chart tools become available. Click the Format tab.

③ Click Format Selection in the Current Selection group.

● The Format Data Series dialog box appears.

④ Click Series Options.

⑤ Click Secondary Axis (◯ changes to ◉).

⑥ Click Close.

● Excel plots the data you chose on a secondary axis.

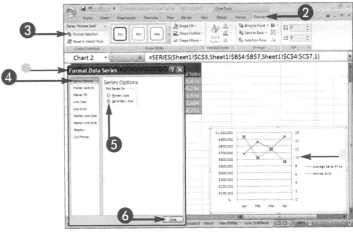

CHANGE CHART TYPE

1 Click a data point in the series for which you want to change the data series.

• The Chart tools become available.

2 Click the Design tab.

3 Click Change Chart Type in the Type group.

• The Change Chart Type dialog box appears.

4 Click a new chart type.

5 Click a new chart subtype.

6 Click OK.

• Excel changes the chart type for the series.

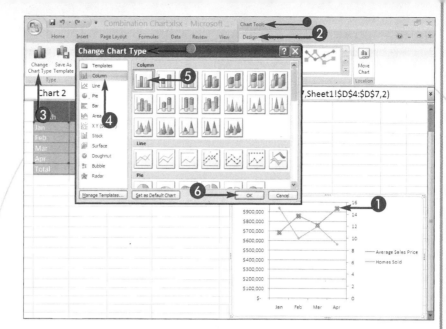

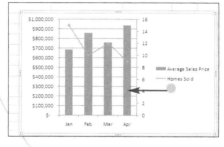

Extra

You can modify the location, style, or layout of a combination chart just as you would any other chart. See the previous tasks in this chapter to learn more about changing a chart location, style, or layout. When you change the chart style, the styles associated with both data series change.

When you create a secondary axis, Excel provides you with options that allow you to modify the axis. To access those options, click anywhere in your chart. The Chart tools become available. Click the Layout tab, and then click Axes or Gridlines in the Axes group.

You can add a title to your secondary axis. Click anywhere in your chart. The Chart tools become available. Click the Layout tab, click Axis Titles in the Labels group, click Secondary Vertical Axis Title, and then choose an option from the menu. Choose None if you do not want to display an axis title. Choose Rotated if you want to display a rotated axis title and you want Excel to resize the chart. Choose Vertical if you want to display vertical text and you want Excel to resize the chart. Choose Horizontal if you want to display horizontal text and you want Excel to resize the chart.

Paste Link into Word

Y ou can use Excel data within other programs, thereby extending your ability to use, analyze, and present your Excel data. In Word, for example, you can use Excel worksheets to present quarterly reports or other financial documents. In PowerPoint, you can use Excel worksheets to illustrate your presentations.

You can add Excel data to Word or PowerPoint by using the Copy and Paste commands. The Copy command copies the Excel data. The Paste command places the copy in another document. When you copy and paste, if you make changes to the original Excel document, you must go into the Word or PowerPoint document and update it as well.

You can also copy Excel data into Word or PowerPoint by using a paste link. When you use a paste link, if you alter Excel data in Word or PowerPoint, Office automatically updates the Excel source document. The

opposite is also true. When you alter paste-linked data in Excel, Office automatically updates the linked Word or PowerPoint document. Paste linking enables you to keep your documents in sync because you do not have to worry about coordinating the changes in one document with changes in the other document. Use the Paste Special command to paste link your document. You can choose to insert your paste-linked file as a picture or an icon. Choosing Picture displays your worksheet. Choosing Icon displays an icon.

To edit a paste-linked Excel worksheet in Word or PowerPoint, double-click the worksheet picture or icon. When you do, Microsoft Word or PowerPoint automatically opens the document in Excel and makes all the Excel commands available as you edit the document.

Paste Link into Word

① Select the range you want to paste link.

② Click the Home tab.

③ Click the Copy button in the Clipboard group.

● Switch to the Word document.

> To paste link an Excel file into PowerPoint, switch to PowerPoint.

④ Click the Home tab.

⑤ Click Paste in the Clipboard group.

⑥ Click Paste Special.

> The Paste Special dialog box appears.

⑦ Click Paste Link (○ changes to ◉).

● Click here if you want to display your document as an icon (☐ changes to ☑) and the Change Icon button appears.

⑧ Click Microsoft Office Excel Worksheet Object.

⑨ Click OK.

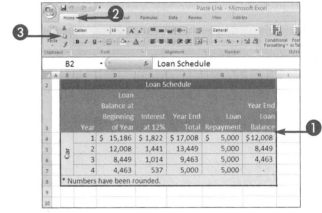

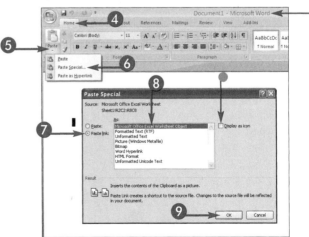

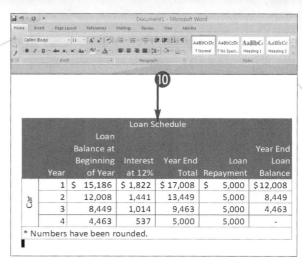

A picture of the worksheet appears in Word.

If you chose Display as Icon, the icon appears.

⑩ Double-click the worksheet to edit it.

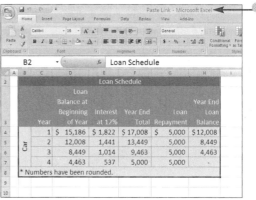

● Your worksheet opens in Excel and you can make any necessary edits.

When you have completed your edits, save and close your Excel document and return to your Word document.

Extra

In Word or PowerPoint, you can use an icon to represent your worksheet. This is useful if your worksheet is large. You choose Display as Icon (☐ changes to ☑) in the Paste Special dialog box. When you do, Excel displays the default icon and a Change Icon button. If you do not want to use the default icon, click the Change Icon button to choose the icon you want.

If you paste linked your worksheet as a picture and you want to display it as an icon instead, or vice versa, right-click the icon or picture. A menu appears. Click Worksheet Object and then click Convert. The Convert dialog box appears. Select Display as Icon to display your worksheet as an icon. Deselect Display as Icon to display your worksheet as a picture.

You can paste link a Word document into Excel. You select the data in Word you want to paste link, click the Home tab, and then click the Copy button. Then move to Excel and click the Home tab, click Paste, and then click Paste Special. The Paste Special dialog box appears. Click Paste Link, click Microsoft Office Word Document Object, and then click OK. Your Word document appears in Excel. You double-click to edit it.

Embed a Worksheet

As you present your PowerPoint presentation or change your Word document, you can edit your Excel worksheets without leaving PowerPoint or Word. This means you can demonstrate different business scenarios as you give your PowerPoint presentation or do sophisticated mathematical calculations while in Word. To use this feature, you must embed your worksheet into your PowerPoint or Word file.

When you embed Excel documents, the embedded Excel worksheet becomes part of the PowerPoint or Word document and is accessible only through PowerPoint or Word. There is no link between the embedded document and the original document and, in that way, embedding differs from paste linking. When you make changes to an embedded Excel document, the changes only affect the PowerPoint or Word file. When you paste link a worksheet into Word or PowerPoint, you can change the original

Excel file from within Word or PowerPoint, and Office automatically updates the Excel worksheet. When you update the Excel worksheet from within Excel, Office automatically updates the PowerPoint or Word file. See the previous task, "Paste Link into Word," for more information on paste linking.

You can embed an existing Excel file or generate a new file entirely within PowerPoint or Word. Use the Insert Object dialog box to embed an Excel file. You can choose to have embedded worksheets display as a picture or as an icon. As with paste-linked worksheets, if you choose Display as Icon, Excel gives you several icons from which to choose. You just click the Change Icon button and then select an icon.

If you choose to embed an existing file, you can use the Insert Object dialog box to browse for the file.

Embed a Worksheet

1 Open the PowerPoint presentation in which you want to include a worksheet.

Note: *This example uses PowerPoint. You can follow similar steps to embed your document in Word.*

2 Click the Insert tab.

3 Click Object in the Text group.

● The Insert Object dialog box appears.

4 Click Create New (○ changes to ◉) to generate a new worksheet.

Alternatively, click Create from File to open an existing workbook.

5 Click Microsoft Office Excel Worksheet.

Alternatively, choose another type of Excel worksheet.

6 Click OK.

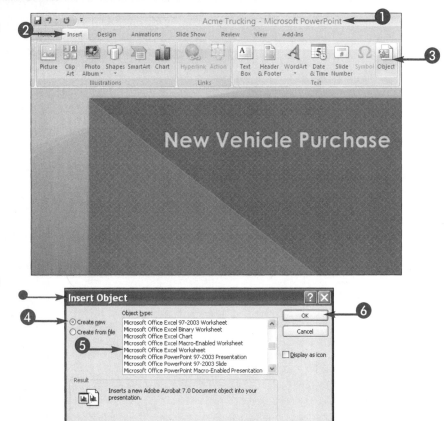

- A blank worksheet appears.

- All of the Microsoft Excel commands are available to you.

7 Create your worksheet.

Click outside the worksheet when you have finished.

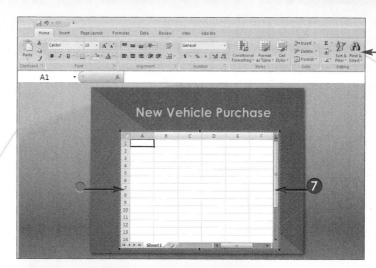

- Your completed worksheet appears in your PowerPoint presentation.

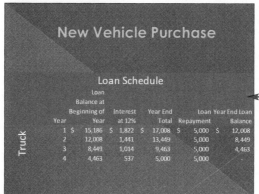

Hyperlink a Worksheet

You may be familiar with the many benefits of hyperlinks on Web pages. When you click a link, you jump to a new Web page with more links, creating an enormous and seamless web of information. Like most Office applications, Excel also lets you create links. These links can take users to a place in the same workbook, to a document created by another Office application, or even to a Web page. For example, creating a hyperlink to a Word document provides an alternative to annotating worksheets by using comments and text boxes. Unlike comments, a linked Word document can be of any length and complexity. Unlike text boxes, hyperlinks do not obstruct worksheets or distract readers.

Hyperlinking a document is different from paste linking. Instead of pulling data created by another application into

Excel, a hyperlink jumps you from a worksheet to a related document.

You use the Insert Hyperlink dialog box to create a hyperlink. In the Text to Display field, you type the text you want to appear in the hyperlinked cell. The ScreenTip button opens the Set Hyperlink ScreenTip dialog box. Use this dialog box to enter the text that appears as users move the mouse pointer over the hyperlink. By default, the address of the linked-to file appears. In the Address field, type the filename of the file to which you want to link or the Web address of the Web page to which you want to link. The Edit Hyperlink dialog box has buttons to help you find the file or Web page you want. Click Current Folder to search the current folder, click Browsed Pages to review files you have browsed, and click Recent Files to review files you have recently opened.

Hyperlink a Worksheet

① Click the cell in which you want the hyperlink to appear.

② Click the Insert tab.

③ Click Hyperlink in the Links group.

   The Insert Hyperlink dialog box appears.

④ Click a Link To location.

   This example uses Existing File or Web Page.

⑤ Type the text you want to display in the field.

⑥ Click here and select a folder.

⑦ Click here to search the current folder.

● Alternatively, click here to search browsed pages.

● Or, click here to search recent files.

⑧ Click a file.

● Click here to enter the text that appears when you run your mouse pointer over your hyperlink.

⑨ Click OK.

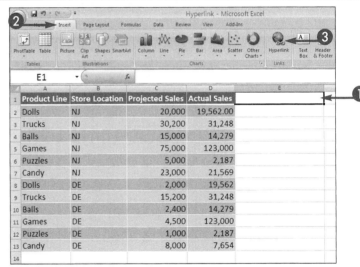

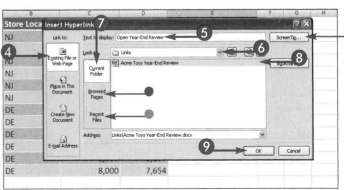

The cell content appears as a hyperlink. You can pass your mouse over the link without clicking to see the name of the linked-to file or the text you entered in the Text to Display field.

⑩ Right-click the link.

A menu appears.

⑪ Click Open Hyperlink.

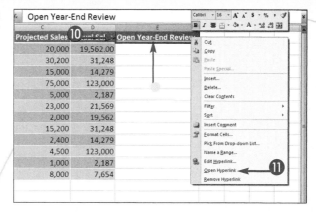

The linked-to document appears.

⑫ Click the Close button to close the document.

Office returns you to your original document.

To remove the hyperlink, right-click the linked worksheet cell and then click Remove Hyperlink.

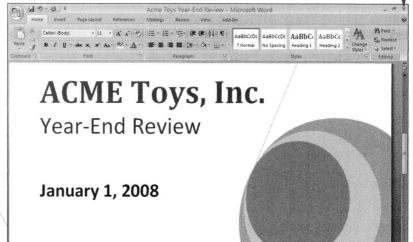

ACME Toys, Inc.

Year-End Review

January 1, 2008

Apply It

Adding a hyperlink to another area of your workbook can help you move around your workbook quickly. For example, if you have sales figures for different regions in a single workbook, you can create a menu of links that will quickly take you to the information you want.

To create an internal workbook hyperlink, move to the cell in which you want to place the link. Click the Insert tab. Click Hyperlink. The Insert Hyperlink dialog box appears. Click Place in This Document in the Link To area. Type the text you want to appear in the cell in the Text to Display field. Type the cell you want to move to in the Type the Cell Reference field. Alternatively, click the sheet name in the Or Select a Place in this Document box to move to cell A1 of a particular sheet. If you have named ranges, you can also click a range name in the Or Select a Place in this Document box. When you have completed your entries, click OK. Excel creates your hyperlink.

Query a
Web Site

With the data in Excel, you have complete access to data analysis and presentation tools, including functions, PivotTables, and charts. Excel gives you two options for opening and using Web-based tabular data. You can click the Office button, click Open, type the Web address in the File Name field, and then click Open again. Or, you can use a Web query.

Both techniques allow you to view and edit numbers, but querying a Web site has advantages. When you import data as a Web query, you can filter the data and view only records of interest. A Web query also lets you refresh data if it is subject to updates.

The New Web Query dialog box works much like any Web browser. You type the address of a Web site and view the associated Web pages. The dialog box analyzes each Web page and breaks it into individual tables of data. Little

yellow arrow buttons display next to each section of the Web page. You use the buttons to identify the portion of the Web page you want to import. The icon changes to a green check button to identify your selections.

Excel only imports the text portion of the Web page. If you want to capture any of the graphics on the Web page, you must do so by using the Copy and Paste commands.

You must tell Excel where to place Web data. By default, Excel selects the active cell. If the existing worksheet contains data, Excel adds enough columns to contain the imported data. Any existing worksheet data moves to the right, into new columns. Alternatively, you can select the New Worksheet option to create a new worksheet for the data. If you create a new worksheet, Excel inserts the worksheet in the current workbook.

Query a Web Site

① Open an Excel worksheet.

② Click the Data tab.

③ Click From Web in the Get External Data group.

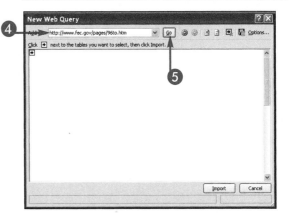

The New Web Query dialog box appears.

④ Type the Web address for the site from which you want data.

This example uses www.fec.gov/pages/96to.htm.

⑤ Click Go.

The Web page appears in the dialog box.

● Click to move through pages you have viewed.

⑥ Click the elements you want to appear in your query.

A check mark indicates you want to query an element.

● An arrow indicates you do not want to query an element.

⑦ Click Import.

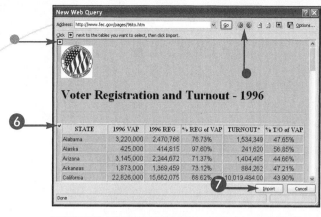

● The Import Data dialog box appears.

⑧ Click to select a location for the imported page (○ changes ◉).

● If you select Existing Worksheet, click the cell that represents the upper-left cell of the data area.

⑨ Click OK.

● The selected Web elements appear within Excel, ready for analysis, charting, and so on.

● Click Refresh All on the Data tab to refresh your data.

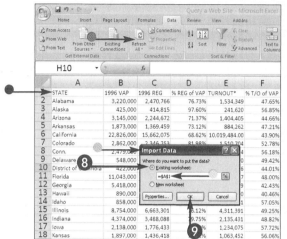

Extra

You can import the text formatting along with the Web page data. Click the Options button in the upper-right corner of the New Web Query dialog box. In the Web Query Options dialog box that appears, select one of the following formatting options.

FORMATTING	DESCRIPTION
None	Imports the text only and applies the Normal format style
Rich Text	Imports the text with the formatting on the Web page
Full HTML	Imports the text with all HTML styles, including links

A *query* is a file containing a definition of the data you import into Excel from an external source. The query definition indicates the data source, the rows to include, how rows added to the source are accommodated by the query, and the frequency with which the data is updated. You can view and modify query properties by clicking the Data tab and then clicking Properties.

Import a Text File

Many software applications have an option you can use to export the application's data to a text file. You can import text files from other applications into Excel by using the Text Import Wizard. You can then use Excel's sophisticated data-analysis capabilities to analyze the data. In fact, once you have imported the data, you can use it in a PivotTable, create charts with it, or manipulate it just as you would any other Excel data.

The Text Import Wizard can handle any delimited or fixed-width file. A *delimited* file uses a comma, semicolon, tab, space, or other character to mark the end of each column. A *fixed-width* file aligns each column and gives each column a defined width. A space usually separates the columns.

You start the import of a text file by using the Import Text File dialog box to locate the file you want to import. Text files created by other software applications may be in one of many popular file formats. You can identify the file format by the file extension. Programs usually use commas to delimit files with a .csv extension. Another popular extension is .txt. The exporting program usually delimits TXT files with tabs.

After you locate your file, Excel opens the Text Import Wizard. You must tell Excel whether you are importing a fixed-width file or a delimited file. If you are importing a fixed-width file, you tell Excel exactly where each column begins by clicking the location in the Data Preview window. Excel inserts a break line. You can adjust the location of the line or delete the line.

Import a Text File

① Click the Data tab.

② Click From Text in the Get External Data group.

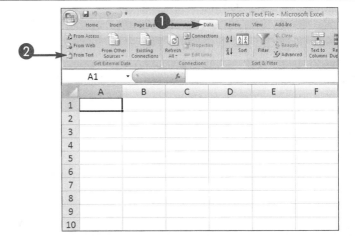

The Import Text File dialog box appears.

③ Click here and locate the folder in which you stored your file.

④ Click the file.

⑤ Click Import.

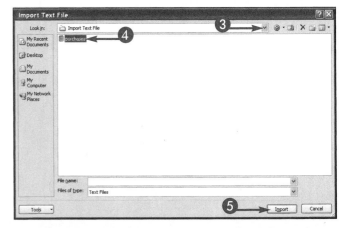

The Text Import Wizard appears.

6 Click to select the file type that best describes your data (○ changes to ◉).

7 Click to select the row at which to begin importing.

8 Click Next.

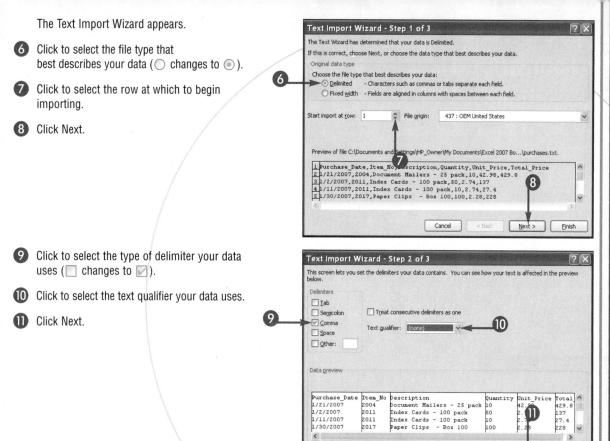

9 Click to select the type of delimiter your data uses (☐ changes to ☑).

10 Click to select the text qualifier your data uses.

11 Click Next.

You may find you want to import Excel data into another application that accepts text files. You can use the following steps to export an Excel file as a text file. Click the Office button. A menu appears. Click Save As. Another menu appears. Click Other Formats. The Save As dialog box appears. In the Save In field, select the folder in which you want to save your file. In the Save as Type field, select a text format such as Formatted Text (Space delimited) (*.prn), CSV (Comma delimited) (*.csv), or any one of the many other text formats, including *.txt formats. Type the filename you want to give the file in the File Name field and then click Save. A dialog box appears telling you Excel will only save the active sheet. Click OK. Another dialog box appears warning you that any feature incompatible with a text file will be lost. Click Yes. Excel saves your file as a text file.

continued →

Import a Text File (continued)

Y ou can use the Start Import at Row field to specify the row in your text file where you want to begin the import. If your data has titles or other information you do not want to import at the top of the file, you can skip those rows. Excel provides you with a preview of the import file. The Preview window numbers each row.

If you are importing a delimited file, you tell Excel the type of delimiters the file uses on the second page of the Text Import Wizard. You can specify more than one delimiter. Some delimited file formats surround text data with a text qualifier, such as single or double quotes. The Import Wizard provides you with the Text Qualifier field in which you can specify whether your data has a text qualifier and, if so, what the qualifier is.

After you have defined the layout of your data, you must define the data type contained in each column. You have three options: general, text, and date. General converts numeric data to numbers, dates to dates, and everything else to text. If you have numeric data that is text, use the text option to have Excel convert the data to text. If you have dates, click the date option and specify the format you want to use. If there is a column you do not want to import, click the Do Not Import Column option.

In the Import Data dialog box, you must tell Excel where you want to place your imported text file. You can choose an existing worksheet or a new worksheet. If you choose Existing Worksheet, you must specify the starting cell. If you choose New Worksheet, Excel places the data starting in cell A1 of a new worksheet.

Import a Text File (continued)

⑫ Click the column head.

⑬ Click to select a data type or to skip a column (○ changes to ◉).

Repeat Steps 12 and 13 for each column.

⑭ Click Finish.

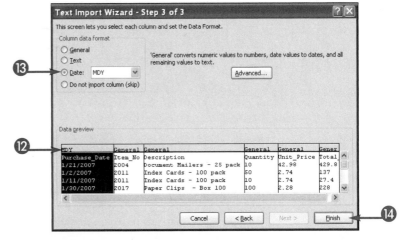

● The Import Data dialog box appears.

⑮ Click to select where you want to put your data (○ changes to ◉).

● If you selected Existing Worksheet, click a cell or type a cell address.

⑯ Click OK.

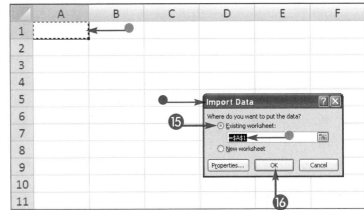

Excel imports the data.

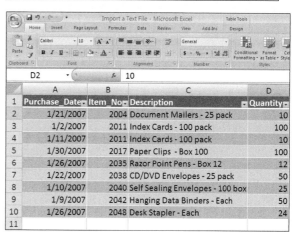

You can format and analyze your data.

Apply It

Excel has an option you can use to break individual cells into columns. The feature works a lot like the Text Import Wizard. You select the field you want to divide and then click the Data tab. In the Data Tools group, click Text to Columns. The Convert Text to Columns Wizard appears. Select whether your field is delimited or of fixed width. Click Next.

If your field is delimited, on page 2, select the delimiter and enter the text qualifier. Click the Treat Consecutive Delimiters as One box (☐ changes to ☑), if that is what you want to do. Click Next. Assign formats to each column, select a destination for the output, and then click Finish. Excel breaks your cell into columns.

If your field is a fixed width, on page 2, click in the Data Preview box to place a line between columns. Click Next. Assign formats to each column, select a destination for the output, and then click Finish. Excel breaks your cell into columns.

Import an Access Database

Many organizations use more than one application to manage tabular data. Excel is best for managing, analyzing, and presenting numbers. Databases such as Access help you store, filter, and retrieve data in large quantities and of every type. With Excel, you can apply easy-to-use data-analysis techniques to complex Access databases.

Instead of using worksheets in Access, you must carefully organize your information into data tables, each of which stores information about one part of the entity of interest to you: customers, products, employees, transactions, and so on. To help keep track of these tables in Access, you create unique identifiers, called *keys*. Access can automatically assign keys to each customer, product, employee, transaction, and so on. The keys link tables to each other.

You can import an Access data table and analyze your Access data in Excel. You start the import process by selecting the Access database from which you want to import data. Excel presents you with a list of the tables found in that database. You select the table you want to import. You then choose how you want to view the data. You can choose from Table, PivotTable Report, and PivotChart and PivotTable Report. The Table option brings the data into your worksheet as a table. See Chapter 6 to learn more about tables. The PivotTable Report option connects to your table and makes your data ready for you to use in a PivotTable report. It does not import the table as a list. See Chapter 7 to learn more about PivotTables. The PivotChart and PivotTable Report option connects to your table and imports your data, ready to be used in a PivotChart and PivotTable. It does not import the table as a list. See Chapter 8 to learn more about PivotCharts.

Import an Access Database

1. Click the Data tab.

2. Click From Access in the Get External Data group.

● The Select Data Source dialog box appears.

3. Click here to select the folder in which your Access database is located.

4. Click to select your database.

5. Click Open.

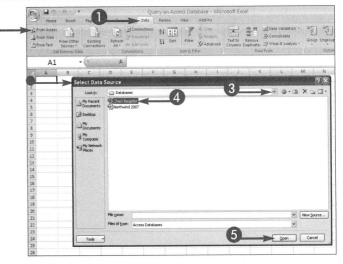

The Select Table dialog box appears.

6. Click the table you want to open.

7. Click OK.

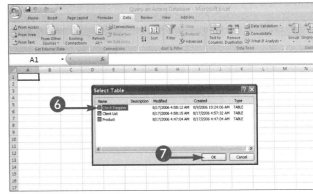

The Import Data dialog box appears.

8 Click to select how you want to view your data (○ changes to ◉).

9 Click to select where you want to put your data (○ changes to ◉).

● If you selected Existing Worksheet, click a cell or type a cell address.

10 Click OK.

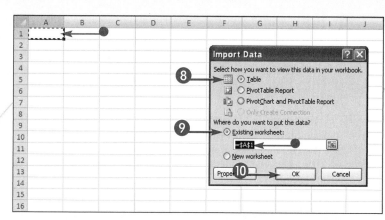

Your data appears in Excel.

Check No	Client ID	Ref No	Check Date
50234	CL-305	11137	3/1/2007
50235	CL-300	11138	3/1/2007
50236	CL-300	11139	3/1/2007
50237	CL-302	11140	3/1/2007
50238	CL-323	11141	3/1/2007
50239	CL-330	11142	3/1/2007
50240	CL-318	11143	3/1/2007
50241	CL-300	11144	3/1/2007
50242	CL-323	11145	3/1/2007
50243	CL-317	11146	3/1/2007
50244	CL-329	11147	3/1/2007
50245	CL-310	11148	3/1/2007
50246	CL-300	11149	3/1/2007

Extra

You can copy and paste Access data into Excel. In Access, click the Home tab, View, and then Datasheet View. Drag your mouse pointer over the column labels to select the columns you want to copy. Click the Copy button. Move to Excel. Click where you want to place your Access table. Click Paste. Excel pastes your data.

Importing your data into Excel has an advantage over copying and pasting your data into Excel. When you import your data, you make a connection between your data and the Access database. You can refresh your data so that any changes made to the Access database appear in Excel. To refresh your data manually, click Refresh All on the Data tab and then click Refresh.

You can tell Excel how you want to refresh your data. Click the Properties button in the Import Data dialog box. The Connection Properties dialog box appears. If you want to be able to use Excel while your data is refreshing, click Enable Background Refresh. If you want to refresh at certain intervals, click Refresh and enter the interval in minutes. If you want to refresh when the file opens, click Refresh Data When Opening File.

Query an Access Database

The Query Wizard is part of Microsoft Query, a separate application that comes with Microsoft Office. Microsoft Query makes it easy for you to generate queries in Structured Query Language (SQL), a standard in the corporate world.

The Query Wizard provides a point-and-click interface for importing tables or selected columns into Excel. You start the process in the Choose Data Source dialog box by selecting MS Access Database as your data source and telling Excel you want to use the Query Wizard to create or edit queries. You then locate the database you want to use. The Query Wizard displays a list of tables and columns found in the database. You can select one or more tables and/or columns to query. You can also preview the data in the individual fields of your tables. Your columns will appear in Excel in the order listed in

the Columns in Your Query field in the Choose Columns dialog box. You can adjust the order of the fields.

Once you have selected the columns or tables you want, you can filter and sort. The Query Wizard provides 16 comparison operators. In addition, you can create multiple filters by using and and or.

Use or when you want the wizard to select data that meets either of the specified conditions. For example, ask the wizard to select all dresses that are blue or all dresses that have red buttons. The wizard returns every blue dress and every dress with red buttons. Alternatively, ask the wizard to select all dresses that are blue and have red buttons. The and selection criteria are more restrictive. The wizard returns only items that meet both selection criteria: blue dresses with red buttons.

Query an Access Database

Note: *You must install the New Database Query button on the Quick Access toolbar. See the Extra section of "Assign a Macro to the Quick Access Toolbar" in Chapter 12 to learn how to install objects on the Quick Access toolbar.*

1. Click the New Database Query button.

● The Choose Data Source dialog box appears.

2. Click the Databases tab.

3. Click MS Access Database.

4. Click OK.

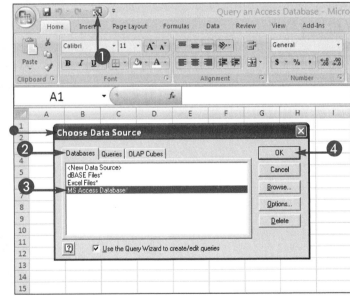

The Select Database dialog box appears.

5. Click to locate the folder in which you stored your database.

6. Click to select your database.

7. Click OK.

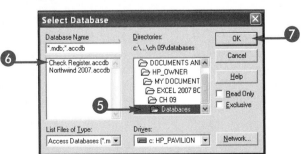

The Query Wizard — Choose Columns dialog box appears.

⑧ Click the table and/or fields you want to import.

⑨ Click the Add button.

If you want to open more than one table, repeat Steps 8 and 9.

⑩ Click Next.

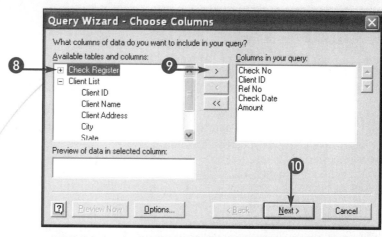

The Query Wizard — Filter Data dialog box appears.

⑪ Click the column by which you want to filter.

⑫ Click here and select a comparison operator.

⑬ Click here and select the criteria by which you want to filter.

● You can apply additional filters.

● You can use And and/or Or (○ changes to ⊙).

⑭ Click Next.

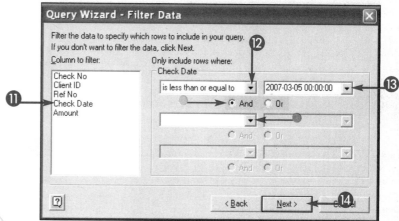

Extra

You use the Choose Data Source dialog box to import an Access database. To open the Choose Data Source dialog box, you click the New Database Query button on the Quick Access toolbar or you click the Data tab, click From Other Sources in the Get External Data dialog box, and then click From Microsoft Query.

If you import fields from more than one table, you may need to tell Microsoft Query how to join the tables. Microsoft Query provides a sophisticated interface to help you. On the final page of the wizard, if you click View Data or Edit Query In (○ changes to ⊙) and then click Finish, the Microsoft Query interface appears. You can use it to edit your query. Click Help on the Microsoft Query menu to learn how to use this function.

Filtering data improves performance when you are working with large databases. Using Microsoft Query can speed up performance. If you work with large databases and want to apply numerous filters and sort orders, MS Query is worth learning.

continued →

With the Query Wizard, you can sort your data and create sorts within sorts. For example, you can alphabetize a list of states, counties, and towns as follows: first in alphabetical order by state, then in alphabetical order by county, and finally in alphabetical order by town.

After you import the data into Excel, you can use Excel's tools to further sort and filter. You can go beyond the wizard and directly manipulate the Access tables from which your query is drawn.

On the final page of the Query Wizard, click View Data or Edit Query in Microsoft Query and then click Finish for a graphical view of the underlying data tables. You can work directly with criteria fields, add tables, and connect tables by shared fields. You can also run and view queries. When you have finished, you can save the query. Saved queries become available in Excel for viewing, analyzing, charting, and so on.

You can choose how you want to view your data in Excel. You can view it as a table, a PivotTable report, or a PivotChart and PivotTable report. The Table option brings the data into your worksheet as a table. See Chapter 6 to learn more about tables. The PivotTable Report option connects to your table and makes your data ready for you to use in a PivotTable report. It does not import the table as a list. See Chapter 7 to learn more about PivotTables. The PivotChart and PivotTable Report option connects to your table and imports your data ready to be used in a PivotChart and PivotTable report. It does not import the table as a list. See Chapter 8 to learn more about PivotCharts.

Query an Access Database (continued)

⑮ Click here and select the column by which you want to sort your data.

⑯ Click Ascending or Descending order (○ changes to ◉).

● Optionally, you can add additional sort criteria.

⑰ Click Next.

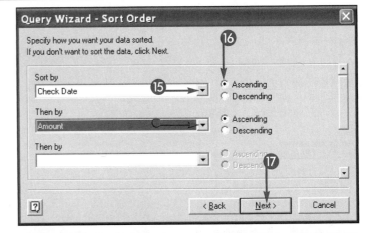

The Query Wizard – Finish dialog box appears.

⑱ Click Return Data to Microsoft Office Excel (○ changes to ◉).

● Click View Data or Edit Query in Microsoft Query and then click Finish for a graphical view of the underlying data tables.

● Click here to save your query.

⑲ Click Finish.

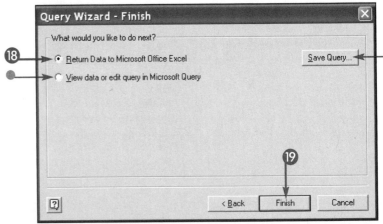

The Import Data dialog box appears.

㉒ Click to select how you want to view your data (○ changes to ⦿).

㉑ Click to select where you want to place your data (○ changes to ⦿).

◉ If you selected Existing Worksheet, click and drag or type a range.

㉒ Click OK.

Your Access data appears in Excel.

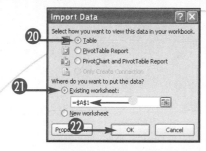

	A	B	C	D	E	F
1	Check No	Client ID	Ref No	Check Date	Amount	
2	50247	CL-324	11150	3/1/2007 0:00	231.69	
3	50236	CL-300	11139	3/1/2007 0:00	605.71	
4	50234	CL-305	11137	3/1/2007 0:00	1015.15	
5	50248	CL-329	11151	3/1/2007 0:00	1461.02	
6	50242	CL-323	11145	3/1/2007 0:00	1817.57	
7	50241	CL-300	11144	3/1/2007 0:00	1852.42	
8	50245	CL-310	11148	3/1/2007 0:00	1996.15	
9	50246	CL-300	11149	3/1/2007 0:00	2941.65	
10	50249	CL-315	11152	3/1/2007 0:00	2979.46	
11	50239	CL-330	11142	3/1/2007 0:00	3143.82	
12	50243	CL-317	11146	3/1/2007 0:00	3284.35	
13	50235	CL-300	11138	3/1/2007 0:00	3379.4	
14	50244	CL-329	11147	3/1/2007 0:00	3606.71	
15	50240	CL-318	11143	3/1/2007 0:00	3928.45	
16	50238	CL-323	11141	3/1/2007 0:00	4691.22	
17	50250	CL-308	11153	3/1/2007 0:00	4770.37	
18	50237	CL-302	11140	3/1/2007 0:00	4810.37	
19	50258	CL-322	11161	3/2/2007 0:00	89.83	

Extra

By saving your query, you can quickly retrieve data. To save, click Save Query on the final page of the Query Wizard. The Save As dialog box appears. In the Save In field, locate the folder in which you want to save your query. Name your query in the File Name field. Click Save. Excel saves your query.

To retrieve a saved query, click the Data tab and then click Existing Connections in the Get External Data group. The Existing Connections dialog box appears. Click the name of your saved query. Click Open. The Import Data dialog box appears. Click to select how you want to view your data. Click to select where you want to place your data. Click OK. Excel imports your data.

Refreshing updates the data so you can see any changes made to your data in Access since the last refresh. To refresh your data, click the Data tab and then click Refresh All. Excel refreshes your data.

To delete a saved query, click the New Database Query button on the Quick Access toolbar to open the Choose Data Source dialog box. Click the Queries tab. Click your query and then click Delete.

Perform What-If Analysis

hen you use a formula or function, your purpose is often to find out how one thing influences another. When you use the IRR function, for example, you can find out how a change in the loan amount, payment amount, or payment date — or some combination of these factors — affects the interest received. You can type in different amounts and different payment dates to see how different scenarios affect the interest rate.

What-if analysis is a systematic way of finding out how a change in one or more variables affects a result. The Scenario Manager lets you vary one or more inputs into any formula or function to see how the result changes.

You can use the Scenario Manager two ways. You can click a scenario in the Scenario Manager dialog box and then click Show. Excel displays the scenario and the result in your worksheet. When you use this method, Excel changes the values in your worksheet to the values in your scenario. If your original worksheet data is not one of your scenario options, it will be lost. You can also create a summary report. A summary report displays each of your scenarios in a different column, in a new worksheet. With a summary report, you can compare scenarios side by side.

The beauty of the Scenario Manager is that it stores a series of values so you can see how each value or combination of values influences the result. You can also present your information as a PivotTable and thereby give yourself all the flexibility a PivotTable offers. To learn more about PivotTables, see Chapter 7.

To create scenarios, you must first enter the values required into a worksheet and type a formula that calculates the answer. The example uses the Internal Rate of Return function.

Perform What-If Analysis

1 Click and drag to select the cells that contain the values you want to vary.

2 Click the Data tab.

3 Click What-If Analysis in the Data Tools group.

4 Click Scenario Manager.

● The Scenario Manager dialog box appears.

5 Click Add.

● The Add Scenario dialog box appears, indicating the cells selected in Step 1.

6 Type a name for your scenario.

7 Click OK.

● The Scenario Values dialog box appears.

8 Type the scenario values.

9 Click Add to create more scenarios.

● The Add Scenario dialog box reappears.

10 Click OK instead of Add when you finish entering scenarios.

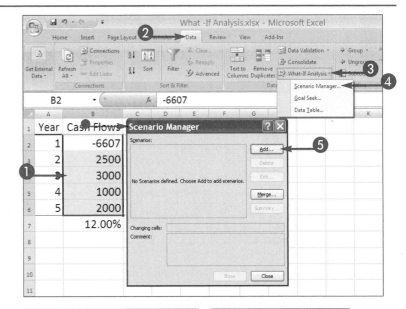

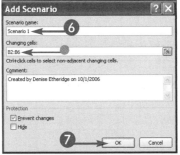

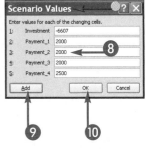

- The Scenario Manager dialog box appears.

⑪ Click Summary.

- Alternatively, click a scenario and then click Show to display the scenario in your worksheet.

- The Scenario Summary dialog box appears.

⑫ Click to select a report type (○ changes to ◉).

Click Scenario Summary for a summary report.

Click Scenario PivotTable Report for a PivotTable report.

⑬ Click the field or type the cell address of the field that calculates the results.

⑭ Click OK.

- The type of report you requested appears in a new worksheet, displaying how each value affects the result.

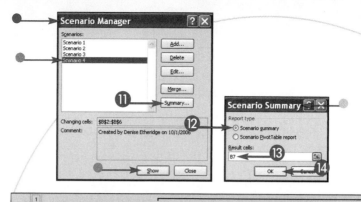

		Current Values:	Scenario 1	Scenario 2	Scenario 3	Scenario 4
Scenario Summary						
Changing Cells:						
	Investment	-6607	-6607	-6607	-6607	-6607
	Payment_1	2500	2000	2500	5000	1000
	Payment_2	3000	2000	2000	1000	1000
	Payment_3	1000	2000	2000	1000	1000
	Payment_4	2000	2500	2000	1500	5000
Result Cells:						
	Interest	12.00%	10.50%	11.36%	15.12%	6.13%

Notes: Current Values column represents values of changing cells at time Scenario Summary Report was created. Changing cells for each scenario are highlighted in gray.

Apply It

If you name the cells in your original worksheet, your Scenario Summary becomes easier to read because Excel displays the cell name instead of the cell address. For example, in this task, cell B2 is named Investment, cells B3 through B6 are named Payment_1 through Payment_4, and cell B7 is named Interest_Earned. To learn how to name cells, see Chapter 2.

If you share copies of a workbook and people add their own scenarios, you can merge these scenarios into a single list. To do so, open the workbooks and click Data and then Scenario Manager. In the Scenario Manager, click Merge. In the Merge Scenarios window, select the workbooks and individual worksheets to consolidate. Click OK when you finish selecting them.

You can use the Scenario Manager dialog box to edit and delete scenarios. Click the Data tab, click What-If Analysis in the Data Tools group, and then click Scenario Manager. The Scenario Manager dialog box appears. Click a scenario and then click Delete to delete a scenario. Click a scenario and then click Edit to edit a scenario.

Optimize a Result with Goal Seek

Excel gives you a powerful tool for finding a way to reach your goals: Goal Seek. With Goal Seek, you tell Excel which value in your formula you want to change; Excel then adjusts that value to give you the result you want. For example, if you need a loan for a new home, your goal might be to make a specific monthly payment. You can use the Goal Seek feature to show how you can reach your goal by adjusting one of the loan terms, such as the interest rate or loan amount.

You can also have Goal Seek find the interest rate required to reach your payment goal, given a certain loan amount, or find the loan amount required to reach your goal, given a specific interest rate. You cannot meet some goals, such as reducing your monthly payment to nothing; the interest rates and loan amounts would be unrealistic.

In the Goal Seek dialog box, the Set Cell field tells Excel which field contains the formula with a value you want to manipulate to achieve your goal. The To Value field tells Excel what your goal is. The By Changing Cell field tells Excel the cell that contains the value you want to change to reach your goal. The cell address you enter in the By Changing Cell field must be included in the formula you reference in the Set Cell field. If you are not getting a result, you can try clicking the Office button, clicking Excel Options, and then clicking Formulas. Then in the Calculations Options area, increase the maximum iterations.

To vary multiple inputs to achieve a specific goal, you need to use Solver. To use the Solver add-in, you must first load it into Excel.

Optimize a Result with Goal Seek

1. Click the cell that contains the value you want to reach.

2. Click the Data tab.

3. Click What-If Analysis in the Data Tools group.

   A menu appears.

4. Click Goal Seek.

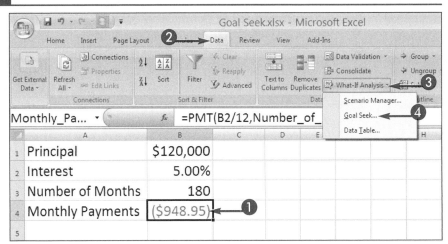

- The Goal Seek dialog box appears.

5. Type the value you want to reach.

6. Click a cell or type the address of the cell whose value you want to change to reach your goal.

7. Click OK.

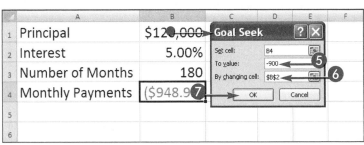

- The results appear in the worksheet.

8 Click OK to accept the change.

- Alternatively, you can click Cancel to restore the original values.

  In this example, the principal remains the same, and the $900 monthly payment can be reached by finding an interest rate of 4.2 percent.

- Repeat Steps 1 to 8 for another value.

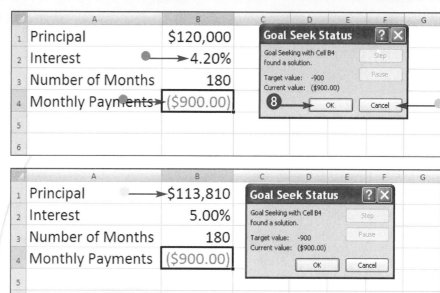

Extra

The example in this task shows the loan amount required to bring the monthly payment down to $900 ($113,810). If your purchase price is $120,000, you would have to contribute a down payment of just over $6,000 to bring the loan down to that amount. You could construct a worksheet in which you could enter various down-payment amounts.

To vary multiple inputs to achieve a specific goal, you must use Solver. To add the Solver add-in to Microsoft Excel, click the Office button. A menu appears. Click Excel options. The Excel Options dialog box appears. Click Add-Ins. The View and Manage Microsoft Office Add-Ins dialog box appears. Click the add-in you want. In this case, click Solver Add-in. Click Go. Click OK. The Solver add-in appears on the Add-Ins tab ready for you to use.

Solve a Formula with a Data Table

W hen you need to find out how changing certain values in your formula affects the outcome, you can use a data table. For example, if you want to create a worksheet that shows how different interest rates affect the amount you must pay monthly on a loan, use a data table. With a data table, you can create your worksheet without having to enter the same formula multiple times.

A data table contains at least two columns or two rows. If you use columns, the first column consists of the values you want to substitute into a formula. The first cell of the second column contains the formula you want to use. The formula must reference the first value in the first column. If you are varying interest rates so you can compare loan payments, and the first column (column A)

contains the interest rate you want to substitute in the PMT function, the Rate argument must reference column A, as shown in the following formula:

=PMT(A5/PeriodsPerYear, LoanTerm, -LoanAmount)

If you use rows to create your data table, place your substitution values in the first row. Place your formula in the first cell of the second row and reference the first cell of the first row in your formula.

If your data is set up in columns, use the Column Input Cell field in the Data Table dialog box to tell Excel the location of the cell referenced in your formula. If your data is set up in rows, use the Row Input Cell field in the Data Table dialog box to tell Excel the location of the cell referenced in your formula.

Solve a Formula with a Data Table

① Type the substitution values in a column.

You can also place values in a row.

② Type the formula in the first cell of the next column.

If your values are in a row, type the formula in the first cell in the row under the values.

③ Select the cells containing substitution values, the formula, and the cells you want to fill.

④ Click the Data tab.

⑤ Click What-If Analysis in the Data Tools group.

A menu appears.

⑥ Click Data Table.

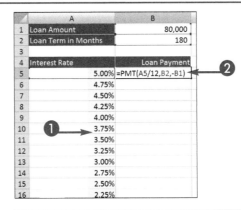

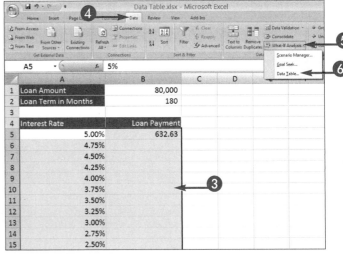

The Data Table dialog box appears.

7 Click the cell, or type the cell reference for the first substitution cell if you are using columns.

● Type the cell reference in this field if you are using rows.

8 Click OK.

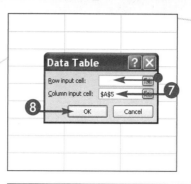

● Excel displays the comparison results in the second column of the data table.

	A	B
1	Loan Amount	80,000
2	Loan Term in Months	180
3		
4	Interest Rate	Loan Payment
5	5.00%	632.63
6	4.75%	622.27
7	4.50%	611.99
8	4.25%	601.82
9	4.00%	591.75
10	3.75%	581.78
11	3.50%	571.91
12	3.25%	562.14
13	3.00%	552.47
14	2.75%	542.90
15	2.50%	533.43

Apply It

If you want to substitute values for two different arguments in a formula, you can create a two-input data table. In a two-input data table, you specify the first set of substitution values in the column under the formula cell and the second set of substitution values in the row to the right of the formula. For example, if you want to see how both interest rates and loan terms affect your payments, you specify the interest rates in the column under the formula and the loan term values in the row next to the formula.

When you create a two-input data table, your formula must initially reference cells located outside the data table. This means if your data table contains interest rates in a column, the formula must initially reference a cell outside the column containing an interest rate value. In the Data Table dialog box, you specify both the row and column initial input cells. To see an example of a two-input data table, refer to Sheet2 of Data Tables.xlsx, which is on the Web site for this book.

Extend a Series with AutoFill

utoFill gives you a way to ensure accurate data entry when a particular data series has an intrinsic order such as days of the week, months of the year, or numeric increments of two.

To use AutoFill, start by typing one or more values from which you will generate other values. Select the cell or cells you want to extend. Selecting two or more cells determines the step size, or increment, by which you want to jump in each cell. For example, selecting 2 in the first cell and 4 in the second cell causes Excel to increment by two, as in 2, 4, 6, 8. With the cells selected, click the fill handle in the lower-right corner of the selected area and drag. When you release the mouse button, Excel fills the cells with values. You can fill a series in any direction: up, down, left, or right.

Your fill can consist of numbers, dates, times, months of the year, days of the week, text, or formulas. When filling, Excel also copies the format. For example, if you type Jan in red and then click and drag the fill handle two cells, Excel fills Jan, Feb, Mar using red text. If you type January in a cell with a green background and white text, Excel fills January, February, March using a green background and white text.

After you fill the cells, the AutoFill button appears. Click the button to open a menu that enables you to change the fill. You can copy the initial value, fill the series one day at a time, or extend it by weekdays, months, or years, depending on the type of fill you create.

Extend a Series with AutoFill

① Type the initial value for the series you want to create.

② Select a cell or cells.

③ Click the fill handle.

④ Drag the desired number of cells and release the mouse button.

● Excel fills the cells with a series.

● The AutoFill Options button appears.

⑤ Click the AutoFill Options button.

A menu appears.

You can use the menu to change the manner in which Excel fills the cells.

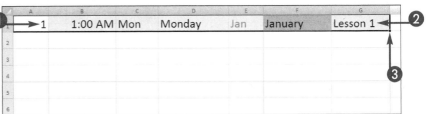

⑥ Type a pattern.

⑦ Repeat Steps 2 to 4.

⑥

	A	B	C	D	E	F	G
1	1	1:00 AM	Mon	Monday	Jan	January	Lesson A
2	3	3:00 AM	Wed	Wednesday	Apr	April	Lesson C
3							
4							
5							
6							

● Excel fills the cells with the pattern.

	A	B	C	D	E	F	G
1	1	1:00 AM	Mon	Monday	Jan	January	Lesson A
2	3	3:00 AM	Wed	Wednesday	Apr	April	Lesson C
3	5	5:00 AM	Fri	Friday	Jul	July	Lesson A
4	7	7:00 AM	Sun	Sunday	Oct	October	Lesson C
5	9	9:00 AM	Tue	Tuesday	Jan	January	Lesson A
6	11	11:00 AM	Thu	Thursday	Apr	April	Lesson C
7	13	1:00 PM	Sat	Saturday	Jul	July	Lesson A
8	15	3:00 PM	Mon	Monday	Oct	October	Lesson C
9	17	5:00 PM	Wed	Wednesday	Jan	January	Lesson A
10	19	7:00 PM	Fri	Friday	Apr	April	Lesson C
11	21	9:00 PM	Sun	Sunday	Jul	July	Lesson A
12	23	11:00 PM	Tue	Tuesday	Oct	October	Lesson C

Extra

When you release the mouse button after creating a series, the AutoFill Options button (🖳▾) appears. Click the button to view a menu of options (○ changes to ◉). If you want to fill with the days of the week, you can click Fill Days or Fill Weekdays to fill with Monday through Friday. You can also click the Fill Formatting Only option to change the formatting of the cell without changing the contents. Click the Fill Without Formatting option to change the contents of the filled cells without changing the formatting.

You can fill cells with a growth trend, such as 1, 3, 9, 27 or 2, 4, 8, 16. Type the first two values of the growth trend. Select the values you typed and all the cells you want to fill. Click the Home tab and then click the Fill button (📄). A menu appears. Click Series. The Series dialog box appears. Click Growth, click Trend, and then click OK. Excel fills the cells with your growth trend. To learn more about growth trends, see the task "Add a Trendline" in Chapter 8.

Work with Multiple Windows

When a worksheet contains a large amount of data, you may not be able to see all of it on-screen at the same time. Excel enables you to open additional copies of your worksheet, each in its own window, so you can view them simultaneously and yet manipulate them independently. By opening multiple copies of a worksheet, you can work with and compare nonadjacent rows and columns. When you have multiple copies of a window open, Excel numbers each copy and places the number after the workbook name.

You can also view worksheets located in multiple workbooks simultaneously. Open the workbooks and then use the Arrange Windows dialog box to choose how you want to view worksheets on-screen.

Once the worksheets are open, you can view them side by side, stacked, tiled, or cascaded. If you want to view your worksheets side by side, choose Vertical in the Arrange Windows dialog box. For a stacked arrangement, choose Horizontal. For a view with your windows displayed in columns and rows, choose Tiled. To view worksheets on top of each other with the title bar for each window displayed, choose Cascade.

Click anywhere in a worksheet window to make the window active. Only one window can be active at a time. The active window has controls you can use to minimize it, maximize it, or close it. You can cut and copy from one window and paste into another window. You can click Switch Windows in the Window group in the Ribbon to move to another window.

The zoom settings control how much of a worksheet appears on your screen. Drag the zoom control to the left to make your worksheet smaller. Drag the zoom control to the right to make your worksheet larger.

Work with Multiple Windows

OPEN MULTIPLE WINDOWS

1 Click the View tab.

2 Click New Window.

● Excel creates a new window, as indicated by the number appended to the filename.

Note: *Excel opens a copy of your worksheet in a new window. The copy may be directly on top of the old window so you may not be able to discern that it is there.*

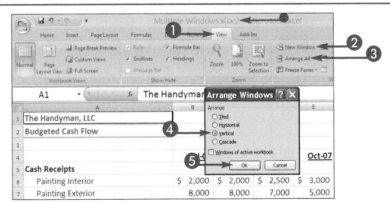

3 Click Arrange All.

4 In the Arrange Windows dialog box, click an option, Vertical in this example.

5 Click OK, and Excel displays all open windows.

6 Click a window to activate it. You can navigate around each window independent of the other windows.

7 Drag to adjust the zoom.

● Excel resizes the contents of the window.

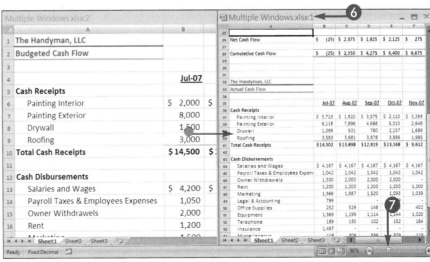

OPEN MULTIPLE WORKBOOKS

1 Open two or more workbooks.

2 Click the View tab.

3 Click Arrange All in the Window group.

4 In the Arrange Windows dialog box, click to select how you want to arrange your windows, Tiled in this example.

● Click here if you have multiple workbooks open, but you only want to see worksheets that are in the active workbook.

5 Click OK.

● Worksheets from multiple workbooks appear.

6 Click Switch Windows.

7 Click a window name to make it the active window.

You can also click anywhere in a window to make that window active.

● Use the document controls to minimize, maximize, or close the window.

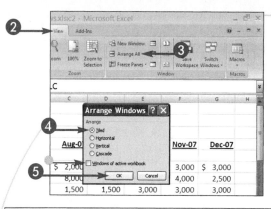

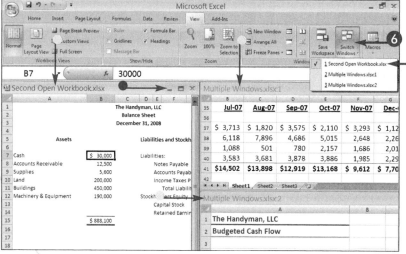

Extra

If you have a large worksheet and want to view different parts of the worksheet at the same time, you can also split the worksheet. Click the View tab and then click the Split button (▣). Excel splits the worksheet into four parts. You can navigate each part independent of the other parts. To remove a splitter, click and drag the splitter off the screen or click the Split button again to toggle off the split feature.

If you have a window open, but you do not want to view it, you can hide it. To hide a window, make it active, click the View tab, and then click the Hide button (▣). If later you want to unhide the window, click the Unhide button (▣). The Unhide dialog box appears. Click the name of the window you want to unhide and then click OK. Excel unhides the window.

Let Excel Read Back Your Data

If you have a large amount of data to enter, especially numbers, you may want to check the accuracy of your data entry by having the data read back to you while you match it against a printed list. Excel can read back your data. All you have to do is specify the data you want to read, click a button, and Excel begins reading. You can choose to have Excel read across the first row and then move to the next row or read down the first column and then move to the next column.

However, before Excel can read your data, you must add the following buttons to the Quick Access toolbar: Speak Cells, Speak Cells – Stop Speaking Cells, Speak Cells by Columns, Speak Cells by Rows, and Speak Cells on Enter.

To learn how to add buttons to the Quick Access toolbar, see the Extra section in the "Assign a Macro to the Quick Access Toolbar" task in Chapter 12. You can find the buttons needed for this task in the Commands Not in the Ribbon section of the Excel Options dialog box.

Before Excel can read your worksheet, you must have speakers attached to your computer and you must set the Speech, Sound, and Audio Devices option in the Control Panel properly. Click the Start button, click Settings, and then click Control Panel to check these device settings in Windows XP; in Windows Vista, click Start, click Control Panel, click Hardware and Sound, and then under the Sound icon, click Manage Audio Devices.

Let Excel Read Back Your Data

1 Click and drag to select the cells you want Excel to read.

2 Click either the Speak Cells by Columns or the Speak Cells by Rows button.

● Click Speak Cells by Columns if you want Excel to read down the columns.

● Click Speak Cells by Rows if you want Excel to read across the rows.

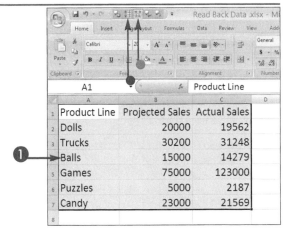

3 Click the Speak Cells button.

Excel reads the cells.

● To stop the reading of cells, click the Speak Cells – Stop Speaking Cells button.

Note: *You can also have Excel read data as you enter it. Click the Speak on Enter button ( ). Excel says, "Cells will now be spoken on Enter." Type data into your worksheet. Excel reads your data as you enter it. Click the Speak on Enter button again. Excel says, "Turn off Speak on Enter." Excel stops reading your data as you type it.*

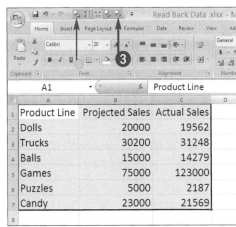

Add a Calculator

O ften you may want to do quick calculations without using a formula or function. In Excel, you can place a calculator on the Quick Access toolbar so it is always available. The Excel calculator is one of many commands you can add to the Quick Access toolbar.

You can use the calculator as you would any electronic calculator. Click a number, choose an operator — such as the plus key (+) to do addition — and then click another number. Press the equal sign key (=) to get a result. Use MS to remember a value, MR to recall it, and MC to clear memory.

Statistical and mathematical functions are available in the calculator's scientific view when you click View and then Scientific. In this view, you can cube a number, find its square root, compute its log, and more. In both standard and scientific views, you can transfer a value from the calculator to Excel by displaying it, copying it, and pasting it into a cell.

For complete instructions on using the Excel calculator, open the calculator. On the calculator's menu, click Help and then click Help Topics. The Calculator dialog box appears. Click the Contents tab and then Calculator. A list of topics appears. Click any topic to learn more about the calculator.

Add a Calculator

① Click the Calculator button.

● The calculator appears in Standard mode.

② Click View.

③ Click Scientific.

The calculator appears in Scientific mode.

Note: Before you can use the calculator, you must add it to the Quick Access toolbar. Click the Office button. A menu appears. Click Excel Options. The Excel Options dialog box appears. Click Customize. The Customize the Quick Access Toolbar pane appears. In the Choose Commands From field, select Commands Not in the Ribbon. In the box below the Choose Commands From field, click Calculator. Click Add. Click OK. The calculator appears on the Quick Access toolbar.

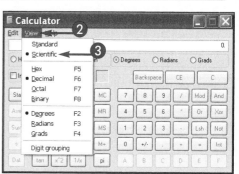

Change Text to Numbers

You can use formulas to perform complex calculations quickly and accurately on numbers, dates, or times. Sometimes, however, your numbers look like numbers but are, in fact, text — mere characters. If a number is left-aligned in a cell, it is probably text; true numbers, by default, are right-aligned. The numbers-as-text problem often occurs when you import data from another application — for example, from an external database such as Access. Chapter 9 covers importing data in detail.

In Excel, text and numbers are different data types. You should use numbers, not text, in mathematical formulas and functions. Trying to include text in a mathematical calculation can result in an error. You can address the problem several ways. You can use the Format Cells dialog box to reformat the text cells to numbers, but this method does not always work. A more reliable technique is to use the Paste Special dialog box to multiply each numeral by 1 to convert the data type from text to a number.

Change Text to Numbers

Note: *The left-aligned numbers in this task are really text. In Excel, the default position for numbers is the right side of the cell.*

● You cannot calculate the average; Excel displays a #DIV/0! error.

① Type **1** into any neighboring cell, and then click in the cell.

② Click the Home tab.

③ Click the Copy button.

④ Click and drag to select the cells you want to convert and then right-click the selected cells.

⑤ In the context menu that appears, click Paste Special.

● The Paste Special dialog box appears.

⑥ Click Multiply (○ changes to ◉).

⑦ Click OK.

● The numbers now appear on the right side of their cells and you can use them in mathematical formulas.

Note: *Excel can convert text-based numbers to actual numbers. Click the Office button and then click Excel Options. The Excel Options dialog box appears. Click Formulas. In the Error Checking Rules section, select Numbers Formatted as Text or Preceded by an Apostrophe (☐ changes to ☑). Excel will now flag cells containing text by placing a green flag in the upper-left corner. Click the menu button appearing alongside any cells with this error and click Convert to Number. If Excel is able to convert the text to a number, the numbers will be right-aligned. This method does not always work.*

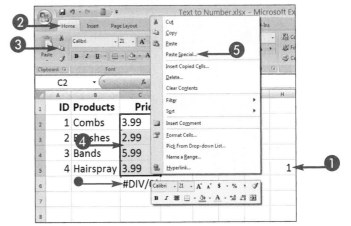

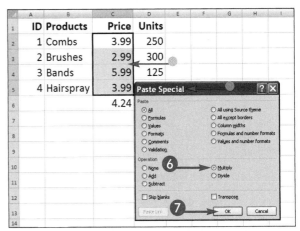

Convert a Row to a Column

When you create a worksheet, Excel gives you flexibility when working with rows and columns. At any time, you can insert new rows or columns, delete rows or columns, and move entire rows or columns while retaining most of their properties. Sometimes, however, you may want to transpose a row into a column — or vice versa.

Transposing comes in handy when you need to create a table, a special kind of worksheet discussed in Chapter 6. A table might consist of rows describing products, with each column describing a feature of the product: its ID, its price, the quantity in inventory, and so on. Tables typically have many rows and fewer columns.

With Excel, you can transpose a row into a column and vice versa by using the Paste Special dialog box. To ensure you have room for new worksheet data, you can place the transposed columns or rows on a different worksheet or in a new workbook.

You can avoid rearranging worksheets by designing them carefully. For long lists of people, things, transactions, and so on, arrange them in columns with descriptive column heads. Excel calls this type of layout a table and provides many tools to help you view and manage tables.

Extra

Using the TRANSPOSE function, you can transpose a grid of cells. Start by selecting an area large enough to hold the new grid. In the Formula bar, type **=TRANSPOSE(** and then click the Insert Function button. The Function Arguments dialog box appears. Select the cells you want to transpose and then press Ctrl+Shift+Enter. Excel transposes the grid.

Convert a Row to a Column

1 Click and drag to select the cells you want to transpose.

Note: Make sure a series of blank cells is available to accommodate the copied data.

2 Click the Home tab.

3 Click the Copy button in the Clipboard group.

4 Click to select the first cell in the new column or row.

Note: Excel removes existing data by copying over it.

5 Click Paste.

A menu appears.

6 Click Transpose.

● The data appears in its new position.

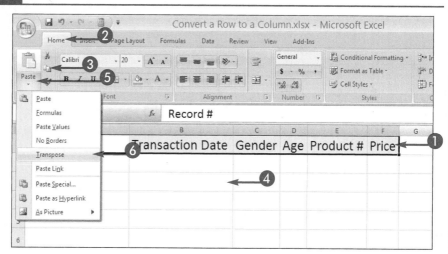

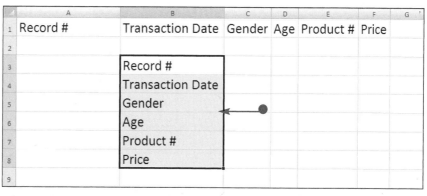

Consolidate Worksheets

If you keep related data in separate worksheets — or for that matter, separate workbooks — you may eventually want to consolidate. For example, if you keep sales information for several regions on separate worksheets, you may want to consolidate the worksheets to find the total sales for all regions. With Excel's Consolidate feature, you can do just that. Excel provides a variety of functions you can use to consolidate, including SUM, COUNT, AVERAGE, MAX, MIN, and PRODUCT.

You start the consolidation process by selecting the location for your consolidated data. You may want to format your cells so the incoming data displays properly. Then select the function you want to use to consolidate your data. The SUM function takes the data from each location you specify and adds it together. You tell Excel

the locations of the data you want to consolidate. You can type the range in the Reference field of the Consolidate dialog box or click and drag to select the area. If you type the range, remember to include the worksheet name in single quotes followed by an exclamation point and the range. For example, to refer to a range on Sheet1 in range $A$1:$C$1, type **'Sheet1'!$A$1:$C$1**. Excel takes the data and consolidates it.

If you want to include data from another workbook in your worksheet, you must open the other workbook. In the Consolidate dialog box, place your cursor in the Reference field. Click the View tab, click Switch Windows, and select the other workbook from the menu that appears. Click and drag to specify the data you want to consolidate. Click Add. Click OK. Excel consolidates the data.

Consolidate Worksheets

① Click in the top-left cell of the range into which you want to consolidate your data.

② Click the Data tab.

③ Click Consolidate in the Data Tools group.

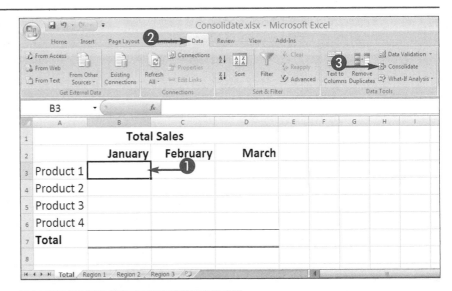

The Consolidate dialog box appears.

④ Click here and select the function you want to use to consolidate your data.

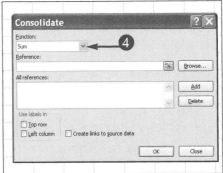

⑤ Click and drag to select the location of your data or type the cell range.

⑥ Click Add.

⑦ Repeat Steps 5 and 6 for each location you want to consolidate.

⑧ Click OK.

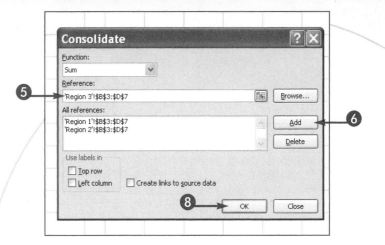

● Excel consolidates your data.

	Total Sales		
	January	**February**	**March**
Product 1	$ 364,414	$ 416,103	$ 393,622
Product 2	307,192	447,774	451,990
Product 3	570,061	575,791	376,203
Product 4	566,924	542,990	307,101
Total	$ 1,784,793	$ 1,956,570	$ 1,508,799

Total / Region 1 / Region 2 / Region 3

Extra

If you click Create Links to Source Data (☐ changes to ☑) in the Consolidate dialog box, Excel updates your consolidated data each time you make a change to the data on which you base your consolidation. If you select this option, you cannot change the cells and ranges included in the consolidation. If you want to update your consolidation, do not select Create Links to Source Data.

If you click Top Row and/or Left Column (☐ changes to ☑) in the Use Labels In section of the Consolidate dialog box, Excels copies the row or column labels in the source ranges to the consolidation. If a label does not match a label already in the consolidation, Excel creates a new column or row. If you have a column or row you do not want to consolidate, give it a unique name. Use this option if you have arranged the data you want to consolidate differently on each worksheet but you have given your data the same column or row labels.

Conditionally Format Your Worksheet

If you want to monitor your data by highlighting certain conditions, Excel's conditional formatting feature can aid you. For example, if your company offers a bonus whenever sales exceed $150,000, you can have Excel highlight cells containing sales figures whenever the value is more than $150,000. You can also have Excel highlight a cell when the entry is less than or equal to a specified value or between specified values. Use Excel's conditional formatting feature to monitor text, dates, duplicate values, the top N, the top N percent, the bottom N, the bottom N percent, above average values, or below average values.

You can use data bars to indicate the relative size of a number in relation to other numbers — the longer the bar, the higher the number. Data bars enable you to do things such as compare sales performance quickly. You can add additional formatting rules. For example, in addition to having Excel add data bars to your cells to indicate the relative sales performance, you can also have Excel format the top two sales performers.

Changes affect conditionally formatted data. If, after a change, a cell no longer meets the condition, Excel removes the highlighting. If, after a change, a cell meets the condition, Excel adds highlighting. You determine exactly what the condition is and what should happen if a cell meets the condition. Excel provides a list of formats from which to choose, and you can create custom formats. You can apply multiple conditional formats to a single group of cells. For example, you can apply data bars and you can highlight the lowest two values.

Conditionally Format Your Worksheet

CREATE A CONDITIONAL FORMAT

1. Click and drag to select the data you want to monitor.

2. Click the Home tab.

3. Click Conditional Formatting in the Styles group.

4. Click to select a menu option, Highlight Cells Rules in this example.

5. Click to select a menu option, Greater Than in this example.

● A dialog box appears.

6. Type your criteria.

7. Click here and select the formatting you want to apply.

   Choose Custom Format if you want to create a custom format.

8. Click OK.

● Excel highlights all of the data that meets your criteria.

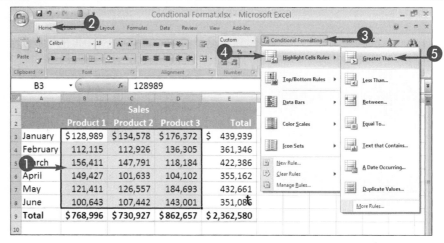

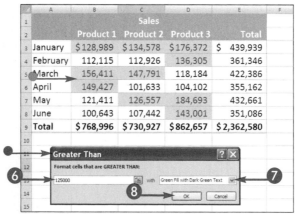

CREATE DATA BARS

1. Repeat Steps 1 to 3 in the section Create a Conditional Format.

● This is the selected data.

2. Click Data Bars.

3. Click the color data bar you want to use.

● Excel applies data bars to the cells you selected.

APPLY A SECOND CONDITION

4. Repeat Steps 1 to 3 in the section Create a Conditional Format.

● This is the selected data.

5. Click to select the options you want. This example uses Top/Bottom Rules → Bottom 10 Items.

● A dialog box appears.

6. Click the number of items you want.

7. Click here and select a format.

8. Click OK.

● Excel applies the rule by formatting the bottom two items in red text.

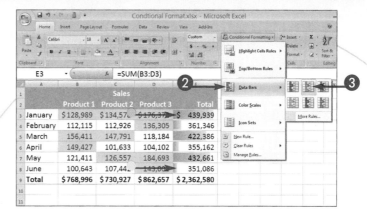

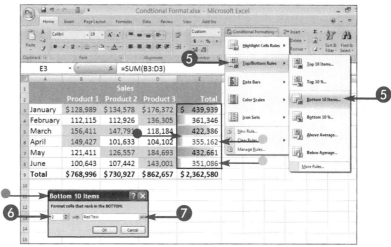

Apply It

In Excel, you can choose from several colors when you add data bars to your worksheet. You can also choose another color. Click the Home tab and then click Conditional Formatting in the Styles group. A menu appears. Click Data Bars and then click More Rules. The New Formatting Rule dialog box appears. Use the Bar Color field to select a new color. Click OK.

You can clear selected cells, an entire sheet, a table, or a PivotTable of conditional formatting. Select what you want to clear. Click the Home tab. Click Conditional Formatting in the Styles group. A menu appears. Click Clear Rules. A menu appears. Select the Clear option you want.

You can use color scales to conditionally format data. Color scales use gradations of color. For example, if you use Excel's yellow and green color scale, yellow represents lower values and green, higher values. To apply a color scale, select the cells to which you want to apply the scale, click the Home tab, click Conditional Formatting, click Color Scales, and then click the color scale you want to apply.

Change Conditional Formatting Rules

A data bar is a colored bar you place in a cell. Data bars enable you to discern at a glance how large a value in one cell is relative to the values in other cells. The length of the bar represents the value of the cell relative to other cells — the longer the bar, the higher the value. Excel provides you with several bars from which to choose, or you can design your own. Color scales and icon sets are similar to data bars, except color scales use gradients of color to represent the relative size of the cell value, and icon sets use icons to represent the relative size of the value.

Data bars, color scales, and icon sets all use rules to determine when to display what. You can use the rules defined by Excel or you can create your own. At the bottom of the data bar, color scale, or icon set submenu, click More Rules to adjust and create rules. You can create rules that format cells based on their values, what they contain, how they rank, whether they are above or below average, and whether they are unique or duplicate values; or you can use a formula to tell Excel how to format the cell.

You can sort and filter by cell color, font color, or icon. Right-click in any cell that has conditional formatting applied to it. A context menu appears. Click Sort and then select the appropriate sort option. See Chapter 6 to learn more about sorting and filtering.

Change Conditional Formatting Rules

1 Click and drag to select the data you want to monitor.

2 Click the Home tab.

3 Click Conditional Formatting in the Styles group.

A menu appears.

4 Click Icon Sets.

Alternatively, you can click Data Bars or Color Scales. Each allows you to change the associated rules.

A submenu appears.

5 Click More Rules.

The New Formatting Rule dialog box appears.

6 Click a rule.

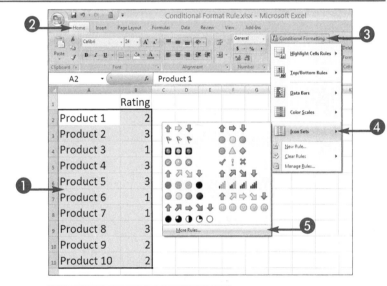

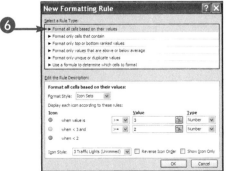

⑦ Click here and select a format style.

⑧ Click here and select an operator.

⑨ Type a value or click in the cell that contains the value you want to use.

⑩ Click here and select a type.

Note: *You can choose Number, Percent, Formula, or Percentile.*

⑪ Click here and select an icon style.

⑫ Click OK.

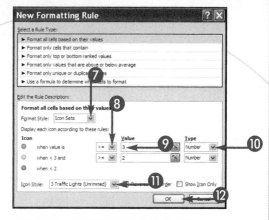

● Excel displays the results of your rule.

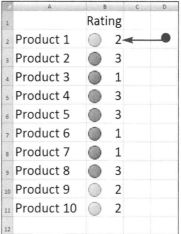

Apply It

To apply an icon set without changing the default rule, select the data you want to format, click the Home tab, and then click Conditional Formatting in the Styles group. A menu appears. Click Icon Sets and then click the icon set you want to use. Excel applies the icon set.

If you click Show Icon Only, Show Bar Only, or Show Color Only in the New Formatting Rule dialog box (☐ changes to ☑), Excel displays icons, bars, or colors but not the values in each cell.

When you apply conditional formatting rules to cells, Excel executes them in order of precedence. By default, rules stack in the order you create them. Excel gives the most recently created rule the highest precedence. If two rules conflict, Excel applies the rule with the highest precedence. For example, if one rule formats text green and another rule formats text blue, Excel applies the rule with the highest precedence. You can click the Home tab, Conditional Formatting, and then Manage Rules to open the Conditional Formatting Rules Manager. The manager lists rules in order, putting the rule with the highest precedence on top. Use the Up and Down arrow keys (⬆ and ⬇) to change the order.

Paste with Paste Special

By clicking the Copy button on the Home tab, pressing Ctrl+C, or clicking Copy on a context menu, you can easily copy the contents of a range of cells so you can paste the contents somewhere else in your worksheet. Cells can contain a lot of information. When you paste with Paste Special, you decide exactly what information you want to paste.

You can choose to paste everything or you can choose to paste just one element of the cell's contents, such as the formula, value, format, comment, validation, or column width. You can use the Paste Special dialog box to choose what you want to paste; however, you do not have to open the Paste Special dialog box to paste formulas and values, to paste without borders, transpose, or paste-link. You can select these options directly from the Paste menu.

When you paste without borders, Excel pastes all of your formatting but does not include any borders. When you transpose, Excel changes a row to a column or vice versa. For more information about transposing, see the task "Convert a Row to a Column" in this chapter. You can use the Paste Link option in the Paste Special dialog box to keep your source and destination data synchronized. If you click the Paste Link button when pasting, Excel automatically updates the destination data when you make changes to the source data.

You can paste more than once. For example, when you paste by clicking Paste on the Home tab, Excel pastes the values, formulas, and formats but does not adjust the column widths. You can remedy this problem by pasting in two steps. In the first step, paste column widths. Excel adjusts the column widths. In the second step, paste your values, formulas, and formats.

Paste with Paste Special

① Click and drag to select the cells you want to copy.

② Click the Home tab.

③ Click the Copy button in the Clipboard group.

④ Place the cursor in the upper-left corner of the cell(s) into which you want to paste.

⑤ Click Paste.

A menu appears.

⑥ Click Paste Special.

● The Paste Special dialog box appears.

⑦ Click Column Widths (○ changes to ◉).

⑧ Click OK.

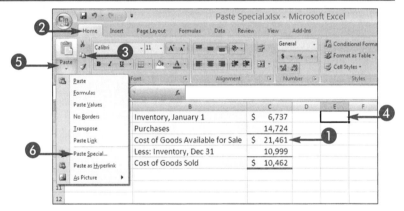

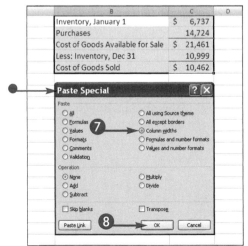

- Excel copies the column widths from the source to the destination.

9 Click Paste.

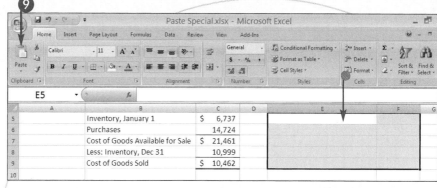

- Excel pastes the contents of the cells.

  You can press Esc to end the copy session.

Extra

The following table lists Paste Special options:

OPTION	FUNCTION
All	Pastes the contents and the formatting of copied cells.
Formulas	Pastes the formulas included in copied cells.
Values	Pastes the results of formulas or the data displayed in a cell.
Comments	Pastes the comments attached to a cell.
Validation	Pastes the validation rules from copied cells.
All using source theme	Pastes the cell contents, using the document theme applied to the copied data.
All except borders	Pastes all of the cell contents except borders.
Column widths	Pastes the column widths of the copied cells.
Formulas and number formats	Pastes only the formulas and number formats.
Values and number formats	Pastes only the values and number formats.

continued →

Paste with Paste Special (continued)

Y ou can use the Format Painter to copy formats from one cell to another. You can also use Paste Special. Simply copy a cell with the format you want, and then use Paste Special to paste the format into other cells. This feature is useful when you want to use the same format but different data in a range of cells. See Chapter 1 to learn more about the Format Painter.

You can use Paste Special to copy formulas or values from one location in your worksheet to another. When you want to use a cell's formula in adjacent cells in your worksheet, you can drag the fill handle to fill adjacent cells with the formula. However, when you want to use a formula in a nonadjacent cell, you must paste the formula with Paste Special. To learn more about using the fill handle, see the task "Extend a Series with AutoFill" in this chapter. When you want the results of a formula but not the formula, paste the value.

You can also use Paste Special to perform simple arithmetic operations on each cell in a range. For example, in a list of prices, you may want to increase every price by 10 percent. You can use Paste Special to make the change quickly. Just type **1.10** in a cell and then select Multiply in the Paste Special dialog box.

You can choose the Skip Blanks option in the Paste Special dialog box if your source data includes any blanks. If you choose this option, Excel will not overwrite a destination cell with a blank if the destination cell has data in it.

Paste with Paste Special *(continued)*

⑩ Click in a cell with the format, formula, or value you want to copy.

This example copies a formula.

⑪ Repeat Steps 3 to 6.

● The Paste Special dialog box appears.

⑫ Click to select a Paste option (○ changes to ◉).

⑬ Click OK.

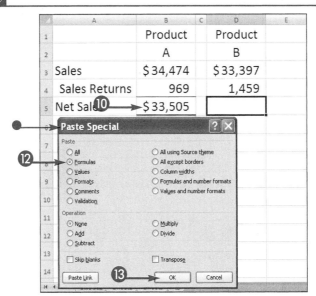

● Excel pastes.

● If you paste a formula, an icon menu appears. Click Formulas and Number Formatting (○ changes to ◉) from this menu to copy the number formatting as well as the formula.

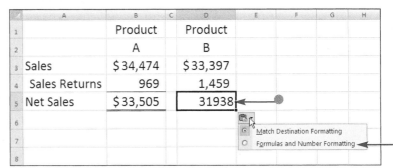

204

⑭ Click in a cell with the number by which you want to add, subtract, multiply, or divide.

⑮ Repeat Steps 3 to 6.

● The Paste Special dialog box appears.

⑯ Click an operation (○ changes to ◉).

⑰ Click OK.

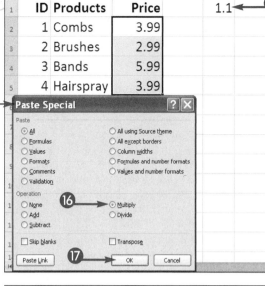

● Excel performs the operation you selected.

Extra

The following table lists Paste Special operations:

OPTION	FUNCTION
None	No mathematical operation.
Add	Adds the copied data to the destination cell.
Subtract	Subtracts the copied data from the destination cell.
Multiply	Multiplies the copied data by the data in the destination cell.
Divide	Divides the copied data by the data in the destination cell.
Skip blanks	Does not overwrite a destination cell with a blank if the destination cell has data in it and the copied cell does not.
Transpose	Changes columns to rows and vice versa.
Paste link	Links the destination cells to the copied data.

Insert Photographs into Your Worksheet

Photographs can enhance your worksheet, illustrate your point, and emphasize your message. Adding a photograph to Excel is easy. Just locate the photograph and insert it.

After you insert your photograph, you can choose from many options to enhance the display of your photo. Use picture styles to angle; add borders, shadows, and reflections; and otherwise stylize your photograph. As you roll your cursor over the various picture styles, Excel provides a preview of how the style appears when applied.

You can change the color of your picture border. Excel can make the border of your picture any color in Excel's palette, including custom colors. You can also adjust your photo's brightness and contrast. These features make it easy for you to correct any deficiencies in your

photograph. You can even crop your photo to show only the portion you want. When you select the Crop option, Excel places black marker on your photograph. To crop either side of your photograph, click and drag either side marker. To crop the top or bottom of your photo, click and drag the top or bottom marker. Click and drag any of the corner markers to crop proportionately.

You can manipulate your photograph the same way you manipulate any other graphic. You can move it, rotate it, and resize it. When resizing, drag the corner handles to resize your photo proportionately. Drag the side handles to make your picture wider. Drag the top and bottom handles to make your picture taller.

If, after making changes to your picture, you want to return it to its original state, you can click the Reset button.

Insert Photographs into Your Worksheet

① Click the Insert tab.

② Click Picture.

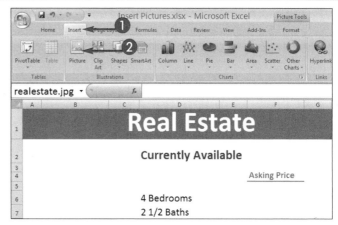

The Insert Picture dialog box appears.

③ Click here and select the folder in which you stored your picture.

④ Click your picture.

⑤ Click Insert.

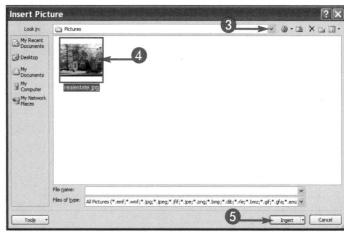

- The picture appears in your worksheet, and the Picture tools become available.

6 Click the Format tab.

7 Click Crop, and black markings appear on your photo.

8 Click and drag the markings to crop your photo.

9 Click here and select a picture style.

10 Click here and select a color for your picture's border.

11 Click here to adjust the brightness or contrast.

- Click here to reset your photograph.

12 Click outside your photo, and Excel applies the option you selected.

13 Click your photo.

- Click and drag to rotate.

- Click and drag to resize.

Excel adjusts your photo.

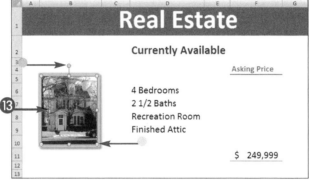

Extra

You can also add clip art to your worksheet. Click the Insert tab and then click Clip Art. The Clip Art dialog box appears. In the Search For field, type the category in which the item for which you are looking falls under and then click Go. Excel finds all the clip art in that category and displays them. Double-click the image you want. It appears in your worksheet.

You can use Excel to colorize your photographs. Click your photo. Click the Format tab and then click Recolor in the Adjust group. Among other choices, you can change your photo to grayscale or to a sepia tone.

You can change the shape of your picture. You can change a rectangular photograph to an oval, arrow, or some other shape. Click your photograph. The Picture tools become available. Click Format and then click a Picture Shape in the Picture Styles group. Excel applies the shape to your picture.

You can apply picture effects to your photograph. For example, you can give your photograph a bevel or a 3-D rotation. Click your photograph. The Picture tools become available. Click Format and then click a Picture Effects in the Picture Styles group. Click a menu option and then roll your mouse pointer over the suboptions. Excel provides you with a preview of how the effect will look when it is applied to your photograph.

Validate with a Validation List

With Excel, you can restrict the values a user can enter in a cell. By restricting values, you help ensure that all worksheet entries are valid and that calculations based on them are valid as well. During data entry, a validation list forces anyone using your worksheet to select a value from a drop-down menu rather than typing it and potentially entering the wrong information. In this way, validation lists save time and reduce errors.

You can use two methods to create a data validation list. Both methods use the Data Validation dialog box. If your list is short and does not change, you can type it into the Source field of the Data Validation dialog box. For example, if your field collects gender, you can type **Male**,

Female in the Source field. You must separate values with commas.

If your list is long or if it changes, you can type the values you want to include into adjacent cells in a column or row. You may want to name the range. See Chapter 2 to learn how to name ranges. After you type your values, use the Source field in the Data Validation dialog box to assign the values to your validation list. Then copy and paste your validation list into the appropriate cells by using the Paste Special Validation option. You may want to place your validation list in an out-of-the-way place on your worksheet or on a separate worksheet. If your list changes, just type the new values into the cells you have designated as the validation list.

Validate with a Validation List

① Click in the cell in which you want to create a validation list.

② Click the Data tab.

③ Click Data Validation in the Data Tools group.

● The Data Validation dialog box appears.

④ Click the Settings tab.

⑤ Click here and then select List.

⑥ Make sure the In-cell Drop-down box is checked.

⑦ Click and drag to select the valid entries, type the range, or type = followed by the range name.

Alternatively, type the list of valid entries, with each entry followed by a comma.

⑧ Click OK.

● Excel creates a validation list in the cell you selected.

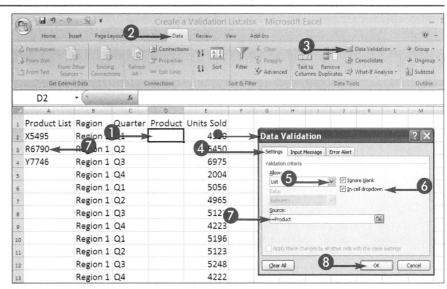

PASTE YOUR VALIDATION LIST

① Click in the cell that contains your validation list.

② Click the Home tab.

③ Click the Copy button in the Clipboard group.

④ Select the cells in which you want to place your validation list.

⑤ Click Paste in the Clipboard group.

A menu appears.

⑥ Click Paste Special.

● The Paste Special dialog box appears.

⑦ Click Validation (○ changes to ◉).

⑧ Click OK.

Excel places the validation list in the cells you selected.

● When you make an entry into the cell, you must pick from the list.

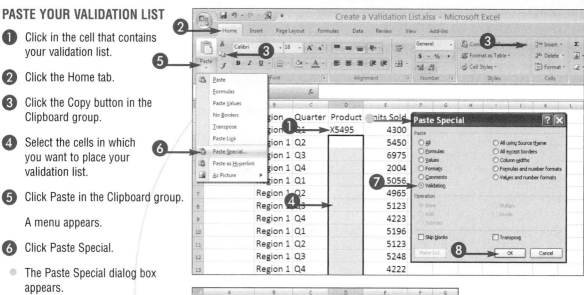

Extra

To remove a validation list, click in any cell that contains the validation list you want to remove, click the Home tab, and then click Find and Select in the Editing group. A menu appears. Click Go To Special. The Go To Special dialog box appears. Click Data Validation, click Same, and then click OK. The Go To Special dialog box closes. Click the Data tab and then click Data Validation in the Data Tools group. The Data Validation dialog box appears. Click the Settings tab. Click Clear All and then click OK.

If you base your validation list on a range of cells and any cell in that range is blank, and if you select the Ignore Blank check box (☐ changes to ☑) on the Settings tab of the Data Validation dialog box, Excel allows you to enter any value into the cells you validate with your list. Otherwise, entry into the cells is restricted to items in your list, and if you try to enter another value, Excel will not allow you to do so.

Validate with Data Entry Rules

You can use data entry rules to ensure data is entered in the correct format, and you can restrict the data entered to whole numbers, decimals, dates, times, or a specific text length. You can also specify whether the values need to be between, not between, equal to, not equal to, greater than, less than, greater than or equal to, or less than or equal to the values you specify.

As with all data validation, you can create an input message that appears when the user enters the cell, as well as an error alert that displays if the user makes an incorrect entry. Error alerts can stop users, provide a warning, or just provide information. For example, when a user makes an incorrect entry, the Stop Error Alert style displays the error message you entered and prevents the user from making an entry that does not meet your criteria. The Warning Alert style and the Information

Alert style display a message but allow the user to enter data that does not meet your criteria. Input messages and error alerts consist of a title and a message. The title appears above the message.

After you create your data entry rule, you can copy and paste it into the appropriate cells by using the Paste Special Validation option. Refer to the section "Paste Your Validation List" in the task "Validate with a Validation List" to learn how to copy and paste your data entry rule. You can also click and drag to select the cells to which you want to apply your data validation rules and then open the Data Validation dialog box and create your data validation. Excel applies your validation to all the cells you selected.

If you use cells to specify your validation criteria, you can change your criteria as needed without changing the validation rule.

Validate with Data Entry Rules

1 Click in the cell in which you want to create a data entry rule.

Alternatively, click and drag to select all the cells in which you want to place your data entry rule.

2 Click the Data tab.

3 Click Data Validation in the Data Tools group.

● The Data Validation dialog box appears.

4 Click the Settings tab.

5 Click here and select a validation criterion.

6 Click here and select another validation criterion.

7 Type the criteria or click and drag to select the cells with the criteria you want to use.

8 Click the Input Message tab.

9 Type a title for your message.

10 Type an input message.

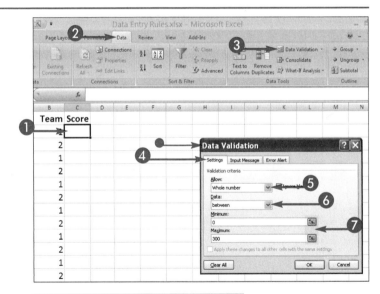

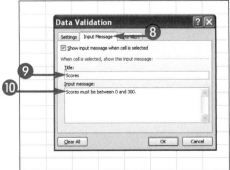

⑪ Click the Error Alert tab.

⑫ Click here and select a style.

Choose Stop if you want to stop the entry of invalid data.

Choose Warning if you want to display a warning to the user but not prevent the data entry.

Choose Information to provide information to the user.

⑬ Type a title.

⑭ Type an error message.

⑮ Click OK.

Excel creates the data entry rule.

● When a user clicks in the cell, Excel displays your input message.

◉ When a user enters invalid data, Excel displays your error alert.

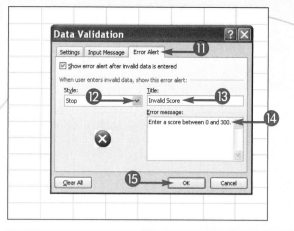

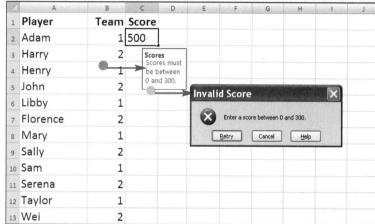

Extra

If you select Custom in the Allow field on the settings tab of the Data Validation dialog box, you can create a formula that validates an entry. Place your formula in the formula field. Your formula must resolve to a logical value.

PURPOSE	FORMULA
Restrict the cell entry to text. B2 is the current cell.	=ISTEXT(B2)
You can only make an entry if cell A2 is less than 1,000.	=AND(A2<1000)
You can only make an entry if cell A2 is less than 1,000 and cell A3 is 0.	=AND(A2<1000, A3=0)
You can only make an entry if your entry is less than cell A2 plus 100. Cell C5 is the current cell.	=IF(C5<A2+100,TRUE,FALSE)

To review these examples, refer to Sheet2 of Data Entry Rules.xlsx, which is on the Web site for this book.

Add Comments to Your Worksheet

A *comment* is a bit of descriptive text that enables you to document your work when you add text or create a formula. If someone else maintains your worksheet, or others use it in a workgroup, your comments can provide useful information. You can enter comments in any cell you want to document or otherwise annotate.

Comments in Excel do not appear until you choose to view them. Excel associates comments with individual cells and indicates their presence with a tiny red triangle in the cell's upper-right corner. View an individual comment by clicking in the cell or passing your cursor over it. View all comments in a worksheet by clicking the Review tab and then clicking Show All Comments.

When you track your changes, Excel automatically generates a comment every time you copy or change a cell. The comment records what changed in the cell, who made the change, and the time and date of the change. To learn more about tracking changes, see the next task, "Track Changes."

When a comment gets in the way of another comment or blocks data, you can move it. Position your cursor over the comment box border until the arrow turns into a four-sided arrow. Click and drag the comment to a better location and then release the mouse button. Your comment will remain in this position until you display all comments again.

When you sort, cut and paste, or copy and paste, comments move with the cell. Once you have created a comment, you can edit or delete it. You can also cycle through the comments in your worksheet by clicking Previous and Next on the Review tab.

Add Comments to Your Worksheet

ADD A COMMENT

① Click in the cell to which you want to add a comment.

② Click the Review tab.

③ Click New Comment in the Comments group.

● A comment box appears. A tiny red triangle appears in the upper-right corner of the cell.

④ Type your comment.

Note: *To apply bold or other formatting, select the text, right-click, click Format Comment, and then make changes as appropriate.*

⑤ Click outside the comment box when you finish.

The comment box disappears.

Move the cursor over the cell to display your comment again.

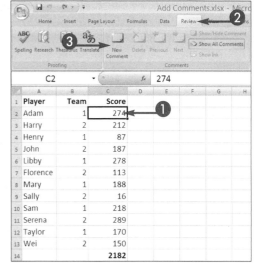

6 Click Edit Comment in the Comments group to edit a comment.

7 Click Delete in the Comments group to delete a comment.

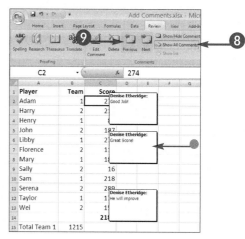

DISPLAY ALL COMMENTS

8 Click Show All Comments.

● You can now see all the comments in the worksheet.

To close the comment boxes, click Show All Comments again.

9 To cycle through comments, click Previous or Next.

Extra

A name displays each time you enter a comment. To set the name that displays, click the Office button, and then click Excel Options. The Excel Options dialog box appears. Click Popular and then, in the User Name field, type the name you want to appear in the comment box.

To delete a name or any other part of a comment, select it and then press the Delete key.

If your worksheet has comments, you can print the comments as they appear in your worksheet or with the comments listed at the end of the sheet. To print the comments, click the Review tab. Click Show/Hide Comments in the Comments group to show your comments. Click the Page Layout tab. Click the launcher in the Page Setup group. The Page Setup dialog box appears. Click the Sheet tab. In the Comments field, click As Displayed on Sheet to print your comments as they appear in your worksheet or click At End of Sheet to print your comments at the end of the sheet. To see how your comments will appear, you can click Print Preview before you print.

Track Changes

If you work with other people, you may need to share your Excel workbook. Sharing your workbook allows more than one person to modify it at the same time. When you share a workbook, Excel records the changes made to the workbook.

Before you share a workbook, enter and format your data, because you cannot change many features in a shared workbook. If several people work on the same workbook, you may need to account for who makes what changes, in which cells, and when. To do so, you can use the Track Changes feature. Tracking changes automatically shares your workbook.

In the Highlight Changes dialog box, use the When, Who, and Where options. Use When to define the time after which edits are tracked — for example, after a specific

date or since you last saved. Use Who to identify the group whose edits you want to track — for example, everyone in the workgroup, everyone but you, or a named individual. Use Where to specify the rows and columns whose data you want to monitor.

When someone makes a change, Excel indicates the change by placing a small purple triangle in the upper-left corner of the changed cell. Excel records cell changes in automatically generated cell comments. You can view these comments by moving your mouse pointer over the cells.

You can review every change made to a worksheet and either accept or reject the change. Click the Review tab, click Track Changes, and then click Accept/Reject Changes. The available options let you restrict your review to changes by certain people and at certain times.

Track Changes

① Click the Review tab.

② Click Track Changes.

A menu appears.

③ Click Highlight Changes.

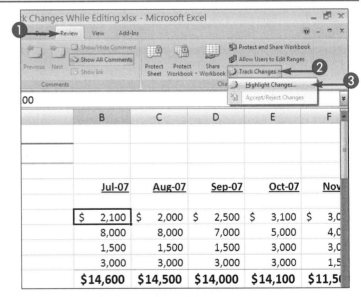

● The Highlight Changes dialog box appears.

④ Click Track Changes While Editing
(☐ changes to ☑).

The optional When, Who, and Where fields become available.

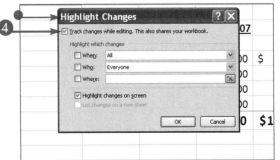

⑤ Click here and select when to track changes.

⑥ Click here and select whose changes to track.

⑦ Type the cell range, or click and drag to select the cells you want to monitor.

⑧ Click Highlight Changes On Screen to insert a purple flag into edited cells (☐ changes to ☑).

⑨ Click OK.

A message informs you that Excel has saved your workbook.

● Purple flags appear in edited cells.

◉ To view a cell's comment, move your cursor over the cell.

Note: *For more about comments, see the previous task, "Add Comments to Your Worksheet."*

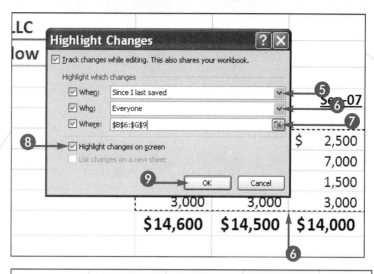

Highlight Changes

☑ Track changes while editing. This also shares your workbook.

Highlight which changes

☑ When: Since I last saved

☑ Who: Everyone

☑ Where: $B$6:$G$9

☑ Highlight changes on screen

☐ List changes on a new sheet

OK   Cancel

	Jul-07	Aug-07	Sep-07	Oct-07	Nov
$	2,200	$ 2,300			
	8,000	8,000			
	1,500	1,500			
	3,000	3,000	3,000	3,000	1,5
	$14,700	**$14,800**	**$14,000**	**$14,100**	**$11,5**

Denise Etheridge, 9/28/2006 9:40 PM:
Changed cell C6 from ' $2,000.00 ' to ' $2,300.00

Extra

When you share a workbook, you cannot modify the following: merged cells, conditional formats, data validations, charts, pictures, objects, hyperlinks, scenarios, outlines, subtotals, data tables, PivotTable reports, workbook and worksheet protection, and macros.

When you use a shared workbook, two or more people can update the workbook at the same time. To make a workbook sharable, click the Review tab and then click Share Workbook in the Changes group. The Share Workbook dialog box appears. Use the Advanced tab to set your shared workbook options, including what you want Excel to do if two people make a change to the same item.

To view all worksheet changes after you or others make edits, open the Highlight Changes dialog box and click the List Changes on a New Sheet option (☐ changes to ☑). For the Who field, click Everyone. Click to deselect the When and Where fields. Click OK. Excel creates a new worksheet called History that shows each change, the type of change, the values changed, the person who made the change, and so on. You can sort and filter the worksheet.

Protect Your Worksheet

If you share your worksheets with others, you can lock them so others can view and print them but can only make changes to the areas you allow them to change. Even if you do not share your worksheets, you may want to lock certain areas so you do not inadvertently make changes. Locking your worksheet enables you to make certain types of changes while disallowing others. For example, you can allow users to make changes to formats; insert or delete columns, rows, or hyperlinks; sort; filter; use PivotTables; and/or edit objects or scenarios.

By default, when you lock a worksheet, Excel locks every cell in the worksheet, and the formulas are visible to anyone who uses the worksheet. You can specify the cells that remain unlocked, and you can hide formulas.

To protect your worksheet, you can enter a password in the Protect Sheet dialog box. To unlock the worksheet, a person must know the password. Adding a password is optional. Keep a list of your worksheet passwords in a safe place because you cannot recover a worksheet password. If you lose or forget your password, you can no longer access the locked areas of your worksheet.

You can also use the Allow Users to Edit Ranges dialog box to specify the ranges users can modify. You just click the New button and complete the fields in the New Range dialog box. By using the Allow Users to Edit Ranges dialog box, you can password-protect each range you allow.

Protect Your Worksheet

① Click and drag to select the cells you want to remain unlocked or whose formulas you want to hide.

② Click the Home tab.

③ Click Format in the Cells group.

A menu appears.

④ Click Format Cells.

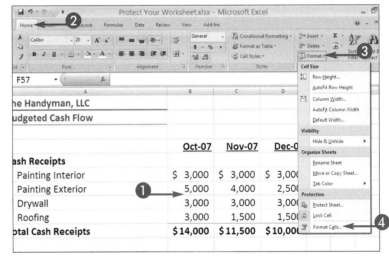

The Format Cells dialog box appears.

⑤ Click the Protection tab.

● By default, Locked is selected.

Selecting Locked enables you to lock the selected cells; deselecting Locked enables you to leave the selected cells unlocked.

● By default, Hidden is deselected; select it if you want to hide the selected formulas.

⑥ Click OK.

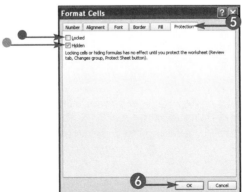

⑦ Click Format in the Cells group.

A menu appears.

⑧ Click Protect Sheet.

● The Protect Sheet dialog box appears.

⑨ Enter a password if you wish to password-protect your worksheet.

⑩ Click to select the options you want to allow the users to perform (☐ changes to ☑).

⑪ Click OK.

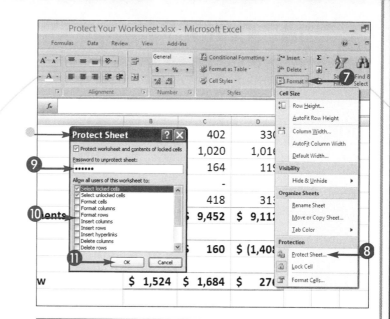

● The Confirm Password dialog box appears.

⑫ Retype your password.

⑬ Click OK.

Excel locks the cells in your worksheet and hides the formulas in the selected cells.

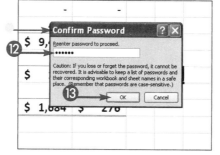

Apply It

You can protect a workbook from unwanted changes. Click the Review tab, click Protect Workbook, and then click Protect Structure and Windows. The Protect Structure and Windows dialog box appears. Select Structure (☐ changes to ☑) to protect your workbook from the moving, addition, and deletion of worksheets. Select Windows (☐ changes to ☑) to protect your workbook from changes in the size and position of windows. Optionally, require a password to remove these protections.

You can use the Allow Users to Edit Ranges dialog box to password-protect specific ranges in your worksheet. To password-protect a range, select the range you want to password-protect, click the Review tab, and then click Allow Users to Edit Ranges in the Changes group. The Allow Users to Edit Ranges dialog box appears. Click New. The New Range dialog box appears. In the Title field, name the range; in the Range password field, assign a password; then click OK. The Confirm Password dialog box appears. Retype your password, click OK, click Apply, and then click OK again. Your sheet must be protected and the range must be locked for this feature to work.

Save Your Workbook as a Template

emplates are special-purpose workbooks you use to create new worksheets. They can contain formats, styles, and specific content such as images, column heads, and date ranges you want to reuse in other worksheets. Templates save you the work of re-creating workbooks for recurring purposes such as filling out invoices and preparing monthly reports.

You create a template by designing a generic workbook that contains the worksheet layouts you want. You can create custom styles, number formats, macros, and formulas and include them in your template. For example, if you regularly use Excel to create and issue invoices, you can create an automatically calculating invoice that includes your logo and other basic information.

Your custom template includes all the changes you have made to your workbook, including formats, formulas,

and such changes as opening multiple windows or deleting tabs. Saving formulas with your template causes your worksheet to calculate automatically. Saving formats saves you from having to re-create them.

When you work with a template, you edit a copy — not the original — so you retain the original template for use in structuring other worksheets. Excel 2007 worksheets ordinarily have an .xlsx file extension. Saving an Excel worksheet as a template creates a file with an .xltx extension.

Excel comes with ready-made templates that serve basic business purposes such as invoicing. To open and use one of these templates, click the Office button and then click New. The New Workbook dialog box appears. Click Installed Templates. Click the template you want to open. Excel provides a preview of the template. Click Create to open the template.

Save Your Workbook as a Template

1 Open the workbook you want to use as a template.

Templates can consist of actual data, column labels, and empty cells with specific number formats such as percentage.

2 Click the Office button.

A menu appears.

3 Click Save As.

4 Click Other Formats.

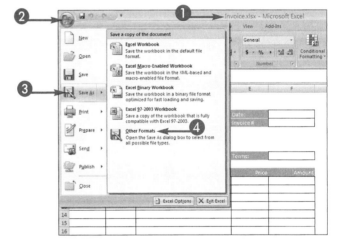

The Save As dialog box appears.

5 Type a name for your template.

6 Click here and select Excel Template (*.xltx).

- The Save In folder changes to Templates.

⑦ Click Save.

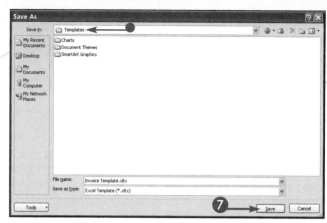

- Excel creates the template.

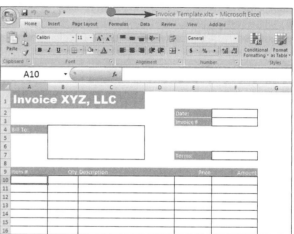

Extra

To use a template you have created, click the Office button and then click New. The New Workbook dialog box appears. Click My Templates. The New dialog box appears. Click the template you want to open and then click OK. Excel opens your template. When you save your modified file, save it as a regular file with an .xlsx extension so you do not overwrite your template.

When you create a new blank workbook, Excel uses the default system settings to create it with the default font settings and three blank worksheets. Excel uses the system default settings as long as a default workbook template does not exist. If you consistently make changes to every new blank workbook, you can make a default workbook template that always loads.

To do so, you first create a workbook that contains all your desired format settings, macros, formulas, and number of worksheets. Save the workbook as a template, name it **Book.xlt** and save it in the XLStart folder, which is typically in the following location: C:\\Program Files\Microsoft Office\Office12\XLStart.

Each time you create a new workbook, Excel uses the default workbook template you modified.

Choose a Format When Saving a Workbook

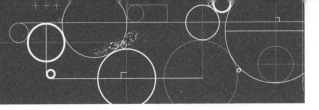

After you create an Excel 2007 worksheet, you may want to share it with others. The file format you choose when you save your file can help you. The default format for Office 2007 is Excel Workbook (*.xlsx). This file format is new to Office 2007. The smaller files it creates are easily accessible in other software programs because they are in Extensible Markup Language (XML) format, which is a data-exchange standard.

Previous versions of Excel did not use XML as the default format. These files have an .xls extension. If you want to share your documents with people who use Excel 97–2003, you can save your file as an Excel 97–2003 workbook (*.xls). Features that are not supported in earlier versions of Excel are lost when you save your file as an Excel 97–2003 workbook.

If you have a computer with Excel 97–2003 installed, you can go to the Office Update Web site and download the

2007 Microsoft Office system Compatibility Pack for Excel. After you install the Compatibility Pack, you can open Excel 2007 files in Excel 97–2003. Excel 2007 formatting and other features may not display in the earlier version, but they are still available when you open the file again in Excel 2007.

If you want to see the XML layout for an Excel 2007 file, change the file extension on the file to .zip and then double-click the file. The file opens and several folders and files appear. Double-click the files to open and view them.

You can also save your worksheet in other file formats, including HTML (a Web page format) and several text-based formats such as Text (tab-delimited), Text (Macintosh), and CSV (comma-delimited). These formats save the worksheet as text, which can be read by other applications, or in Hypertext Markup Language (HTML), which can be read by browsers.

Choose a Format When Saving a Workbook

① Click the Office button.

A menu appears.

② Click Save As.

③ Click Other Formats.

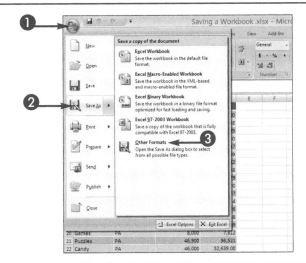

The Save As dialog box appears.

④ Click here and select the folder in which you want to save your file.

⑤ Type a filename.

⑥ Click here and select a file type.

⑦ Click Save.

Excel may warn you about incompatibilities.

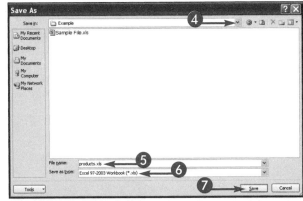

Excel saves your worksheet in the format you specify.

● This example shows the worksheet saved in Office 2003.

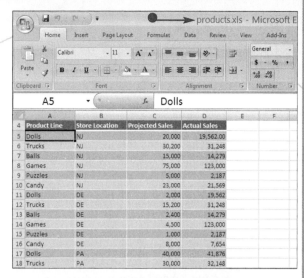

● This example shows the file saved in CSV format.

products.csv - Notepad

File Edit Format View Help

```
Product Line,Store Location,Projected Sales,Actual Sales
Dolls,NJ,"20,000","19,562.00"
Trucks,NJ,"30,200","31,248"
Balls,NJ,"15,000","14,279"
Games,NJ,"75,000","123,000"
Puzzles,NJ,"5,000","2,187"
Candy,NJ,"23,000","21,569"
Dolls,DE,"2,000","19,562"
Trucks,DE,"15,200","31,248"
Balls,DE,"2,400","14,279"
Games,DE,"4,500","123,000"
Puzzles,DE,"1,000","2,187"
Candy,DE,"8,000","7,654"
Dolls,PA,"40,000","41,876"
Trucks,PA,"30,000","32,148"
Balls,PA,"150,000","114,369"
Games,PA,"8,000","7,812"
Puzzles,PA,"46,900","96,521"
Candy,PA,"46,000","52,639.00"
```

Extra

To save your workbook as an .xlsx file, click the Office button and then click Save. The Save As dialog box appears. In the Save In field, locate the folder in which you want to save your file, type a filename in the File Name field, and then click Save.

Before you distribute a document to others, you may want to save it in a fixed format — one that others cannot easily modify. For example, say you create an invoice you want to e-mail to a client, but you do not want to e-mail an Excel workbook. For cases such as this, Microsoft has a free add-in titled Microsoft Save As PDF or XPS. You can download the add-in from the Microsoft Web site to save your files as PDF or XPS files. PDF stands for Portable Document Format; XPS stands for XML Paper Specification. When you save files as PDF or XPS files, they retain the formatting you have applied and others cannot easily modify your files.

Print Your Workbook

The most common way to share a workbook with others is to print the worksheets and distribute paper copies. Excel has several features to help you format and print your worksheets. You can select the worksheet's margin size, orientation, paper size, print area, page breaks, and much more. If you want to see a live view of how print settings affect your report, use Page Layout view.

You can print part of your worksheet or your entire worksheet. If you want to print part of your worksheet, you can use the Set Print Area option on the Page Layout tab to tell Excel the area you want to print.

On the Page Layout tab, the Size to tell Excel the size of your paper. When you click Size, the most commonly

used paper sizes appear on the menu. If you do not see the paper size you are using, click More Paper Sizes and select a size from the Page tab of the Page Setup dialog box. While in the Page Setup dialog box, you can select the orientation of your worksheet: Landscape or Portrait. Selecting Portrait makes the shortest edges of your paper the top and bottom and the longest edges of your paper the sides. Selecting Landscape makes the longest edges of your paper the top and bottom and the shortest edges of your paper the sides.

If at any time during the process of setting up your document for printing, you want to see a preview of how your printed document will look, you can click the Print Preview button, which is located on every tab in the Page Setup dialog box.

Print Your Workbook

① Click and drag to select the area you want to print.

② Click the Page Layout View button on the status bar.

Excel changes to Page Layout view.

● Click here to return to Normal view.

③ Click the Page Layout tab.

④ Click Print Area in the Page Setup group.

A menu appears.

⑤ Click Set Print Area.

Excel sets the print area.

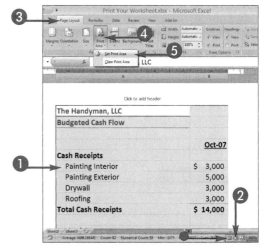

⑥ Click the Page Layout tab.

⑦ Click Size in the Page Setup group.

⑧ Click More Paper Sizes.

● Alternatively, select a paper size from the menu.

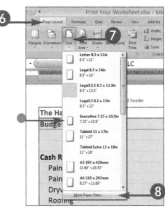

The Page Setup dialog box appears.

9 Click here and select a paper size.

10 Click here and select an orientation
(○ changes to ◉).

● Click Print Preview if you want to see a preview of
how your document will look when it is printed.

11 Click the Margins tab.

Alternatively, you can access the Margins tab
by clicking the Page Layout tab on the Ribbon,
Margins, and then Custom Margins.

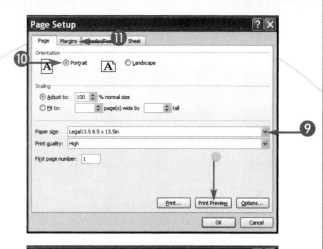

The Page options appear.

12 Set your margin sizes, including the area you want
to reserve for headers and footers.

13 Click if you want to center the print range
horizontally and/or vertically (☐ changes to ☑).

14 Click OK.

The Page Setup dialog box closes.

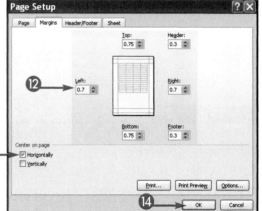

Extra

In the Ribbon, clicking the launcher in the Page Setup, Scale to Fit, or
Sheet Options group on the Page Layout tab opens the Page Setup
dialog box. If you want to see a preview of how your document will
look when you print it, click the Print Preview button. You can use the
Next Page and Previous Page buttons to scroll through your document.
If you want to view the margins, select the Show Margins check box
(☐ changes to ☑). To zoom in and out, click the Zoom button. Click
the Page Setup button to open the Page Setup dialog box. Use the
Page Setup dialog box to adjust your settings. When you are ready to
print, click the Print button. The Print dialog box appears. Select your
options and then click OK to print your document.

On the Ribbon, you can click
Breaks in the Page Setup group
of the Page Layout tab to
specify where a new page is to
begin in your printed copy.
Select where you want to place
the break. Click the Breaks
button and then click Insert
Page Break. Excel inserts a page
break above and to the left of
your selection.

continued →

Print Your Workbook
(continued)

Margins define the amount of white space that surrounds your document. You can apply Excel's predefined margins by selecting them from the Margins menu, or you can open the Page Setup dialog box to define your margins. By default, Excel places your data in the upper-right corner of the page. The Margins tab in the Page Setup dialog box has options you can choose to center your worksheet horizontally and/or vertically.

A header is text that prints across the top of every page of your worksheet. A footer is text that prints across the bottom of every page of your worksheet. You can set the amount of margin space Excel reserves for headers and footers on the Margins tab.

When you click in the header or footer area while in Page Layout view, the Header and Footer tools become available. You can use the Design tab to tell Excel what data you want to include in your header and/or footer. Header and Footer provide you with a list of predefined headers and footers. In the Header & Footer Elements group, you can select the options you want to place in your header or footer. You can choose from Page Number, Number of Pages, Current Date, Current Time, File Path, File Name, Sheet Name, or Picture.

If your data does not fit on the number of pages you want, you can scale your data. You can use a percentage to make your data larger or smaller. For example, setting the scale to 110 makes your data 10 percent larger than its normal size. Setting the scale to 90 makes your data 90 percent of its normal size. You can also scale your data by selecting the number of pages on which you want your data to fit.

Print Your Workbook *(continued)*

⑮ Click the left, right, or center of the header area in Page Layout view.

Click in the left area to place information on the left side of the page.

Click in the center area to place information in the center of the page.

Click in the right area to place information on the right side of the page.

● The Header & Footer tools become available.

⑯ Click the Design tab.

⑰ Click an option in the Header & Footer Elements group.

● Excel places the option in the area you selected.

This example adds a page number in the center.

● Click here to use a predefined header or footer.

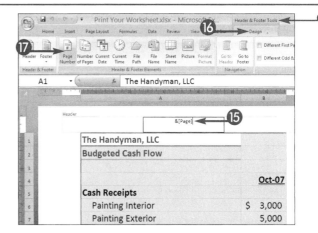

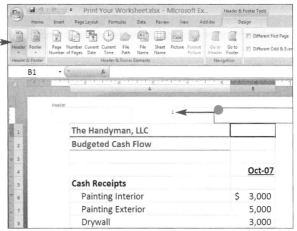

⑱ Click a cell in your data area.

⑲ Click the Page Layout tab.

⑳ Type the number of pages wide you want your document to be.

㉑ Type the number of pages long you want your document to be.

Excel scales your document.

Alternatively, click here and scale your document.

㉒ Press Ctrl+P.

The Print dialog box appears.

㉓ Click here and select the number of pages.

㉔ Click to tell Excel what you want to print.

㉕ Click Preview to see a preview.

㉖ Click OK.

Excel prints your worksheet.

Extra

If you have many rows of data, you may want the column headings to print at the top of each page of your printed worksheet. If you have many columns of data, you may want the row labels to print on the left side of each page of your printed worksheet. To print column headings and row labels, click the Page Layout tab in the Ribbon and click the launcher in the Sheet Options group. The Page Setup dialog box opens to the Sheet tab. In the Rows to Repeat at Top field, click and drag to select, or type the range of, the rows you want to appear at the top of each page. In the Columns to Repeat at Left field, click and drag to select, or type the range of, the columns you want to appear on the left and then click OK.

Gridlines separate the columns and rows in your data. To see the gridlines in your printed document, select the Print check box in the Sheet Options group on the Page Layout tab in the Ribbon. To see gridlines on-screen, select the View check box in the Sheet Options group on the Page Layout tab.

Print Multiple Areas of Your Worksheet

You can print noncontiguous areas of your worksheet, thereby limiting your printing to the information that is of relevance. This feature involves little more than selecting the cells you want to print.

There are many reasons why you may want to print noncontiguous areas of your worksheet. For example, if you have sales data for several products, each in a column, you can select and print only the columns in which you are interested. You select noncontiguous areas of the worksheet by pressing and holding Ctrl as you click and drag. After you select areas, you set them as the print area. Print areas stay in effect until you clear them. You can add to the print area by selecting a range and clicking Page Layout, Print Area, or Add to Print

Area. To clear the print area, click Page Layout, click Print Area, and then click Clear Print Area.

Excel places the ranges you selected in the Print Area field of the Sheet tab in the Page Setup dialog box. A comma follows each range. Use the same format if you want to enter your print ranges manually into the Print Area field.

When printing noncontiguous areas of your worksheet, you may have column headings or row labels you want to print with each selection. You can specify the rows you want to repeat at the top or the columns you want to repeat down the side of every page you print.

When you print a worksheet with multiple selected areas, each area prints on its own page.

Print Multiple Areas of Your Worksheet

① Press and hold the Ctrl key as you click and drag to select each area you want to print.

② Click the Page Layout tab.

③ Click Print Area.

④ Click Set Print Area.

Excel sets the print area.

⑤ Click Print Titles.

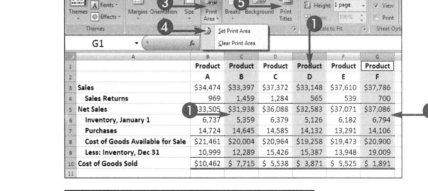

The Page Setup dialog box appears.

⑥ Click the Sheet tab.

⑦ Click and drag the columns or rows you want to repeat or type the range.

⑧ Click Print Preview.

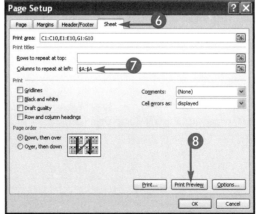

- The Print Preview window shows the first page of the printout containing an area you selected in Step 1.

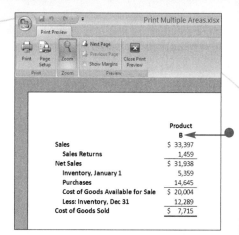

9 Click the Next Page and Previous Page buttons to view subsequent and previous pages.

- The Print Preview window shows the next page of the printout containing an area you selected in Step 1.

10 Click Print when you are satisfied with the layout.

Excel prints the selected areas.

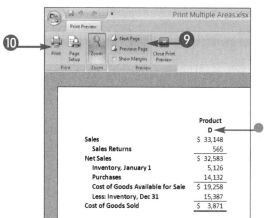

Extra

To open the Page Setup dialog box, click the launcher in the Page Setup group. You can use the Header/Footer tab in the Page Setup dialog box to add page numbers as well as a header and a footer. Click Custom Header or Custom Footer to create dates and page numbers on each page, or even add an image to the header or footer.

To print several workbooks at the same time, click the Office button and then click Open. In the Open dialog box, press and hold the Ctrl key and click the workbooks you want to print. Click the Tools drop-down menu in the lower-right corner and then click Print.

You can print row numbers and column letters on every page. Click the launcher in the Page Setup group on the Page Layout tab to open the Page Setup dialog box. On the Sheet tab, click Row and Column Headings (☐ changes to ☑) before printing your worksheet. Alternatively, click the Page Layout tab and then click the Print check box under Headings (☐ changes to ☑) in the Sheet Options group.

Add a Form Control to a Worksheet

You can add controls to a worksheet to make it easier to enter data into a cell. Form controls can aid users who are not familiar with Excel and can increase the accuracy of data entry by limiting the options a user has. For example, you can add check boxes to your worksheet so your worksheet looks like a paper form. You can also add a list box from which users can select an entry.

Excel provides nine controls you can add to a worksheet. You add controls by selecting the control you want from the Form Controls menu. After you add a control, you can adjust its size by dragging the side or corner handles. When you add a control or right-click a control to edit,

you are in design mode. In design mode, you can modify the properties and size of the control, but you cannot test its functionality.

When you place a control on a worksheet, it sits on top of the worksheet. You can size it so it appears to be located in a cell, but controls are separate from cells and you can place them anywhere on the worksheet. A control can cover any portion of a cell or range of cells.

After you add a control to a worksheet, you can assign it values. See the next task, "Assign Values to a Form Control," to learn how. Form control options are located on the Developer tab. See Chapter 12 to learn how to display the Developer tab.

Add a Form Control to a Worksheet

① Click the Developer tab.

Note: *See Chapter 12 to learn how to display the Developer tab.*

② Click Insert in the Controls group.

The Form Controls menu appears.

③ Click to select the control you want to add; this example uses list box.

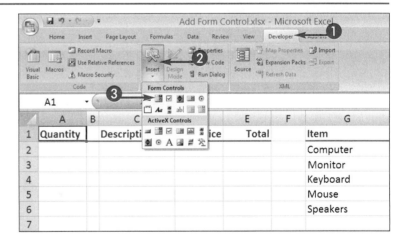

④ Drag the mouse pointer to create the control.

⑤ Drag the handles on the sides and corners to adjust the size.

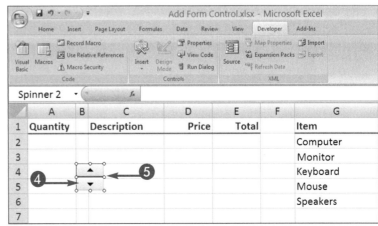

6 Place your mouse pointer on the border of a control and drag the control to change the control's location.

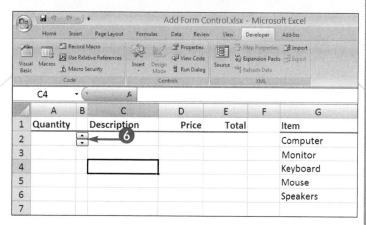

The control appears on the worksheet.

● Right-click the control to place it in design mode.

● To cancel design mode, click any cell in the worksheet.

● To remove a control, right-click the control to select it and then press the Delete key.

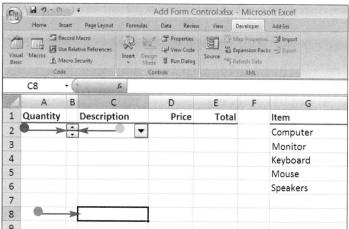

Extra

You can add the controls listed in the following table to your worksheets.

CONTROL	CONTROL NAME	DESCRIPTION
	Button	Runs an associated macro when clicked.
	List box	Displays a list of items for selection.
	Check box	Selects or deselects an option.
	Spinner	Scrolls up and down through a list of numeric values.
	Combo box	A menu that displays a list of items.
	Radio button	Selects one of a group of items.
	Group box	Places related controls together.
	Label	Provides information about an associated control.
	Scroll bar	Increases or decrease a value when the user clicks the arrows or drags the bar.

Assign Values to a Form Control

After you add a control to a form, you can assign it the values. For example, if your worksheet contains a list box, you can assign the list of values that will appear when users access the list box. Some controls enable you to define a range of valid numeric values for the control. For example, if you use a spinner, you define the starting value and the maximum value for the control. For combo boxes and list boxes, you can place the options associated with the control in a range of cells. For example, if you use a combo box, you tell Excel the list of values used by the control by entering the range of cells containing the values. The values can be located on another worksheet or even in another workbook, as long as Excel can access the workbook when users view the worksheet that contains the control.

You can link a cell to a control. If you link a cell to a control, whatever value users select when utilizing the control becomes the value in the linked cell. If you use a combo box control or list box control, the value in the linked cell is a number that represents the user's selection. Excel assigns the number based on the position of the selected value in your list. If the list is Computer, Monitor, Keyboard, and the user selects Monitor, the linked cell receives the value 2, because Monitor is second in the list.

With a control, such as a check box, you can tell Excel whether you want the option initially selected or unselected. Both options — selected and unselected — have a value associated with it.

Assign Values to a Form Control

① Right-click the selected control.

    A menu appears.

② Click Format Control.

③ Click the Control tab.

    The available fields are different depending on the control type.

    This example uses a list box.

④ Click and drag to select, or type the range that lists, the valid values.

⑤ Click a cell to assign a linked cell.

    The value associated with your selection appears in the linked cell.

⑥ Type the number of values in your list.

⑦ Click OK.

The Format Object dialog box appears.

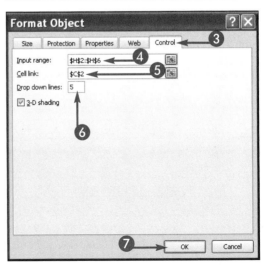

8 Select the desired control value.

C	D	E	F	G	H	I
Item #	Description	Price	Total		Item	Cost
	Monitor ▼				Computer	1,295.00
	Computer				Monitor	995.00
	Monitor				Keyboard	55.00
	Keyboard				Mouse	75.00
	Mouse				Speakers	55.00
	Speakers					

8

● Excel places a numeric value representing the control selection in the linked cell.

C	D	E	F	G	H	I
Item #	Description	Price	Total		Item	Cost
2	Monitor ▼				Computer	1,295.00
					Monitor	995.00
					Keyboard	55.00
					Mouse	75.00
					Speakers	55.00

Apply It

When working with a value selected from a list box or combo box control, you may want to use the value in the linked cell to set the value of another cell. For example, assume you have the following Excel list in cells H2:I4:

```
Computer      $1295
Monitor        $995
Keyboard        $55
```

You can use the INDEX function to determine the price based on the equipment selection. For example, if the user selects Monitor from the control, Excel places a value of 2 in the linked cell. If you want users to find the cost of the selection, you type a formula similar to the following, assuming that C2 is the linked cell:

```
=INDEX($H$2:$1$4,C2,2)
```

When the user selects Monitor, the INDEX function returns $995. The INDEX function actually creates an array of the Excel list and uses the control selection to determine which element in the array to return. The function uses three arguments: Array, Row_num, and Column_num.

Add a Macro to a Form Control

You can use macros to automate the tasks you perform in Excel. See Chapter 12 to learn more about macros. You can assign a macro to any form control on a worksheet. For example, if a user clicks a radio button control, you can have Excel add a postage amount to an invoice.

You can create one macro for each control on a worksheet. You create a macro either by recording a series of keystrokes or by writing a Visual Basic for Applications (VBA) procedure. This book does not cover writing procedures. When you select the Assign Macro menu option, Excel automatically creates a new macro name by using the name of the control followed by an underscore and an event name, such as _Click. Excel assigns the control name to the control when you add it to a worksheet. For example, the first OptionButton control that you add to a worksheet is named OptionButton1.

If you create a macro for the option button, Excel gives the macro the name OptionButton1_Click. Every time you add a new control, Excel gives the control a unique name by adding a sequential number to OptionButton; for example, OptionButton2_Click, Option Button3_Click, and so on.

The portion of the macro name following the underscore character corresponds to an action, commonly referred to as an event. For example, with an OptionButton control, the user clicks the radio button to select the option, so the event is Click. If you create a macro for a combo box control, Excel assigns Change to the name of the event because you want to execute the macro when the value of the control changes. The event extension tells Excel to monitor the control and execute the macro whenever a user clicks the control.

Add a Macro to a Form Control

① Right-click your control.

A menu appears.

② Click Assign Macro.

The Assign Macro dialog box appears.

Excel assigns a default macro name for the selected control.

③ Click Record and then record your macro.

Note: See Chapter 12 to learn how to record a macro.

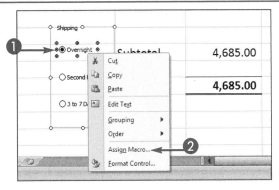

4 Click the control with the assigned macro.

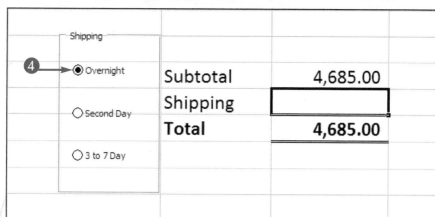

Excel executes the associated macro.

● In the example, Excel assigns postage to the invoice.

Extra

The macros that you assign to a control only execute when the corresponding event occurs for the control. For example, you may have a macro assigned to a control that computes the total amount to be paid when the user clicks the control. If you change the values needed to compute the total amount after a user clicks the control, Excel does not update the total until the user clicks the control again.

If you no longer want a macro to be assigned to a control, right-click the control and then click the Assign Macro option. In the Assign Macro dialog box, clear the macro name from the Macro Name field and then click OK. Excel removes the macro assignment from the control, but the macro remains as part of the workbook.

To remove the macro from the workbook, click the View tab and then click Macros in the Macros group to display the Macro dialog box. Select the macro you want to delete and then click Delete.

You create a macro either by recording a series of keystrokes or by writing a VBA procedure in Visual Basic Editor. This book does not cover writing procedures; refer to *Excel Programming: You visual blueprint for creating interactive spreadsheets to learn VBA* (Wiley, 2007).

Introducing Macros

You can use macros to automate many of the tasks you perform in Excel. For example, if you frequently format your data in a particular way, you can use Excel's macro recorder to record the steps you use to format your data. You can then play back the recorded steps whenever you want to apply your format. Any series of commands you can execute in Excel, you can also record and play back.

The commands you use to create and execute macros are located on the Developer tab. By default, the Developer tab does not display in Excel. To display it, you must choose Show Developer Tab in the Ribbon in the Excel Options dialog box.

You begin recording macros by clicking Record Macro on the Developer tab or by clicking the Record Macro button on the status bar. Both options open the Record Macro

dialog box. For detailed instructions on how to use the Record Macro dialog box, see the task "Record a Macro."

When you record a macro, you can record it using an absolute reference or a relative reference. If you record using an absolute reference, when Excel plays back your macro, it plays back the exact cells you clicked when you recorded the macro. If you record using a relative reference, Excel plays back the relative location of the cells you used when you recorded your macro. Click Use Relative References on the Developer tab to record using a relative reference. To learn more about absolute and relative references, see the task "Record a Macro."

When you save a workbook that has macros, you must save it as a macro-enabled workbook. Excel gives macro-enabled workbooks an .xlsm extension.

Introducing Macros

SHOW THE DEVELOPER TAB

① Click here and then select More Commands.

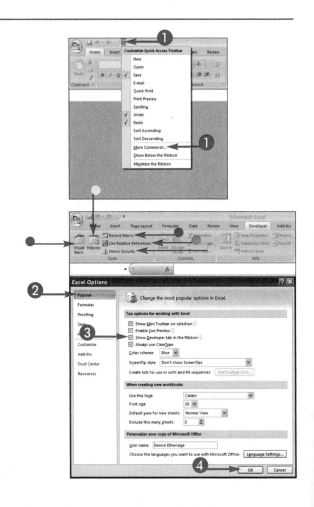

The Excel Options dialog box appears.

② Click Popular.

③ Click Show Developer Tab in the Ribbon (☐ changes to ☑).

④ Click OK.

The Developer tab appears on the Ribbon.

● Click to record a macro.

● Click to record with a relative reference.

● Click to change macro security.

● Click to run macros.

● Click to open Visual Basic Editor.

SAVE A WORKBOOK

① Click the Office button.

A menu appears.

② Click Save As and then Excel Macro-Enabled Workbook.

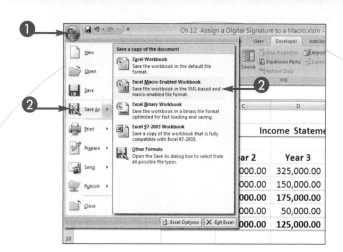

The Save As dialog box appears.

③ Click here and then select the folder in which you want to save your workbook.

④ Type the name you want to give your workbook.

⑤ Click Save.

Excel saves your workbook as a macro-enabled workbook.

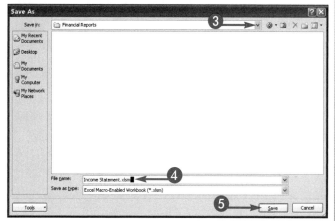

Extra

Because of problems with macro viruses, by default Excel disables all macros when you open a workbook. You can click Macro Security on the Developer tab to change the default setting. To learn more about macro security, see the tasks "Set Macro Security," "Create a Digital Signature," and "Assign a Digital Signature to a Macro."

You can use the Macro dialog box to run a macro. To open the Macro dialog box, click Macros button on the Developer tab, press Alt+F8, or place the View Macros button on the Quick Access toolbar. To place the View Macros button on the Quick Access toolbar, click the Office button, and then click Excel Options. The Excel Options dialog box appears. Click Customize. The Customize the Quick Access Toolbar page appears. In the Choose Commands From field, choose Popular Commands and then click View Macros. Click the Add button. Click OK. The View Macros button appears on the Quick Access toolbar.

If you have programming experience or aptitude, you can edit Excel macros by using Visual Basic Editor, available by clicking Visual Basic on the Developer tab.

Set Macro Security

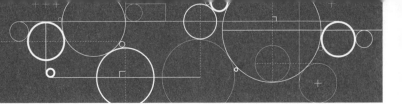

Because of increasing problems with computer viruses, specifically macro viruses, the default Excel macro security setting disables all macros when you open a workbook and allows you to decide on a case-by-case basis whether you want to enable them. This is true whether you created the macros or someone else created them.

You can change the Excel macro security setting. Excel provides four options:

- **Disable all macros without notification:** This option disables all macros and does not provide you with any security alerts to let you know macros exist.

- **Disable all macros with notification:** This is the default setting. It notifies you if macros are present so you can enable them on a case-by-case basis.

- **Disable all macros except digitally signed macros:** This option disables all macros except those digitally

signed by a trusted publisher. If the publisher has digitally signed the macro but you have not opted to trust the publisher, you can enable the macro or trust the publisher. See the Extra section of the task "Run a Macro" to learn how to trust a publisher.

- **Enable all macros (not recommended; potentially dangerous code can run):** This option allows you to run all macros. Because potentially dangerous code can run, Microsoft does not recommend this option.

Changes you make to macro security in Excel do not change the macro security in other Office programs.

Macro creators use digital signatures to verify the safety of the macros they create. You can create your own digital signature by using the Microsoft Selfcert.exe tool or you can obtain a digital certificate from a commercial certificate of authority. For more information on the Microsoft Selfcert.exe tool, see the next task, "Create a Digital Signature."

Set Macro Security

① Click the Developer tab.

Note: See the task "Introducing Macros" to learn how to display the Developer tab.

② Click Macro Security in the Code group.

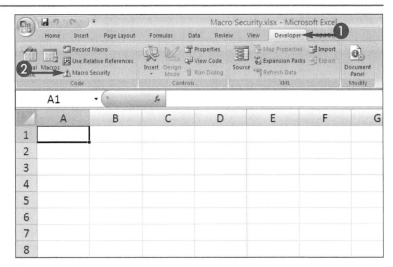

The Trust Center dialog box appears.

③ Click to select a macro setting (○ changes to ◉).

④ Click OK.

Excel changes your macro security setting.

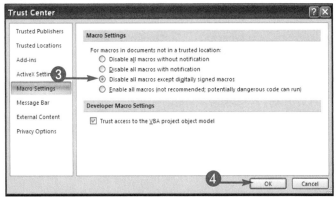

Create a Digital Signature

I f you create a workbook that contains macros, you should consider using a digital signature. A digital signature provides assurance that the workbook file is valid and no one has altered it. You can create a personal digital signature by using the Microsoft Selfcert.exe tool. Projects signed with digital signatures created with the Selfcert.exe tool only work on computers that have the certificate in their Personal Certificates store.

Digital signatures that you create with the SelfCert.exe tool work well for personal workbooks; however, if you plan to distribute your workbook to users outside your workgroup, you should consider acquiring a commercial digital signature file. When you use a commercial digital signature file, the digital ID attaches to the macro and remains with it; if anyone alters the macro in any way, Excel notifies the user that someone has changed the macro and therefore the macro should not be trusted.

The most common provider of commercial digital certification is VeriSign, Inc. To obtain a commercial certification, you must submit an application and pay a fee. You can find out more about obtaining a commercial certification from VeriSign at www. verisign.com. You can also obtain a digital signature from Thawte Consulting. You can find out more about their digital signature options at www.thawte.com.

Extra

To view the certificates in your Personal Certificate store, open Windows Internet Explorer. On the Internet Explorer menu, click Tools and then click Internet Options. The Internet Options dialog box appears. Click the Content tab. Click the Certificates button. The Certificates dialog box appears. Click the Personal tab. All of your personal certificates appear.

Create a Digital Signature

① Click the Start button.

② Click All Programs → Microsoft Office → Microsoft Office Tools → Digital Certificate for VBA Projects.

The Create Digital Certificate dialog box appears.

③ Type the name you want to give your certificate.

④ Click OK.

Excel creates a Personal Digital Certificate.

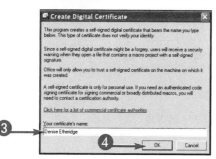

Record a Macro

A macro enables you to automate common tasks. You can use a macro to record any series of commands you can execute in Excel. For example, if you frequently apply a certain format to your worksheet, you can record the steps for creating the format and then play them back each time you want to apply the format.

Clicking the Macro Recorder button opens the Record Macro dialog box in which you can name your macro, assign your macro to a shortcut key, and tell Excel where you want to store your macro. You can name your macro anything you want; however, the name must start with a letter; only contain letters, numbers, and underscores; and not contain any spaces. You can assign any upper- or lowercase letter to act as the shortcut key.

In the Record Macro dialog box, the Store Macro In field tells Excel where to store your macro. You can choose to store your macro in the Personal Macro Workbook, a New Workbook, or This Workbook. Use the Personal Macro Workbook option if you want to make your macro available to all Excel files. After you have stored a least one macro in the Personal Macro Workbook, the workbook opens whenever you open an Excel file. Use the New Workbook option if you have specialized macros that you want to use with multiple files. If you store your macro in a New Workbook, you can use the macros whenever that workbook is open. Use the This Workbook option if you want your macro to be in the workbook in which you are currently working.

Record a Macro

① Click the Developer tab.

Note: See the task "Introducing Macros" to learn how to display the Developer tab.

● Alternatively, click the Record Macro button on the status bar and skip Step 2.

② Click Record Macro in the Code group.

The Record Macro dialog box appears.

③ Type the name you want to give your macro.

④ Type the shortcut key you want to assign to your macro.

Press Shift as you type to assign an uppercase key.

⑤ Click here and then select the workbook in which you want to store your macro.

⑥ Type a description of your macro.

⑦ Click OK.

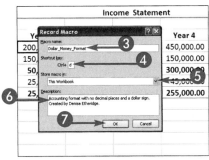

You are now ready to record your macro.

⑧ Perform the steps you want to record.

Note: *This example changes the number format using the following steps. Click the Number Group launcher. Click Accounting. Set Decimal Place to 0. Select $ as Symbol. Click OK.*

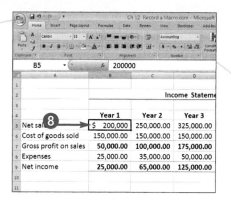

⑨ Click the Developer tab.

● Alternatively, click the Stop Recording button on the status bar and skip Step 10.

⑩ Click Stop Recording in the Code group.

Excel stops recording your macro.

Your macro is ready for you to use.

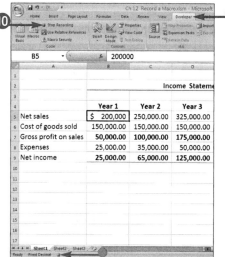

Extra

A macro you create in Excel can have a relative, an absolute, or a mixed reference. If you use a relative reference, Excel performs the macro based on a relative location. For example, suppose you move up two cells from cell A3 to A1 when creating your macro. When you run your macro, if you are in cell C3, Excel will move up two cells from cell C3 to C1. If you use an absolute reference, however, Excel performs the macro based on the exact cell addresses. For example, suppose again that you move up two cells from cell A3 to A1. When you run your macro, if you are in cell C3, Excel moves from there to the cells you used when you recorded your macro. That is, Excel moves from cell A3 to cell A1.

By default, Excel creates macros with an absolute reference. To create a macro with a relative reference, click Use Relative References in the Code group on the Developer tab to toggle the relative reference option on. To create a macro with both a relative and an absolute reference — a mixed reference — toggle the Use Relative References button on and off as needed as you create your macro.

Assign a Digital Signature to a Macro

A digital signature provides assurance that a workbook file is valid and no one has altered it. There are two types of digital signatures: personal digital signatures and commercial digital signatures. You can create a personal digital signature by using the Microsoft Selfcert.exe tool, or you can purchase a digital signature. Refer to the task "Create a Digital Signature" to learn how to create digital signatures. After you create a digital signature, you must attach it to your workbook. Attaching a digital signature is similar to sealing an envelope. If an envelope arrives sealed, you have some level of assurance that no one has tampered with its contents.

Use the Digital Signature dialog box to attach a digital signature. Visual Basic Editor is a separate Excel module that you can use to edit your macro. Access the Digital Signature dialog box by opening Visual Basic Editor. The Digital Signature dialog box lists valid certificates. You can use the Digital Signature dialog box to view certificates and to select the one you want to use.

Unless you have on your compucter a valid digital signature certificate for the signature used to sign a macro, Excel removes the digital signature when you modify a macro and you must reattach it. If you are not sure if a workbook has a digital signature, you can check the signature by reviewing the Digital Signature dialog box. If a workbook has a digital signature, the name of the signature appears in the Certificate Name field. If you click the Remove button in the Digital Signature dialog box, Excel removes the digital signature.

Assign a Digital Signature to a Macro

① Click the Developer tab.

Note: See the task "Introducing Macros" to learn how to display the Developer tab.

② Click Visual Basic in the Code group.

Visual Basic Editor appears.

③ Click Tools → Digital Signature.

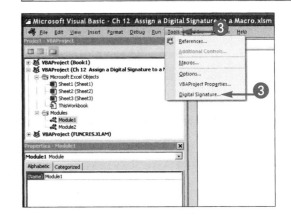

The Digital Signature dialog box appears.

④ Click Choose.

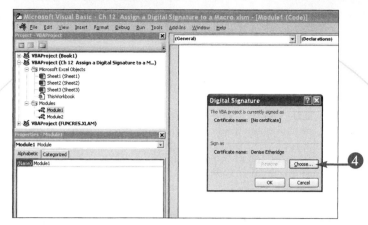

● The Select Certificate dialog box appears.

Note: See the task "Create a Digital Signature" to learn how to create a digital signature.

⑤ Click the signature you want to apply.

⑥ Click OK to close the Select Certificate dialog box.

⑦ Click OK to close the Digital Signature dialog box.

Excel attaches the digital signature to your workbook.

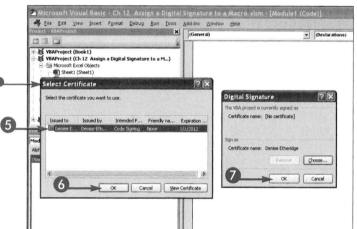

Extra

If you have macro security enabled, Excel displays a warning just below the Ribbon when you open a workbook containing a signed macro. You can click the Options button located beside the warning to open the Microsoft Office Security Options dialog box, where you can indicate that you trust the publisher. Excel then saves the name of the publisher in the Trusted Publishers section of the Trust Center.

If you click Macro Security on the Developer tab, the Trust Center dialog box appears. Click Trusted Publisher to display a list of your trusted publishers. If you no longer want to trust macros from a publisher listed on the Trusted Publishers page, click the name of the publisher and then click Remove. The next time you open a workbook with a macro from a removed publisher, Excel again warns you about its macros.

Unless you have your macro settings set to enable all macros, Excel checks all documents you open for macros. See the task "Set Macro Security" for more information. If you have a file that you do not want Excel to check, you can store it in a trusted location. In the Trust Center dialog box, click Trusted Locations to define a trusted location.

Run a
Macro

Macros enable you to quickly perform tasks that would normally take multiple steps. When you run a macro, Excel replays the steps you recorded when you created the macro. You can run any macro located in any workbook as long as the workbook in which the macro is located is open. To run a macro, you can press the shortcut key you assigned when you created the macro or you can select the macro from the Macro dialog box.

When you create a macro, you can choose to store it in one of three locations: the current workbook, a new workbook, or the Personal Macro Workbook. By default, the Macro dialog box lists all the macros in open workbooks. If a macro is stored in the Personal Macro Workbook, the macro opens as a hidden file each time

you open a file. By default, the files in the Personal Macro Workbook always appear in the Macro dialog box.

You can use the Macros In field to limit the number of macros listed in the Macro dialog box. To see the macros in any open workbook, including the Personal Macro Workbook, select the All Open Workbooks option. To see the macros from a specific workbook, select the name of the workbook from the Macros In drop-down list. To see global macros stored in the Personal Macro Workbook, select the Personal.xlsb option.

To run a macro from another workbook, the macro must be from a signed source or you must enable all macros. You can set the security setting for macros. See the task "Set Macro Security" to learn more about macro security.

Run a Macro

① Select the cells to which you want to apply your macro.

② Click the Developer tab.

Note: See the task "Introducing Macros" to learn how to display the Developer tab.

③ Click Macros in the Code group.

Alternatively, click Alt+F8.

The Macro dialog box appears.

④ If your macro does not appear in the Macro dialog box, click here and then select the workbook that contains your macro.

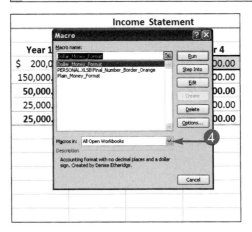

⑤ Click the name of the macro you want to run.

⑥ Click Run.

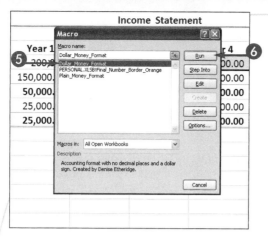

● Excel runs the macro.

You can also run your macro by pressing the shortcut key you assigned when you created your macro.

	A	B	C	D	E	F	G
1							
2				Income Statement			
3							
4		Year 1	Year 2	Year 3	Year 4	Year 5	
5	Net sales	$ 200,000	$ 250,000	$ 325,000	$ 450,000	$ 600,000	
6	Cost of goods sold	150,000.00	150,000.00	150,000.00	150,000.00	150,000.00	
7	Gross profit on sales	50,000.00	100,000.00	175,000.00	300,000.00	450,000.00	
8	Expenses	25,000.00	35,000.00	50,000.00	45,000.00	55,000.00	
9	Net income	25,000.00	65,000.00	125,000.00	255,000.00	395,000.00	
10							
11							

Extra

Excel differentiates between macros listed in the Macro dialog box by placing the name of the workbook that contains the macros in front of the macro name. For example, Excel lists a macro named Sum_Expenses in the Personal Macro Workbook as PERSONAL.XLSB!Sum_Expenses. If the macro Sum_Cells exists in both the Budget.xlsm and Expenses.xlsm workbooks, Excel treats them as two different macros. The Macro dialog box lists them as Budget.xlsm!Sum_Cells and Expenses.xlsm!Sum_Cells.

If you have macro security enabled, the Office Trust Center checks the macros when you open a workbook to see if the macros are valid. If there are any problems, Excel displays a warning just below the Ribbon. You can click the Options button located beside the warning to open the Microsoft Office Security Options dialog box.

In the Microsoft Office Security Options dialog box, click Help Protect Me from Unknown Content (Recommended) to disable the macros, click Enable the Content to enable the macros, or click Trust All Documents from this Publisher to add the macro publisher to the Trusted Publisher list. Excel does not display a warning when you open workbooks with macros if the publisher is on the Trusted Publisher list.

Create and Launch a Keyboard Shortcut

A keyboard shortcut is a combination of keys you press to execute a command. You can use a keyboard shortcut to launch an Excel macro command. You can assign an upper- or lowercase key to a macro when you create it or assign one later by using the Macro Options dialog box. You execute a macro keyboard shortcut by pressing the Ctrl key along with that upper- or lowercase key. Refer to the task "Record a Macro" to learn how to create a macro.

Keyboard shortcuts are case sensitive. For example, Excel interprets a lowercase *m* and an uppercase *M* as two different keys. To execute a macro you have assigned to a lowercase letter, press Ctrl plus the letter, such as Ctrl+m. To execute a macro you have assigned to an uppercase letter, press the Ctrl key and the Shift key plus the letter, such as Ctrl+Shift+M.

If you give the same keyboard shortcut to macros in two different workbooks, you may execute the wrong macro if you use the shortcut while you have both workbooks open. Excel cannot discern from which workbook you want the macro. You can use the Macro Options dialog box to reassign one of the conflicting macros to a new key.

You should also be careful not to assign the macro to a keyboard shortcut that Excel uses. If you do, Excel will execute your macro instead of the command it created. For example, by default, Ctrl+o opens the Open dialog box. If you assign *o* to a macro, your macro will override Excel's assignment.

Create and Launch a Keyboard Shortcut

CREATE A KEYBOARD SHORTCUT

1. Click the Developer tab.

2. Click Macros in the Code group.

   The Macro dialog box appears.

3. Click the desired macro.

4. Click the Options button.

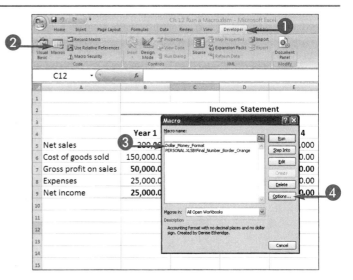

   The Macro Options dialog box appears.

5. Type the desired shortcut key.

   Press Shift as you type to assign an uppercase key.

6. Type a description.

7. Click OK.

8. Click Close.

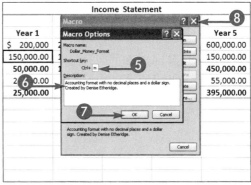

LAUNCH A KEYBOARD SHORTCUT

1 Select the cells in which you want the macro to execute.

2 Press Ctrl and the shortcut key.

	B	C	D	E	F
			Income Statement		
	Year 1	**Year 2**	**Year 3**	**Year 4**	**Year 5**
	$ 200,000	$ 250,000	$ 325,000	$ 450,000	$ 600,000
	150,000.00	150,000.00	150,000.00	150,000.00	150,000.00
	50,000.00	100,000.00	175,000.00	300,000.00	450,000.00
	25,000.00	35,000.00	50,000.00	45,000.00	55,000.00
	25,000.00	65,000.00	125,000.00	255,000.00	395,000.00

● The macro executes.

3 Repeat Steps 1 and 2 to execute the macro again.

	B	C	D	E	F
			Income Statement		
	Year 1	**Year 2**	**Year 3**	**Year 4**	**Year 5**
	$ 200,000	$ 250,000	$ 325,000	$ 450,000	$ 600,000
	150,000	150,000	150,000	150,000	150,000
	50,000.00	100,000.00	175,000.00	300,000.00	450,000.00
	25,000.00	35,000.00	50,000.00	45,000.00	55,000.00
	25,000.00	65,000.00	125,000.00	255,000.00	395,000.00

Extra

If you do not use a macro shortcut frequently, it is easy to forget the keyboard shortcut you assigned to your macro. If you forget your keyboard shortcut, you can view it in the Macro Options dialog box.

You can execute a macro by assigning the macro to a picture, clip art, shape, or smart art. For example, if you want to assign a macro to a picture, you start by inserting the picture into your worksheet by clicking the Insert tab and then clicking Picture. The Insert Picture dialog box appears. In the Look In field, select the folder in which you stored the picture you want to insert. The pictures in that folder appear. Click the picture you want to insert and then click the Insert button. The picture appears in the worksheet. Click and drag the picture to place it where you want it and then double right-click the picture. A menu appears. Click Assign Macro. The Assign Macro dialog box appears. Click the macro you want to assign to the picture and then click OK. Excel assigns the macro to the picture. Click the picture when you want to execute the macro.

Assign a Macro to the Quick Access Toolbar

You can assign a macro to the Excel Quick Access toolbar. You can execute macros assigned to the Quick Access toolbar using a shortcut key or the Macro dialog box; however, using the Quick Access toolbar means you can access the macros by simply clicking the appropriate button.

When you add a button to the Quick Access toolbar, you can specify whether it should appear on the toolbar of all Excel workbooks or only on the Quick Access toolbar in the workbook you specify. By default, the button will appear in all workbooks. If you have placed your macro in the Personal Macro Workbook, you will probably want your macro button to appear in all workbooks because the macro will be available to all workbooks. If your macro will only be available to a single workbook, your

macro button should only appear on the Quick Access toolbar for that workbook.

You use the Customize the Quick Access Toolbar page of the Excel Options dialog box to add a macro button to the Quick Access toolbar. You can use the Modify button to specify the button you want to use to represent your macro. You can specify where on the Quick Access toolbar your button appears and whether the Quick Access toolbar appears above or below the Ribbon. You can click the Reset button to return the Quick Access toolbar to its default state.

Deleting a macro does not remove the macro button from the Quick Access toolbar. When you press the button for a deleted macro, you receive an error message. Use the Remove button on the Customize the Quick Access Toolbar page of the Excel Options dialog box to remove a macro button.

Assign a Macro to the Quick Access Toolbar

① Click here and then select More Commands.

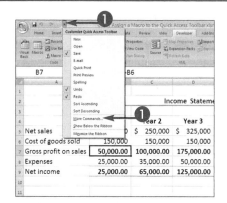

The Excel Options dialog box appears.

② Click here and then select Macros.

③ Click here and then select the workbook in which the button should appear.

④ Click the macro you want to assign to the Quick Access toolbar.

⑤ Click Add.

● The macro appears in the box on the right. Macros display on the Quick Access toolbar in the order shown here.

● Click to move the macro up.

● Click to move the macro down.

⑥ Click Modify.

● Click if you want the Quick Access toolbar to appear below the Ribbon (☐ changes to ☑).

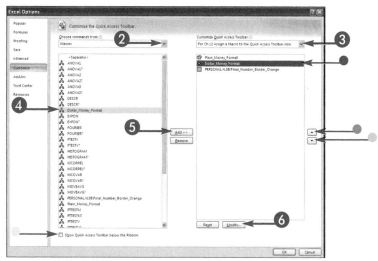

The Modify Button dialog box appears.

⑦ Click the button you want to use to represent your macro.

⑧ Click OK to close the Modify Button dialog box.

⑨ Click OK to close the Excel Options dialog box.

● Click to return the Quick Access toolbar to its default state.

● Click the macro and then click the Remove button to remove a macro.

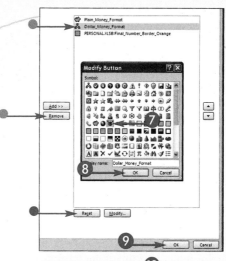

● The button appears on the Quick Access toolbar.

⑩ Click the button to execute your macro.

	A	B	C	D
1				
2			Income Stateme	
3				
4		Year 1	Year 2	Year 3
5	Net sales	$ 200,000	$ 250,000	$ 325,000
6	Cost of goods sold	150,000	150,000	150,000
7	Gross profit on sales	50,000.00	100,000.00	175,000.00
8	Expenses	25,000.00	35,000.00	50,000.00
9	Net income	25,000.00	65,000.00	125,000.00
10				

Extra

You can add commands you frequently use to the Quick Access toolbar. Click the Office button. A menu appears. Click the Excel Options button located in the bottom-right corner. The Excel Options dialog box appears. Click Customize. The Customize the Quick Access Toolbar page appears. Click the down arrow next to the Choose Commands From field and select All Commands. Click the command you want to add to the Quick Access toolbar and then click the Add button. Click OK. Excel returns you to your workbook, and the command you chose appears on the Quick Access toolbar.

You can add commands you cannot find in the Ribbon by choosing Commands Not in the Ribbon in the Choose Commands From field. If a command from a previous version of Excel is not in the Ribbon, you may find it listed under Commands Not in the Ribbon. For example, in previous versions you could format your documents quickly by using AutoFormat. Excel 2007 uses styles, but you can still access AutoFormat via Commands Not in the Ribbon.

Delete a Macro

You can delete macros you no longer need by clicking the Delete button in the Macro dialog box. Because the Macro dialog box only displays macros in open workbooks, the workbook that contains the macro must be open before you can delete it.

The Personal Macro Workbook stores macros you want to make available to all workbooks. Excel creates the Personal Macro Workbook when you choose to store your first macro in it. After Excel creates the Personal Macro Workbook, the workbook opens as a hidden file every time you open Excel. To learn more about storing macros in the Personal Macro Workbook, see the task "Record a Macro."

If your macro is in a hidden workbook such as the Personal Macro Workbook, you must unhide the workbook before you can delete the macro. If you try to

delete a macro from the Personal Macro Workbook prior to unhiding it, Excel displays the following message: "Cannot edit a macro on a hidden workbook, Unhide the workbook using the Unhide command." You unhide the Personal Macro Workbook and other hidden workbooks by executing the Unhide command on the View tab.

If you unhide the Personal Macro Workbook, make sure you hide it again using the Hide command on the View tab after you delete the macros. Hiding the workbook prevents you from making inadvertent changes to it.

You cannot undo the deletion process. If you delete a macro by mistake, you can close the workbook without saving. Of course, if you close without saving, you will lose all the work you have done since saving. Your only other alternative is to re-create the macro.

Delete a Macro

UNHIDE A WORKBOOK

1. Click the View tab.

2. Click Unhide in the Window group.

The Unhide dialog box appears.

3. Click the workbook you want to unhide.

4. Click OK.

Excel unhides the workbook.

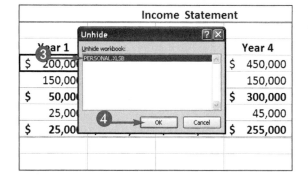

DELETE A MACRO

1. Click the Developer tab.

2. Click Macros in the Code group.

   ● The Macro dialog box appears.

3. Click the macro you want to delete.

4. Click Delete.

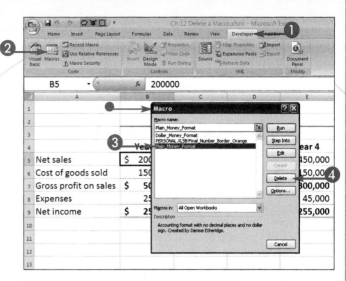

A message box appears, asking you to confirm you want to delete the macro.

5. Click Yes.

Excel deletes the macro.

Income Statement			
Year 1	Year 2	Year 3	Year 4
$ 200,000	$ 250,000	$ 325,000	$ 450,000
150,000	150,000	150,000	150,000
$ 50,000	$ 100,000	$ 175,000	$ 300,000
25,000	35,000	50,000	45,000
$ 25,000	$ 65,000	$ 125,000	$ 255,000

Extra

Typically, you do not share the Personal Macro Workbook with other users. Excel creates a different Personal Macro Workbook for each username on a machine. If you have multiple users on your computer with different usernames, Excel creates a different Personal Macro Workbook for each. You can copy a Personal Macro Workbook from one user to another. The Personal Macro Workbook is stored in the XLStart folder and is named PERSONAL.XLSB. In Windows XP, you can usually find the XLStart folder by following this path: C:\Documents and Settings*username*\Application Data\Microsoft\Excel\XLStart. In Windows Vista, you can usually find the XLStart folder by following this path: C:\Users*username*\Application Data\Microsoft\Excel\XLStart.

Each user can only have one PERSONAL.XLSB file. If a user already has a Personal Macro Workbook, you should rename the old PERSONAL.XLSB file and place the new PERSONAL.XLSB file in the user's XLStart folder. All files stored in the XLStart folder open when you open Excel, so both files will be available each time the user opens Excel. If you have other files you want to open when you open Excel, place them in the XLStart folder.

Using Keyboard Shortcuts with the Ribbon

You can execute Ribbon commands without using the mouse or taking your hands off the keyboard. This enables you to work quickly. This is particularly true if you are an excellent typist. The process is simple. You press the Alt key; when you do, Excel displays KeyTips — letters or numbers you can press to display more KeyTips or to execute a command. If, after you press a KeyTip, a menu or dialog box appears, use the arrow keys to move to your selection. Press the Enter key or the spacebar to make your selection. For example, you can activate KeyTips and then use the keyboard to change the color of your type by clicking the keys shown in the KeyTip and then using the arrow keys to select the color you want. To cancel your access to KeyTips, press F10 or press the Alt key again.

Using Keyboard Shortcuts with the Ribbon

1 Select the cells to which you want to apply your command.

This example changes the font color.

2 Press the Alt key.

KeyTips display on the Ribbon.

3 Press the letter or the number that represents the KeyTip you want to use.

Additional KeyTips may appear.

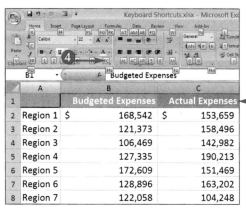

4 Continue pressing KeyTips until Excel executes the command you want.

If two letters appear, press the first letter and then press the second letter.

In this example, press F and then C to change the font color.

5 Use the arrow keys to navigate menus and dialog boxes.

6 Press Enter or the spacebar to make your selection.

● Excel executes your command.

Note: *If you want to see more of your worksheet on your screen, you can minimize the Ribbon by pressing Ctrl+F1 or right-clicking while in the Ribbon and selecting Minimize the Ribbon from the menu that appears. To restore the Ribbon, you can right-click while in the Ribbon and then deselect Minimize the Ribbon or press Ctrl+F1 again.*

Excel Keyboard Shortcuts

Data Entry Shortcut

SHORTCUT	RESULT
Enter	Completes the cell entry and moves to the next cell.
Alt+Enter	Starts a new line within the same cell.
Shift+Enter	Completes the cell entry and moves up to the cell above.
Tab	Completes the cell entry and moves to the next cell on the right.
Shift+Tab	Completes the cell entry and moves to the next cell on the left.
Esc	Cancels the cell entry and restores original cell contents.
Ctrl+D	Fills the active cell with the contents of the cell above it. Fills the selected range with the first cell in the range.
Ctrl+R	Fills the active cell with the contents of the cell to the left of it.
Ctrl+F3	Displays the Name Manager dialog box.
Ctrl+K	Displays the Insert Hyperlink dialog box.
F2	Gives you the ability to edit the active cell by placing the insertion point at the end of the cell contents and in the formula bar.

Editing Shortcuts

SHORTCUT	RESULT
Ctrl+C	Copies the selection to the Office Clipboard.
Ctrl+X	Cuts the selection and places it on the Office Clipboard.
Ctrl+V	Pastes the information on the Office Clipboard.
Backspace	Deletes entire contents of a cell, or deletes the character on the left of the insertion point if you are editing the cell contents.
Delete	Deletes entire contents of a cell, or deletes the character on the right of the insertion point if you are editing the cell contents.
Ctrl+Delete	Deletes text from the insertion point to the end of the cell contents.
Ctrl+Z	Undoes an action.
Ctrl+Y	Repeats an action (Redo).
F4	Repeats an action (same as Ctrl+Y).
Ctrl+-	Opens the Delete dialog box.
Ctrl+Shift++	Opens the Insert dialog box.

continued →

Excel Keyboard
Shortcuts (continued)

Formatting Shortcuts

SHORTCUT	RESULT
Alt+'	Opens the Style dialog box.
Ctrl+1	Opens the Format Cells dialog box.
Ctrl+B	Applies or removes bold formatting.
Ctrl+I	Applies or removes italic formatting.
Ctrl+U	Applies or removes underlining.
Ctrl+5	Applies or removes strikethrough formatting.
Ctrl+Shift+~	Applies the General number format.
Ctrl+Shift+$	Applies the Currency format with two decimal places and negative numbers in parentheses.
Ctrl+Shift+^	Applies the Exponential format with two decimal places.
Ctrl+Shift+#	Applies the Date format with dates formatted as dd-mm-yy.
Ctrl+Shift+@	Applies the Time format with hour, minute, and AM or PM.
Ctrl+Shift+!	Applies the Number format with two decimal places, a thousands separator, and minus sign for negative numbers.
Ctrl+Shift+%	Applies the Percent format.
Ctrl+Shift+&	Applies outside borders.
Ctrl+Shift+_	Removes outside borders.
Alt+Shift+Right Arrow	Displays the Group dialog box.
Alt+Shift+Left Arrow	Displays the Ungroup dialog box.
Ctrl+9	Hides the selected rows.
Ctrl+Shift+(	Unhides the hidden rows within the range selection.
Ctrl+0	Hides the selected columns.
Ctrl+Shift+)	Unhides the hidden columns within the range selection.

Formula Shortcuts

SHORTCUT	RESULT
Ctrl+Shift+Enter	Enters a formula as an array.
Ctrl+Shift+A	Inserts the argument names in parentheses for the specified function name.
F3	Opens the Paste Name dialog box when you have range names defined.
Shift+F3	Opens the Function Arguments dialog box.
=	Starts a formula.
Alt+=	Inserts the AutoSum formula.
Ctrl+;	Enters the current date.
Ctrl+Shift+:	Enters the current time.
Ctrl+Shift+"	Copies the value in the cell above the active cell into the formula bar.
Ctrl+`	Alternates between displaying the value of the cell and the cell formula.

General Program Shortcuts

SHORTCUT	RESULT
Ctrl+N	Creates a new workbook.
Ctrl+O	Opens the Open dialog box.
Ctrl+F12	Opens the Open dialog box (same as Ctrl+O).
Ctrl+S	Saves a workbook (the Save As dialog box opens if you have not previously saved the workbook).
Shift+F12	Saves a workbook (same as Ctrl+S).
F12	Opens the Save As dialog box.
Ctrl+W	Closes the active workbook; if it is the only workbook open, it also closes Excel.
Alt+F4	Closes the active workbook (same as Ctrl+W).
F1	Opens Excel Help.
F7	Runs the spell checker.
F10	Turns KeyTips on and off.
Shift+F10	Opens a context menu containing options related to the current worksheet selection. This is the same as clicking the right mouse button.

continued →

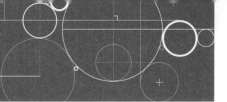

Excel Keyboard
Shortcuts (continued)

SHORTCUT	RESULT
F9	Calculates all worksheets in all open workbooks.
Ctrl+F9	Minimizes the workbook.
Ctrl+F10	Restores or maximizes the workbook.
Ctrl+P	Opens the Print dialog box.
Ctrl+Shift+F12	Opens the Print dialog box (same as Ctrl+P).
Alt+F8	Opens the Macro dialog box.
Alt+F11	Opens Visual Basic for Applications.

Selection Shortcuts

SHORTCUT	RESULT
Shift+Right Arrow	Expands the selection one cell to the right.
Shift+Left Arrow	Expands the selection one cell to the left.
Shift+Up Arrow	Expands the selection up one cell.
Shift+Down Arrow	Expands the selection down one cell.
Ctrl+Shift+*	Selects the current region or cells containing values, around the active cell.
Ctrl+Shift+Right Arrow	Expands the selection right to the next nonblank cell in the row.
Ctrl+Shift+Left Arrow	Expands the selection left to the next nonblank cell in the row.
Ctrl+Shift+Up Arrow	Expands the selection up to the next nonblank cell in the column.
Ctrl+Shift+Down Arrow	Expands the selection down to the last nonblank cell in the column.
Shift+Home	Expands selection to the beginning of the row.
Ctrl+Shift+Home	Expands selection to the beginning of the worksheet.
Ctrl+Shift+End	Expands selection to the end of the active area of the worksheet.
Ctrl+Spacebar	Selects the entire column.
Shift+Spacebar	Selects the entire row.
Ctrl+A	Selects the entire worksheet.
Shift+Page Down	Expands the selection down one screen.
Shift+Page Up	Expands the selection up one screen.
Ctrl+Shift+Spacebar	If an object is selected, selects all objects.
Ctrl+6	Alternates between hiding objects, displaying objects, and displaying object placeholders.
Shift+F8	Adds another range of cells to the selection.

SHORTCUT	RESULT
Up Arrow	Moves the active cell up one row.
Down Arrow	Moves the active cell down one row.
Left Arrow	Moves the active cell left one column.
Right Arrow	Moves the active cell right one column.
Home	Moves to the beginning of the current row.
Ctrl+Home	Moves to the beginning of the worksheet (typically cell A1).
Ctrl+End	Moves to the last cell in the worksheet (the cell at the intersection of the last used row and column in the worksheet).
Page Up	Scrolls up one screen.
Page Down	Scrolls down one screen.
Alt+Page Up	Scrolls right one screen.
Alt+Page Down	Scrolls left one screen.
Ctrl+Page Up	Moves to the previous worksheet in the workbook.
Ctrl+Page Down	Moves to the next worksheet in the workbook.
Ctrl+F6	Switches to the next open workbook.
Ctrl+Shift+F6	Switches back to the previously viewed open workbook.
F6	Moves the focus from status bar, Ribbon, worksheet, and if the worksheet is split, the split panes.
F5	Opens the Go To dialog box.
Shift+F5	Opens the Find and Replace dialog box.
Shift+F4	Repeats the last Find command.
Tab	Moves between unlocked cells of a protected worksheet.
Ctrl+.	Moves clockwise to the next corner of the selected range of cells.

Excel Function
Quick Reference

Legend:

Plain courier text = required   [] = optional

Italics = user-defined   . . . = list of items

Database Functions

FUNCTION	DESCRIPTION
DAVERAGE(*database, field, criteria*)	Averages the values in a column that match the specified criteria.
DCOUNT(*database, field, criteria*)	Counts the numeric values in the column that match the specified criteria.
DCOUNTA(*database, field, criteria*)	Counts the nonblank cells that match the specified criteria.
DGET(*database, field, criteria*)	Finds the value in the selected list that matches the specified criteria.
DMAX(*database, field, criteria*)	Finds the maximum value in the column that matches the specified criteria.
DMIN(*database, field, criteria*)	Finds the minimum value in the column that matches the specified criteria.
DPRODUCT(*database, field, criteria*)	Multiplies the values in the column that match the specified criteria and returns the product.
DSTDEV(*database, field, criteria*)	Estimates the standard deviation of a sample using the numbers in the column that match the specified criteria.
DSTDEVP(*database, field, criteria*)	Estimates the standard deviation of the entire population using the numbers in the column that match the specified criteria.
DSUM(*database, field, criteria*)	Totals the numbers in the column that match the specified criteria and returns the sum.
DVAR(*database, field, criteria*)	Estimates the variance of a sample using the numbers in the column that match the specified criteria.
DVARP(*database, field, criteria*)	Estimates the variance of the entire population using the numbers in the column that match the specified criteria.

FUNCTION	DESCRIPTION
DATE(*year*, *month*, *day*)	Creates a date by combining the specified year, month, and day values.
DATEVALUE(*date_value*)	Converts a date written as a text value into the serial number used by Excel to store the date.
DAY(*serial_number*)	Returns the day portion of a date.
DAYS360(*start_date*, *end_date*[, *method*])	Calculates the number of days between two dates using a 360-day year.
EDATE(*start_date*, *months*)	Returns the date that is the specified number of months before the start_date.
EOMONTH(*start_date*, *months*)	Returns the last day in the month that is the specified number of months before or after the date.
HOUR(*serial_number*)	Returns the hour portion of a time.
MINUTE(*serial_number*)	Returns the minute portion of a time.
MONTH(*serial_number*)	Returns the month portion of a date.
NETWORKDAYS(*start_date*, *end_date*[, *holidays*])	Determines the number of work days between two dates by excluding any weekend dates and any specified holidays.
NOW()	Returns the current date and time.
SECOND(*serial_number*)	Returns the second portion of a time.
TIME(*hour*, *minute*, *second*)	Creates a time by combining the specified hour, minute, and second values.
TIMEVALUE(*time_text*)	Converts a time value into the serial number used by Excel to store the time.
TODAY()	Returns the current date.
WEEKDAY(*serial_number*[, *return_type*])	Returns a number from 1 to 7, indicating the day of the week that a date falls on.
WEEKNUM(*serial_number*[, *return_type*])	Returns the week number representing the week when the date occurs in the year.
WORKDAY(*start_date*, *days*[, *holidays*])	Finds the date that is the specified number of workdays before the date.
YEAR(*year*, *month*, *day*)	Returns the year portion of a date.
YEARFRAC(*start-date*, *end_date*[, *basis*])	Returns a decimal value that represents the fraction of a year represented by the number of days between two dates.

continued →

Excel Function Quick Reference (continued)

FUNCTION	DESCRIPTION
BESSELI(x, n)	Returns the modified Bessel function In(x).
BESSELJ(x, n)	Returns the Bessel function Jn(x).
BESSELK(x, n)	Returns the modified Bessel function Kn(x).
BESSELY(x, n)	Returns the Bessel function Yn(x).
BIN2DEC(number)	Converts a binary number to a decimal number.
BIN2HEX(number[, places])	Converts a binary number to a hexadecimal number.
BIN2OCT(number[, places])	Converts a binary number to an octal number.
COMPLEX(real_num, i_num[, suffix])	Converts real and imaginary coefficients into complex numbers.
CONVERT(number, from_unit, to_unit)	Converts a number from one measurement system to another, such as converting meters to feet.
DEC2BIN(number[, places])	Converts a decimal number to a binary number. Unless specified, uses the minimum number of characters.
DEC2HEX(number[, places])	Converts a decimal number to a hexadecimal number. Unless specified, uses the minimum number of characters.
DEC2OCT(number[, places])	Converts a decimal number to an octal number. Unless specified, uses the minimum number of characters.
DELTA(number1[, number2])	Determines if two numbers are equal. If the second number is omitted, it compares the first number to zero.
ERF(lower_limit[, upper_limit])	Returns the error function integrated between the specified limits.
ERFC(x)	Returns the complementary error function.
GESTEP(number[, step])	Checks if a number is larger than the threshold value.
HEX2BIN(number[, places])	Converts a hexadecimal number to a binary number. Unless specified, uses the minimum number of characters.
HEX2DEC(number)	Converts a hexadecimal number to a decimal number.

FUNCTION	DESCRIPTION
HEX2OCT(*number*[, *places*])	Converts a hexadecimal number to an octal number. Unless specified, uses the minimum number of characters.
IMABS(*inumber*)	Returns the absolute value of a complex number.
IMAGINARY(*inumber*)	Returns the imaginary coefficient of a complex number.
IMARGUMENT(*inumber*)	Returns the argument q for an angle measurement expressed in radians.
IMCONJUGATE(*inumber*)	Returns the complex conjugate of a complex number.
IMCOS(*inumber*)	Determines the cosine for a complex number.
IMDIV(*inumber1*, *inumber2*)	Finds the quotient of two complex numbers.
IMEXP(*inumber*)	Finds the exponential of a complex number.
IMLN(*inumber*)	Determines the natural logarithm of a complex number.
IMLOG10(*inumber*)	Finds the base-10 logarithm of a complex number.
IMLOG2(*inumber*)	Finds the base-2 logarithm of a complex number.
IMPOWER(*inumber*, *number*)	Returns the result of a complex number raised to the specified power.
IMPRODUCT(*inumber1*, *inumber2*, . . .)	Returns the product of two or more complex numbers. The function allows a maximum of 255 complex numbers.
IMREAL(*inumber*)	Returns the real coefficient of a complex number.
IMSIN(*inumber*)	Determines the sine for a complex number.
IMSQRT(*inumber*)	Finds the square root of a complex number.
IMSUB(*inumber1*, *inumber2*)	Subtracts two complex numbers.
IMSUM(*inumber1*[, *inumber2*, . . .])	Adds complex numbers.
OCT2BIN(*number*[, *places*])	Converts an octal number to a binary number. Unless specified, uses the minimum number of characters.
OCT2DEC(*number*)	Converts an octal number to a decimal number.
OCT2HEX(*number*[, *places*])	Converts an octal number to a hexadecimal number. Unless specified, uses the minimum number of characters.

continued →

Financial Functions

FUNCTION	DESCRIPTION
ACCRINT(*issue, first_interest, settlement, rate*)	Finds the accrued interest for a security.
ACCRINTM(*issue, maturity, rate[, par, basis]*)	Finds the total amount of interest paid at maturity of an investment.
AMORDEGRC(*cost, date_purchased, first_period, salvage, period, rate, basis*)	Uses the French accounting system to find the depreciation of an asset. Uses a depreciation coefficient.
AMORLINC(*cost, date_purchased, first_period, salvage, period, rate, basis*)	Uses the French accounting system to find the depreciation of an asset.
COUPDAYBS(*settlement, maturity, frequency[, basis]*)	Finds the number of days between the start of the coupon period and the settlement date.
COUPDAYS(*settlement, maturity, frequency[, basis]*)	Finds the number of days in the coupon period that includes the settlement date.
COUPDAYSNC(*settlement, maturity, frequency[, basis]*)	Finds the number of days from the settlement date to the next coupon date.
COUPNCD(*settlement, maturity, frequency[, basis]*)	Finds the next coupon date after the settlement date.
COUPNUM(*settlement, maturity, frequency[, basis]*)	Finds the number of coupons payable between the settlement date and the maturity date.
COUPPCD(*settlement, maturity, frequency[, basis]*)	Finds the previous coupon date before the settlement date.
CUMIPMT(*rate, nper, start_period, end_period, type*)	Determines the cumulative interest paid on a loan between the specified dates.
CUMIPRINC(*rate, nper, start_period, end_period, type*)	Determines the cumulative principal paid on a loan between the specified dates.
DB(*cost, salvage, life, period[, month]*)	Finds the depreciation of an asset using fixed-declining depreciation.
DDB(*cost, salvage, life, period[, month]*)	Finds the depreciation of an asset using double-declining depreciation.
DISC(*settlement, maturity, pr, redemption[, basis]*)	Determines the discount rate for a security.
DOLLARDE(*fractional_dollar, fraction*)	Converts a dollar price from a fraction to a decimal value.

FUNCTION	DESCRIPTION
DOLLARFR(*decimal_dollar*, *fraction*)	Converts from a dollar price decimal value to a fraction.
DURATION(*settlement*, *maturity*, *coupon*, *yld*, *frequency*[, *basis*])	Returns the Macauley duration for an assumed par value $100.00.
EFFECT(*nominal_rate*, *npery*)	Finds the effective annual interest rate on an investment.
FV(*rate*, *nper*, *pmt*[, *pv*, *type*])	Finds the future value of an investment.
FVSCHEDULE(*principal*, *schedule*)	Finds the future value of an investment. Applies compound interest rates.
INTRATE(*settlement*, *maturity*, *investment*, *redemption*[, *basis*])	Finds the interest rate on a security.
IPMT(*rate*, *per*, *nper*, *pv*[, *fv*, *type*])	Finds the interest payment on an investment for a specific period.
IRR(*values*[, *guess*])	Finds the internal rate of return.
ISPMT(*rate*, *per*, *nper*, *pv*)	Finds the interest payment for a specific period.
MDURATION(*settlement*, *maturity*, *coupon*, *yld*, *frequency*[, *basis*])	Finds the Macauley modified duration value for a security.
MIRR(*values*, *finance_rate*, *reinvest_rate*)	Finds the modified internal rate of return.
NOMINAL(*effect_rate*, *npery*)	Finds the nominal annual interest rate.
NPER(*rate*, *pmt*, *pv*[, *fv*, *type*])	Finds the number of payments on an investment.
NPV(*rate*, *value1*[, *value2*, . . .])	Calculates the net present value of an investment.
ODDFPRICE(*settlement*, *maturity*, *issue*, *first_coupon*, *an abnormal rate*, *yld*, *redemption*, *frequency*[, *basis*])	Calculates the price of an investment with an odd first period.
ODDFYIELD(*settlement*, *maturity*, *issue*, *first_coupon*, *rate*, *pr*, *redemption*, *frequency*[, *basis*])	Calculates the yield of an investment with an odd first period.
ODDLPRICE(*settlement*, *maturity*, *issue*, *last_interest*, *rate*, *yld*, *redemption*, *frequency*[, *basis*])	Calculates the price of an investment with an odd first period.
ODDLYIELD(*settlement*, *maturity*, *issue*, *last_interest*, *rate*, *pr*, *redemption*, *frequency*[, *basis*])	Calculates the yield of an investment with an odd first period.
PMT(*rate*, *nper*, *pv*[, *fv*, *type*])	Calculates a loan payment.
PPMT(*rate*, *per*, *nper*, *pv*[, *fv*, *type*])	Finds the amount applied to the principal for a payment period.
PRICE(*settlement*, *maturity*, *rate*, *yld*, *redemption*, *frequency*[, *basis*])	Calculates the price of a security with periodic interest.

continued →

Financial Functions

FUNCTION	DESCRIPTION
PRICEDISC(*settlement, maturity, discount, redemption*[, *basis*])	Calculates the price of a discounted security.
PRICEMAT(*settlement, maturity, issue, rate, yld*[, *basis*])	Calculates the price of a security with interest paid at maturity.
PV(*rate, nper, pmt*[, *fv, type*])	Finds the present value of an investment.
RATE(*nper, pmt, pv*[, *fv, type, guess*])	Finds the interest rate per period of an annuity.
RECEIVED(*settlement, maturity, investment, discount*[, *basis*])	Calculates the amount received at the maturity of a security.
SLN(*cost, salvage, life*)	Finds the straight-line depreciation of an asset.
SYD(*cost, salvage, life, per*)	Finds the sum-of-the-years-digits depreciation of an asset.
TBILLEQ(*settlement, maturity, discount*)	Finds the bond-equivalent yield for a treasury bill.
TBILLPRICE(*settlement, maturity, discount*)	Finds the price for a treasury bill.
TBILLYIELD(*settlement, maturity, pr*)	Finds the yield for a treasury bill.
VDB(*cost, salvage, life, start_period, end_period*[, *factor, no_switch*])	Finds the depreciation of an asset over multiple periods.
XIRR(*values, dates*[, *guess*])	Calculates the internal rate of return for non-periodic cash flows.
XNPV(*rate, values, dates*)	Calculates the present value of non-periodic cash flows.
YIELD(*settlement, maturity, rate, pr, redemption, frequency*[, *basis*])	Calculates the yield of a security.
YIELDDISC(*settlement, maturity, pr, redemption*[, *basis*])	Calculates the yield of a discounted security.
YIELDMAT(*settlement, maturity, issue, rate*[, *basis*])	Calculates the annual yield of a security with interest paid at maturity.

Information Functions

FUNCTION	DESCRIPTION
CELL(*info_type*[, *reference*])	Determines formatting, location, or contents of the specified cell.
ERROR.TYPE(*error_val*)	Determines the error type for the selected cell.
INFO(*type_text*)	Finds information about the current operating system.
ISBLANK(*value*)	Checks for a blank cell.
ISERR(*value*)	Checks for any errors except #N/A.
ISERROR(*value*)	Checks for any errors.
ISEVEN(*number*)	Checks to see if a number is even.
ISLOGICAL(*value*)	Checks for a logical value.
ISNA(*value*)	Checks for an #N/A value.
ISNONTEXT(*value*)	Checks for any non-text value.
ISODD(*number*)	Checks if a number is odd.
ISREF(*value*)	Checks for a reference.
ISTEXT(*value*)	Checks for text.
N(*value*)	Converts a value to a number.
NA()	Returns an error value of #N/A.
TYPE(*value*)	Finds the data type for a specified value.

Logical Functions

FUNCTION	DESCRIPTION
AND(*logical1*[, *logical2*, . . .])	Returns a value of TRUE if all arguments evaluate to true.
FALSE()	Returns a value of FALSE.
IF(*logical_test*, *value_if_true* [, *value_if_false*])	Performs conditions based on whether a condition is true or false.
NOT()	Reverses the value of an argument.
OR(*logical1*[, *logical2*, . . .])	Returns a value of TRUE if any of the arguments evaluate to true.
TRUE()	Returns a value of TRUE.

continued →

Lookup and Reference Functions

FUNCTION	DESCRIPTION
ADDRESS(*row_num, column_num, abs_num*[, *a1, sheet_text*])	Creates a reference to a specific cell.
AREAS(*reference*)	Finds the number of areas in reference.
CHOOSE(*index_num, value1* [, *value2, . . .*])	Selects a value from a list based upon the index value.
COLUMN(*reference*)	Determines the column number for the reference.
COLUMNS(*array*)	Finds the number of columns in an array.
GETPIVOTDATA(*data_field, pivot_table*[, *field1, item1, field2, item2, . . .*])	Allows you to capture specific data values from a PivotTable report.
HLOOKUP(*lookup_value, table_array, row_index_num*[, *range_lookup*])	Finds the value in the specified row of the matching column.
HYPERLINK(*link_location* [, *friendly_name*])	Creates a shortcut to a document.
INDEX(*reference*[, *row_num, column_num, area_num*])	Returns a reference to specified cells within a reference.
INDIRECT(*ref_text*[, *a1*])	Returns a value or a reference to a value.
LOOKUP(*lookup_value, array*)	Finds the specified value within an array.
MATCH(*lookup_value, lookup_array* [, *match_type*])	Locates a matching value in the array.
OFFSET(*reference, rows, cols* [, *height, width*])	Locates the range that is the specified number of columns and rows from the referenced range.
ROW(*reference*)	Determines the row number for the reference.
ROWS(*array*)	Finds the number of rows in an array.
TRANSPOSE(*array*)	Transposes the selected range from vertical to horizontal, or vice versa.
VLOOKUP(*lookup_value, table_array, col_index_num*[, *range_lookup*])	Finds the value in the specified column of the matching row.

FUNCTION	DESCRIPTION
ABS(*number*)	Finds the absolute value of a number.
ACOS(*number*)	Finds the arccosine of a number.
ACOSH(*number*)	Finds the inverse hyperbolic cosine.
ASIN(*number*)	Finds the arcsine of a number.
ASINH(*number*)	Finds the inverse hyperbolic sine.
ATAN(*number*)	Finds the arctangent of a number.
ATAN2(*x_num*, *y_num*)	Finds the arctangent using two coordinates of an angle.
ATANH(*number*)	Finds the inverse hyperbolic tangent.
CIELING(*number*, *significance*)	Rounds a number up to a specific multiple.
COMBIN(*number*, *number_chosen*)	Finds the number of unique combinations for the specified number of items.
COS(*number*)	Finds the cosine of an angle.
COSH(*number*)	Finds the hyperbolic cosine.
DEGREES(*angle*)	Converts a number from radians to degrees.
EVEN(*number*)	Rounds the number to the nearest even integer.
EXP(*number*)	Raises the constant to the power of the specified number.
FACT(*number*)	Finds the factorial of the number.
FLOOR(*number*, *significance*)	Rounds a number down to a specific multiple.
GCD(*number1*[, *number2*, . . .])	Finds the greatest common divisor for the specified numbers.
INT(*number*)	Rounds a number to the nearest integer.
LCM(*number1*[, *number2*, . . .])	Finds the least common multiple.
LN(*number*)	Finds the natural logarithm of the specified number.
LOG(*number*[, *base*])	Finds the logarithm of a number to the specified base.
LOG10(*number*)	Finds the logarithm of a number to base-10.
MDETERM(*array*)	Finds the determinant of an array.
MINVERSE(*array*)	Finds the inverse of a square matrix.
MMULT(*array1*, *array2*)	Determines the product of two matrixes.
MOD(*number*, *divisor*)	Finds the remainder of the division.
MROUND(*number*, *multiple*)	Rounds a number to the specified integer multiple.
MULTINOMIAL(*number1*[, *number2*, . . .])	Divides the sum by the product of factorials.

continued →

Math & Trig Functions (continued)

FUNCTION	DESCRIPTION
ODD(*number*)	Rounds the number to the nearest odd integer.
PI()	Returns the value of PI.
POWER(*number, power*)	Raises the number to the specified power.
PRODUCT(*number1[, number2, . . .]*)	Multiplies the specified numbers.
QUOTIENT(*numerator, denominator*)	Returns the integer result of division.
RADIANS(*angle*)	Converts a radian measurement to degrees.
RAND()	Creates a random number between 0 and 1.
RANDBETWEEN(*bottom, top*)	Creates a random number between the specified values.
ROMAN(*number[, form]*)	Creates a roman numeral.
ROUND(*number, num_digits*)	Rounds a number to the specified number of digits.
ROUNDDOWN(*number, num_digits*)	Rounds a number down to the specified number of digits.
ROUNDUP(*number, num_digits*)	Rounds a number up to the specified number of digits.
SERIESSUM(*x, n, m, coefficients*)	Sums a power series.
SIGN(*number*)	Determines if a number is positive, negative, or zero.
SIN(*number*)	Finds the sine of an angle.
SINH(*number*)	Finds the hyperbolic sine.
SQRT(*number*)	Determines the square root of a number.
SQRTPI(*number*)	Determines the square root of a number multiplied by PI.
SUBTOTAL(*function_num, ref1[, ref2, . . .]*)	Performs a subtotal function on a portion of a list.
SUM(*number1[, number2, . . .]*)	Sums the specified numbers.
SUMIF(*range, criteria[, sum_range]*)	Sums the cells in the range that match the criteria.
SUMPRODUCT(*array1[, array2, array3, . . .]*)	Sums the products of the arrays.
SUMSQ(*number1[, number2, . . .]*)	Sums the squares of the values.

Math & Trig Functions

FUNCTION	DESCRIPTION
SUMX2MY2(*array_x*, *array_y*)	Sums the differences of the squares of two arrays.
SUMX2PY2(*array_x*, *array_y*)	Sums the squares of two arrays.
SUMXMY2(*array_x*, *array_y*)	Returns the sum of squares for the two arrays.
TAN(*number*)	Finds the tangent of an angle.
TANH(*number*)	Finds the hyperbolic tangent.
TRUNC(*number*[, *num_digits*])	Truncates a number to the specified decimal digits.

Statistical Functions

FUNCTION	DESCRIPTION
AVEDEV(*number1*[, *number2*, . . .])	Finds the average deviation of data points from the mean.
AVERAGE(*number1*[, *number2*, . . .])	Finds the average of the numbers.
AVERAGEA(*value1*[, *value2*, . . .])	Finds the average of numeric, logical, and text values.
BETADIST(*x*, *alpha*, *beta*[, *A*, *B*])	Finds the distribution using the cumulative beta probability density function.
BETAINV(*probability*, *alpha*, *beta*[, *A*, *B*])	Finds the inverse distribution using the cumulative beta probability density function.
BINOMDIST(*number_s*, *trials*, *probability_s*, *cumulative*)	Finds the probability of a number of successes in a specified number of trials.
CHIDIST(*x*, *degrees_freedom*)	Finds the chi-squared distribution.
CHIINV(*probability*, *degrees_freedom*)	Finds the inverse chi-squared distribution.
CHITEST(*actual_range*, *expected_range*)	Compares the expected range of cells to the actual range of cells.
CONFIDENCE(*alpha*, *standard_dev*, *size*)	Finds the confidence mean for a population mean.
CORREL(*array1*, *array2*)	Determines the correlation coefficient of two arrays.
COUNT(*value1*[, *value2*, . . .])	Counts the number of numeric values.
COUNTA(*value1*[, *value2*, . . .])	Counts the number of cells that contain values.
COUNTBLANK(*range*)	Counts the number of empty cells in the selected range.
COUNTIF(*range*, *criteria*)	Counts the number of cells that meet the criteria within the specified range.
COVAR(*array1*, *array2*)	Finds the covariance of two arrays.

continued →

Statistical Functions

FUNCTION	DESCRIPTION
CRITBINOM(*trials, probability_s, alpha*)	Finds the smallest value for the cumulative binomial distribution.
DEVSQ(*number1[, number2, . . .]*)	Sums the squares of the deviations between the specified values.
EXPONDIST(*x, lambda, cumulative*)	Finds the exponential distribution.
FDIST(*x, degrees_freedom1, degrees_freedom2*)	Finds the F probability distribution.
FINV(*probability, degrees_freedom1, degrees_freedom2*)	Finds the inverse of the F probability distribution.
FISHER(*x*)	Calculates the Fisher transformation of the specified value.
FISHERINV(*y*)	Calculates the inverse of the Fisher transformation of the specified value.
FORECAST(*x, known_y's, known_x's*)	Predicts a future value based upon the existing values.
FREQUENCY(*data_array, bins_array*)	Determines the number of times specific values occur within a range.
FTEST(*array1, array2*)	Compares two arrays and determines if the variances are equal.
GAMMADIST(*x, alpha, beta, cumulative*)	Finds the gamma distribution.
GAMMAINV(*probability, alpha, beta, cumulative*)	Finds the inverse of the gamma distribution.
GAMMALN(*x*)	Finds the natural logarithm of the gamma function.
GEOMEAN(*number1[, number2, . . .]*)	Determines the geometric mean of the specified values.
GROWTH(*known_y's[, known_x's, new_x's, const]*)	Finds the future exponential growth.
HARMEAN(*number1[, number2, . . .]*)	Determines the harmonic mean of the specified values.
HYPGEOMDIST(*sample_s, number_sample, population_s, number_population*)	Determines that probability of the specified number of successes based upon the population size.
INTERCEPT(*x, known_y's, known_x's*)	Determines the point where the line crosses the y-axis.
KURT(*number1[, number2, . . .]*)	Determines the kurtosis of the specified values.
LARGE(*array, k*)	Finds the value that is the specified number within an array based upon its size.
LINEST(*known_y's[, known_x's, const, stats]*)	Finds the best-fitting straight line using the least squares method.

FUNCTION	DESCRIPTION
LOGEST(*known_y's*[, *known_x's*, *const*, *stats*])	Finds the exponential curve the fits the specified values.
LOGINV(*probability*, *mean*, *standard_dev*)	Finds the inverse of the lognormal cumulative distribution.
LOGNORMDIST(*x*, *mean*, *standard_dev*)	Finds the lognormal cumulative distribution.
MAX(*number1*[, *number2*, . . .])	Finds the largest numeric value.
MAXA(*value1*[, *value2*, . . .])	Finds the largest value in the list by comparing numbers, text, and logical values.
MEDIAN(*number1*[, *number2*, . . .])	Finds the median value for a list.
MIN(*number1*[, *number2*, . . .])	Finds the smallest numeric value.
MINA(*value1*[, *value2*, . . .])	Finds the smallest value in the list by comparing numbers, text, and logical values.
MODE(*number1*[, *number2*, . . .])	Finds the most frequently occurring value in a list.
NEGBINOMDIST(*number_f*, *number_s*, *probability_s*)	Determines the probability of the specified number of failures.
NORMDIST(*x*, *mean*, *standard_dev*, *cumulative*)	Finds the normal distribution of the specified mean and standard deviation.
NORMINV(*probability mean*, *standard_dev*)	Finds the inverse of the normal cumulative distribution using the specified mean and standard deviation values.
NORMSDIST(*z*)	Finds the normal distribution with a mean of 0 and a standard deviation of 1.
NORMSINV(*probability*)	Finds the inverse of the standard normal cumulative distribution with a mean of 0 and a standard deviation of 1.
PEARSON(*array1*, *array2*)	Finds the Pearson product moment coefficient r.
PERCENTILE(*array*, *k*)	Finds the value that is the specified percentile of values in the list.
PERCENTRANK(*array*, *x*[, *significance*])	Finds the percentage rank of a number within a list.
PERMUT(*number*, *number_chosen*)	Calculates the number of permutations created from the specified number of objects.
POISSON(*x*, *mean*, *cumulative*)	Calculates the Poisson distribution.
PROB(*x_range*, *prob_range*, *lower_limit*[, *upper_limit*])	Determines the probability that a range of values is within the specified limits.
QUARTILE(*array*, *quart*)	Finds the quartile for a list of values.
RANK(*number*, *ref*, *order*)	Finds the rank of a number within a list.
RSQ(*known_y's*, *known_x's*)	Finds the square of the Pearson product moment correlation coefficient through the specified data points.
SKEW(*number1*[, *number2*, . . .])	Finds the degree of asymmetry for a series of numbers.

continued →

Statistical Functions *(continued)*

FUNCTION	DESCRIPTION
SLOPE(*known_y's, known_x's*)	Finds the slope of a linear regression line.
SMALL(*array, k*)	Finds the value that is the specified number within an array based upon its size.
STANDARDIZE(*x, mean, standard_dev*)	Finds the value when you know the mean and the standard deviation.
STDEV(*number1[, number2, . . .]*)	Estimates the standard deviation of numeric values based upon a sample.
STDEVA(*value1[, value2, . . .]*)	Estimates the standard deviation of numeric, text, and logical values based upon a sample.
STDEVP(*number1[, number2, . . .]*)	Estimates the standard deviation of numeric values based upon the entire population.
STDEVPA(*value1[, value2, . . .]*)	Estimates the standard deviation of numeric, logical, and text values based upon the entire population.
STEYX(*known_y's, known_x's*)	Finds the standard error for each y-value.
TDIST(*x, degrees_freedom, tails*)	Finds the Student t-distribution probability for the specified value.
TINV(*probability, degrees_freedom, tails*)	Finds the inverse of Student t-distribution probability for the specified value.
TREND(*known_y's[, known_x's, new_x's, const]*)	Finds the values that match a linear trend using the method of least squares.
TRIMMEAN(*array, percent*)	Finds the mean of the interior of a list of numeric values.
TTEST(*array1, array2, tails, type*)	Determines if two samples are from the same population.
VAR(*number1[, number2, . . .]*)	Estimates the variance of numeric values based upon a sample.
VARA(*value1[, value2, . . .]*)	Estimates the variance of numeric, text, and logical values based upon a sample.
VARP(*number1[, number2, . . .]*)	Estimates the variance of numeric values based upon the entire population.
VARPA(*value1[, value2, . . .]*)	Estimates the variance of numeric, logical, and text values based upon the entire population.
WEIBULL(*x, alpha, beta, cumulative*)	Finds the possibilities of a Weibull distribution.
ZTEST(*array, x[, sigma]*)	Finds the two-tailed P-value of a Z-test.

FUNCTION	DESCRIPTION
BAHTEXT(*number*)	Converts a number to Thai.
CHAR(*number*)	Returns the specified character value.
CLEAN(*text*)	Removes all nonprintable characters from text.
CODE(*text*)	Finds the character code for the first character in a text string.
CONCATENATE(*text1, text2, . . .*)	Joins the specified text strings.
DOLLAR(*number*[, *decimals*])	Converts a number to a currency value.
EXACT(*text1, text2*)	Determines if two strings are the same.
FIND(*find_text, within_text*[, *start_num*])	Locates one text string within another text string.
FIXED(*number*[, *decimals, no_commas*])	Rounds a number to the specified number of decimal places.
LEFT(*text*[, *num_chars*])	Returns the specified number of characters from the left side of a text string.
LEN(*text*)	Finds the length of a text string.
LOWER(*text*)	Converts a string to lowercase characters.
MID(*text, start_num, num_chars*)	Returns the specified number of characters from the center of the text string.
PROPER(*text*)	Capitalizes the first character in a string and converts the remaining characters to lowercase.
REPLACE(*old_text, start_num, num_chars, new_text*)	Replaces text at the specified location with the new text.
REPT(*text, number_times*)	Repeats a text string the specified number of times.
RIGHT(*text*[, *num_chars*])	Returns the specified number of characters from the right side of a text string.
SEARCH(*find_text, within_text* [, *start_num*])	Determines the starting position of one text string within another text string.
SUBSTITUTE(*text, old_text, new_text*[, *instance_num*])	Replaces the specified text within a string.
T(*value*)	Returns the specified value.
TEXT(*value, format_text*)	Converts a value to the text with the specified format.
TRIM(*text*)	Removes all extra spacing from a text string.
UPPER(*text*)	Converts all letters in a string to uppercase.
VALUE(*text*)	Converts a text string to a number.

Formula Basics

Formulas are the building blocks of data analysis in Excel. They enable you to calculate and compare the values in cells. This section serves as a reference for users who are not familiar with Excel.

Formulas contain two basic elements: an *equal sign*, followed by an *expression*, which tells Excel what to do. You can use any combination of functions, cell references, named ranges, constants, and operators to create a formula. If Excel cannot properly evaluate your formula, an error message appears.

Excel provides a large variety of operators you can use to create formulas, most of which are the arithmetic operators; however, Excel also provides comparison operators, reference operators, and a text operator.

Arithmetic Operators

You use arithmetic operators to perform numeric calculations, such as addition or subtraction. If you use arithmetic operators on text, Excel returns an error message. Excel provides addition (+), subtraction (–), multiplication (*), division (/), percent (%), and exponential (^) operators. Placing the subtraction operator in front of a number makes that number a negative number.

Comparison Operators

You use comparison operators between two expressions to determine if they are equal (=), greater than (>), greater than or equal to (>=), less than (<), less than or equal to (<=), or not equal to (<>) each other. When you use comparison operators in a formula, Excel returns a logical value of either TRUE or FALSE.

Text Operator

You can use the text operator to join or concatenate two or more strings of text together to form one string. You concatenate strings together using the ampersand (&). Excel merges the two strings together without adding any extra spacing. If you want spaces between the strings, you must insert the spaces yourself by placing the amount of space you want in quotation marks. For example, if you want to leave a space between the two strings, where APPLE is in cell A1, and SAUCE is in cell A2, you type:

```
=A1&" "&A2
```

When you use the text operator to combine values in cells, the result is a text value. This is true even if the combined values are numeric. For example, if you combine the values 14 and 92 with the text operator, Excel creates the value 1492. Although it is a number, Excel treats 1492 as a text string because you created it using the text operator. If you attempt to use the value in a mathematical calculation, Excel ignores the value and treats it as zero, because it is text. In some instances, Excel may return an error message. For example, if you use the value of a concatenated string as the denominator of a division formula, Excel returns a !DIV/0 error. This indicates that you divided by zero because Excel interprets a text string as zero.

Reference Operators

You specify a range of cells for your formula with one of three different operators. See Chapter 1 for more information on selecting cell ranges. The following table describes each of the operators:

OPERATOR	SYMBOL	PURPOSE	EXAMPLE
Range	:	Specifies a range of cells from the cell reference before the operator to the cell reference after the operator.	A1:A15 specifies all cells from A1 to A15.
Union	,	Combines multiple ranges in one reference.	=SUM(A1:A10, C1:C10) sums cells in A1 through A10, and C1 through C10.
Intersection	(space)	References the cells that are common between two ranges.	(A1:C10 B1:D10) specifies the common cells in the range A1:C10 and B1:D10. In the formula =SUM(A1:C10 B1:D10), Excel sums only the values in cells B1 through C10.

When Excel evaluates a formula that contains operators, it uses a specific order to determine which part of the formula it evaluates first. This is known as the *precedence order*. For example, the following formula has a result of 19 because Excel calculates 4^2 first and then adds 16 to 3: =3+4^2. To change the order of precedence, you can place parentheses around 3+4 so that the following formula gives a result of 49 (7 raised to the second power): =(3+4)^2.

The following table shows the precedence order, from highest to lowest, that Excel uses to evaluate operators in formulas. If the operators in the formula all have the same order of precedence, Excel evaluates the equation from left to right.

PRECEDENCE	OPERATORS	SYMBOL
1	Parentheses	( )
2	Reference operators	: , (space)
3	Minus sign	– (negates a number before any calculations)
4	Percent sign	%
5	Exponentiation	^
6	Multiplication and division	*, /
7	Addition and subtraction	+, –
8	Concatenation	&
9	Comparison operators	=, <, >, <=, >=, <>

continued →

Functions provide an invaluable means of analyzing data in Excel because they are pre-built formulas. Instead of writing a complex formula, you can use a function to perform a specific task, such as calculating an average, retrieving a value from a database, or performing a comparison. For example, the AVERAGE function can determine the average of the numbers in a range of cells, such as =AVERAGE(A1:A15).

Arguments are the values you must provide for the function to return the result. For example, if you select the FV function to determine what the future value is on an investment, you must specify values for the interest rate, number of payments, payment amount, present value, and future value, such as in =FV(Rate, Npes, Pmt, PV, Type).

Built-In Functions

You can use Excel's built-in functions to analyze your data. You can either type the function name manually into your equation, or you can insert it via the Insert Function dialog box. See Chapter 3 for more information. The Insert Function dialog box has various function categories that are listed in the following table. See Appendix B for a complete list of the available Excel functions.

CATEGORY	DESCRIPTION
Financial	Calculates financial information such as the depreciation amount on an asset or the interest rate on a security.
Date & Time	Use these functions to compare dates, retrieve times from the system clock, or return a portion of a date or time.
Math & Trig	Performs common mathematical and trigonometric calculations such as finding the cosine of a value or generating a random number.
Statistical	Performs statistical calculations such as the variance and standard deviation.
Lookup & Reference	Allows you to search for or reference specific values within your workbook, such as creating references to specific cells or finding the location of a value.
Database	Allows you to work with values in lists or databases.
Text	Allows you to manipulate text values; for example, you can change the capitalization of a text label.
Logical	Returns a value of TRUE or FALSE or performs a calculation based on whether a value is true or false.
Information	Returns information about your worksheet or your computer system. For example, =ISODD(A1) determines if cell A1 contains an odd number, and =INFO("directory") returns the directory location of the current workbook.

Add-In Functions

Excel uses a unique reference or address to identify every cell on a worksheet. This identification process, called the *cell reference*, allows you to specify the cell or range of cells you want to use in a formula.

Default Style

By default, Excel identifies all columns with letters and all rows with numbers, giving each cell a unique address. The cell reference forms from the column and row that intersect in the cell. For example, the top-left cell of a worksheet is A1 because Column A and Row 1 intersect in that cell.

R1C1 Reference Style

Excel also provides another cell reference style, called *R1C1*. With this style, Excel identifies the cell with a C, for column, followed by the column number, and an R for row, followed by the row number. The top-left cell is R1C1, the second row in the first column is R2C1, and so on. If you prefer this format, you can change the setting in the Options dialog box. Although this format is available, the examples in the book use the default cell reference style.

Absolute or Relative

When you reference a cell in a formula, you can either use a relative or absolute cell reference. With an absolute cell reference, no matter where you copy and paste the formula, it always refers back to the original cell. You make a reference absolute by placing a $ before both the column and row references. For example, if you copy the formula =SUM($A$1:$A$5) in cell A6 to cell B6, the formula in cell B6 still returns the sum of cells A1 through A5.

If you want to copy a formula and have the cell reference change depending on where you paste the formula, use a relative cell reference. The formula keeps track of the referenced cell's location in relation to the formula cell. So if you copy the formula =SUM(A1:A5) in cell A6 to cell B6, Excel pastes the formula =SUM(B1:B5).

When you create cell references, you can use a combination of absolute and relative references. For example, you can make a column reference absolute while the row reference is relative, or vice versa. For example, the reference A$2 has a relative column reference and an absolute row reference. If you copy the cell reference to another cell, the column reference changes relative to the new cell, but the row reference remains the same.

Errors

If you create a formula that Excel cannot properly evaluate, an error message displays in the formula cell. For example, if you attempt to add two cells that contain text, the #VALUE! error message displays in the formula cell. The following table shows the formula error messages.

ERROR	DESCRIPTION
#####	Either the column is not wide enough to display the result, or an argument contains a negative date or time value.
#VALUE!	An argument contains the wrong type of value; for example, an attempt to add cells containing text.
#DIV/0	Excel attempted to divide a number by zero.
#NAME?	Excel does not recognize the name of a function or range. This typically occurs when you misspell a function name.
#N/A	A specified cell reference is not available to the formula.
#REF!	A cell reference is not valid.
#NUM!	A formula contains invalid numeric values. This can occur when a number is specified with another character, such as a dollar sign, as the value for a formula that requires a number.
#NULL!	The cell ranges do not intersect.

INDEX

INDEX

INDEX

INDEX

INDEX

INDEX

INDEX

X

Z

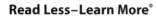
Read Less–Learn More®

There's a Visual book
for every learning level...

Simplified®

The place to start if you're new to computers. Full color.

- Computers
- Mac OS
- Office
- Windows

Teach Yourself VISUALLY™

Get beginning to intermediate-level training in a variety of topics. Full color.

- Computers
- Crocheting
- Digital Photography
- Dog training
- Dreamweaver
- Excel
- Guitar
- HTML
- Knitting
- Mac OS
- Office
- Photoshop
- Photoshop Elements
- Piano
- Poker
- PowerPoint
- Scrapbooking
- Sewing
- Windows
- Wireless Networking
- Word

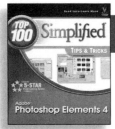

Top 100 Simplified® Tips & Tricks

Tips and techniques to take your skills beyond the basics. Full color.

- Digital Photography
- eBay
- Excel
- Google
- Internet
- Mac OS
- Photoshop
- Photoshop Elements
- PowerPoint
- Windows

Build It Yourself VISUALLY™

Do it yourself the visual way and without breaking the bank. Full color.

- Game PC
- Media Center PC